In *James Baldwin and the American Schoolhouse*, Carl Grant writes with fervor and conviction of an urgent need for teachers to be exposed to the writings of James Baldwin. Grant eloquently contends that Baldwin's work can influence educators to transform schooling, particularly in this moment of racial awakening. The analyses in *James Baldwin and the American Schoolhouse* make a convincing case for how all teachers can show that Black Lives Matter.

> Brian D. Schultz, Professor and Chair of Teacher Education, Miami University, and author of *Spectacular Things Happen Along the Way: Lessons from an Urban Classroom*

Professor Grant's book, in which he develops a soliloquy story of James Baldwin's self-identity discovery, thoughtful analytical writings, and passionate speeches, which dissected systemic racism is a must read for all teachers and teacher educators. Professor Grant has revealed through his thorough and intriguing research of Baldwin's extensive papers and other artefacts that "knowledge is socially distributed, that what you know is what you have been allowed to know." What Professor Grant uncovers in his book for the reader is an enormous amount of written thoughts and ideas shared by Baldwin as he connected with teachers and students. Most significantly, unfortunately his ideas for combatting systemic racism in our schools, especially schools serving "Negro Students" have not received the distribution they deserved. Professor Grant's extensive research, and collection of references and resources incorporated into this book demonstrates a superior scholarly resource for all of us engaged in combatting racism in the United States of America.

My deep appreciation to Professor Grant for providing a book with such enlightening knowledge of Mr. James Baldwin.

> H. Prentice Baptiste, Regents Professor, Multicultural and Science Education Founder, President, National Association for Multicultural Education and Co-Editor of *Visioning Multicultural Education*

James Baldwin and the American Schoolhouse demonstrates how Baldwin's lessons are simultaneously timely and timeless – why we need Baldwin just as much in 2020 as we did in 1963 – why we need Baldwin just as much in the field of education as we do in Black Studies. With extreme care and consideration, Grant explores Baldwin's writings and speeches, meticulously delineating Baldwin's messages to teachers and students alike. Baldwin believed that teachers must recognize the ways white supremacy and anti-blackness necessitate the miseducation of Black students, and "go for broke" in their relentless charge to help students refuse and resist. While Grant effectively interrogates the myriad ways Baldwin calls attention to students' racialized oppression, this book is even more powerful in its articulation of Baldwin's desire for education to empower and inspire a revolution – the way his message is crafted through a lens of "hope and love." Despite Baldwin not considering himself a teacher, Grant's latest must read work illuminates why Baldwin is one of the best educators of past and present, why his words are an absolute necessity in schools of education across the country, and why anyone who desires to be an effective teacher of Black students must first be a student of Baldwin.

> Kihana miraya ross, Assistant Professor, African American Studies, Northwestern University

A compelling story, deeply researched, and richly textured that is simultaneously challenging and inviting to know more about this man, James Baldwin, and to join him in his advocacies and journeys toward the full liberation and humanization of African Americans. Grant often writes about Baldwin in the first person, and in the moment of occurrence such that the reader feels like being THERE when the events happen, yet still in the here and now. Analyses of concerns, explanations, and suggested resolutions of raced-based problems in the U. S. "travel" seamlessly between when Baldwin lived and the present, while maintaining a resolute level of relevance. Both the artist (Baldwin) and the analyst (Grant) are masterful teachers in promoting the humanity, dignity, resilience, and competence of African Americans in the face of persistent and pervasive racism. A must read for gaining historical, personal, and collective perspectives on the necessity of reality-based anti-racist and culturally relevant education for African Americans in schools and society at large.

Geneva Gay, Professor Emeritus, College of Education,
University of Washington, Seattle

What we learn about the inimitable James Baldwin's incomparable genius, his humanity and fearlessness through this illumination of his incisive social analysis, and what we learn also about Carl Grant's painstaking contributions to Black intellectual thought are nothing less than a "balm in Gilead" for our wounded souls. *James Baldwin and the American Schoolhouse* is the book that every educator needs to read and take to heart.

Joyce E. King, Georgia State University

In the Fall of 2020, I taught a newly developed graduate-level course focused on Black intellectual thought in education. The course was motivated by a text of the same name that was written by Carl Grant and his colleagues, Keffrelyn Brown and Anthony Brown. That course, the first of its kind for me and all of the students–proved to be to be transformative for all of us. Not only did it help us discover the thoughts and ideas of powerful Black thinkers and activists, and consider those thoughts and ideas in historical and contemporary context, it helped us to cope with the societal fires that were burning at that time–COVID-19 and intensified anti-Black racism. In this new text: *James Baldwin and The American School House*, Carl Grant continues digging into the reservoirs of Black intellectual thought to re-surface and re-articulate James Baldwin as teacher, teacher educator, and critical race theorist of education. Drawing on the speeches and commentaries of Baldwin, Grant skillfully demonstrates how Baldwin was, and remains, an important source to help educators and policy makers understand some of the most persistent and pressing issues in the field, especially in relation to Black learners. Professor Grant presents Baldwin without equivocation, and tells hard truths that need to heard, especially by white educators. This text will be a valuable companion for all educators when we face the fires next time.

Danny Bernard Martin, University of Illinois at Chicago

JAMES BALDWIN AND THE AMERICAN SCHOOLHOUSE

This book – written for teacher educators, teachers and admirers of James Baldwin – employs his essays and speeches to discuss how the effects of race and racism enter the souls of African American students and become attached and difficult to dislodge. Yet, his essays also provide educators and students with purpose, meaning and suggestions for how to stand up against racism, develop an authentic self and fight oppression. Whereas this book takes advantage of the full body of Baldwin's work – fiction, nonfiction, interviews, lectures, speeches and letters – its foundation is three speeches James Baldwin gave in the 1960s on the education of African American children and African American and European American race relations in the United States. The purpose of education, defying myths, freedom, willful ignorance and developing identity are discussed through a Baldwinian lens. African American and European American teachers are encouraged to "Go for Broke" as this book explores the important role Baldwin's work can play in schools and universities.

Carl A. Grant is Hoefs-Bascom Professor in the Department of Curriculum and Instruction and former Chair of the Afro American Studies Department at the University of Wisconsin-Madison.

JAMES BALDWIN AND THE AMERICAN SCHOOLHOUSE

Carl A. Grant

NEW YORK AND LONDON

First published 2021
by Routledge
52 Vanderbilt Avenue, New York, NY 10017

and by Routledge
2 Park Square, Milton Park, Abingdon, Oxon OX14 4RN

Routledge is an imprint of the Taylor & Francis Group, an informa business

© 2021 Carl A. Grant

The right of Carl A. Grant to be identified as author of this work has been asserted by him in accordance with sections 77 and 78 of the Copyright, Designs and Patents Act 1988.

All rights reserved. No part of this book may be reprinted or reproduced or utilised in any form or by any electronic, mechanical, or other means, now known or hereafter invented, including photocopying and recording, or in any information storage or retrieval system, without permission in writing from the publishers.

Trademark notice: Product or corporate names may be trademarks or registered trademarks, and are used only for identification and explanation without intent to infringe.

Library of Congress Cataloging-in-Publication Data
Names: Grant, Carl A., author.
Title: James Baldwin and the American schoolhouse / Carl A. Grant.
Description: New York, NY : Routledge, 2021. | Includes bibliographical references and index.
Identifiers: LCCN 2020049255 (print) | LCCN 2020049256 (ebook) |
ISBN 9780367709716 (hardback) | ISBN 9780367709709 (paperback) |
ISBN 9781003148746 (ebook)
Subjects: LCSH: Baldwin, James, 1924-1987--Political and social views. |
African Americans--Education. | Education--United States--Philosophy. |
Education--Aims and objectives--United States.
Classification: LCC LC2731 .G72 2021 (print) | LCC LC2731 (ebook) |
DDC 371.829/96073--dc23
LC record available at https://lccn.loc.gov/2020049255
LC ebook record available at https://lccn.loc.gov/2020049256

ISBN: 978-0-367-70971-6 (hbk)
ISBN: 978-0-367-70970-9 (pbk)
ISBN: 978-1-003-14874-6 (ebk)

Typeset in Bembo
by Taylor & Francis Books

To (In Memoriam)

Alvin Grant Jr ... brother

Robert Crumpton ... like a blood brother

Robert A. Saddler ... like a blood brother

My mom told me when I was very young and we were discussing friends and friendship: "Carl," she said, "if you have one really good friend in life, you are lucky." I had two, along with three brothers Alvin, Ernest and Shelby who were at all times good friends. Mom, your son was lucky.

CONTENTS

Acknowledgments	*x*
Exercising a New Voice?	*xiii*
Preface	*xv*

1	Welcome to America's Schoolhouse, James Arthur Baldwin	1
2	The Teacher Within Him, James Arthur Baldwin	40
3	Baldwin and Education: Purpose, Freedom, Defying Myth-making, Truth and Innocence	65
4	"Go for Broke"	108
5	Students be You: Developing Identity, Defying Place, Taking Role	143

Index	*183*

ACKNOWLEDGMENTS

Writing a book can be so all involving in small and big ways. A word here or there with someone, or a full discussion about an idea you are covering, can all play an important role. Such has been the case in my writing of *James Baldwin and The American Schoolhouse*. That I was writing about the famed Baldwin and education, invited discussion about what I was doing and how I was doing it. Out of those discussions came pointed suggestions, references to how Baldwin had affected their lives and what he meant to them. Baldwin reminiscings, and what and how to write served as a great deal of encouragement.

I am indeed indebted to several graduate students, Jalessa Bryant, Emma Gorski, Brittany Johnson and, Laura Roeker, who not only took my Baldwin class, spring 2019–2020, but met with me as a group during the summer of 2019 to offer feedback on drafts of chapters. That was a great "learning and collegial" time.

A special thanks to Rosette Cirillo for her insightful observations and comments.

Terri Pope was always there with a smile and fast response to my many requests of an administrative nature. Thanks Terri.

Much gratitude is directed toward Erika Bullock, my friend and colleague, who read chapter drafts at different points in time and offered valuable suggestions and encouragement.

Many thanks to Davis W. Houck for sending me Baldwin's speech at Castlemont High School.

When I was developing the idea for the book, and wondering about the worth of the idea, I spent four days from opening to closing at the National Museum of African American History and Culture. My purpose was to discover how Jimmy was recognized and positioned at the museum. Upon entering the museum and seeing a statement by Baldwin hanging high up on the wall, I smiled. Throughout those four days, the pest, that I am, I interacted with numerous museum staff members; they all were wonderful. Thank you!

Visiting archives, the Schomburg Center for Research and Black Culture in this case, to me is special; such a privilege to "touch" the material of the person you are studying ... arguably developing a friendship – a connection. My days at the Schomburg reviewing Baldwin's boxes of material were indeed special. Each and every Schomburg staff person made me feel at home during my research visit. Much appreciated!

Matt Friberg, was more than an "editor." Our discussions were always humane, fully thoughtful and caring; and while we discussed business, I always felt the purpose of the project, to help teachers successfully teach African American children and other children of color, always remained centered. Thanks Matt!

Thanks Alex Allweiss. You are always terrific and so darn thoughtful.

When James Baldwin and The American Schoolhouse was in an early draft form, a good friend and colleague, Dr. Louise (Weez) M. Tomlinson read Chapter One of the manuscript and asked me, "Why don't you use African American and European American, instead of Black, white, etc. etc." I asked why and she told me in elaborate, compelling detail. In addition, her reasoning is appropriate and timely, and buoyed by the racial moment we are in ... and have been in for centuries. I took Dr. Tomlinson's advice and changed the wording in the manuscript, except within quoted material. I called Louise ... she likes to be called Weez ... when I began to write the acknowledgments and told her I had followed her advice and asked, if she would succinctly put into two sentences why she recommended the change so I could let the reader know and to know from whence that good idea came. Weez writes:

> If we speak of four out of five groups of people so as to indicate their continent or countries of origin as well as their current nationality (e.g., African American with African indicating African origins and American indicating nation of birth, citizenship or residence, and the same for Asian American, Hispanic American and Native American) then we should consistently categorize the fifth group with parallel terms, thus – European American.
>
> At this point in the evolution of history and current events, it is imperative that we use a nomenclature in the most equitable and realistic ways possible with regard to cultural identity – ways that acknowledge each individual's ancestry such that they are reminded of their heritage and such that no one, grounded on American soil, becomes part of a collective psyche wherein another can tell them to "go back where they came from" – as if the other was always here and is subject to the burden of intrusion – when in reality we should all (with the exception of the Native American) own our immigrant heritage whether voluntary or involuntary.

Louise (Weez) M. Tomlinson, 8/25/2020

Similarly, Tony Morrison contends "In this country American means white. Everybody else has to hyphenate" (In Chavez, Monforti and Michelson, 2015, p. 16).

I wanted one more reading of the manuscript before I sent it to Routledge, someone who really knows the real world of teaching and teacher education and who would not hesitate to get in my face if she thought I was not doing justice to Baldwin and education. Dr. Kathleen Nichols performed that task with excellence. Thanks, Kat, my good friend and colleague.

My brothers, Alvin and Shelby, my nephew Paul and my son Carl were muses. Carl especially would listen to me hash over about something or the other with the book almost every day. I looked to his: "Dad. How is Baldwin going today?" That question, which was more an opportunity, for me to talk to him about Baldwin and the chapter I was working on. Often, he pushed me about what I was saying, making me reframe or think deeper. Super thanks, Carl.

Finally, Alicia, daughter, Gavin and Amaya, grandson and granddaughter are very much appreciated for the questions and encouragement about what I am writing and for serving as good listeners when I quizzed them about their take on a student problem or issue before I wrote it. Thanks!!!

EXERCISING A NEW VOICE?

Several colleagues and friends have said to me that over the past several years, my work (books, articles and lectures) has shifted to center "Black Intellectual Thought." I have not pushed back on the observation, as this is a critical and radical moment for "Black Intellectual Thought," but I also see this work as connected to multicultural education.

During the early days of the last decade, Anthony Brown, Kefferlyn Brown and I engaged in numerous discussions about "centering" or bringing an additional "voice" to our respective scholarship. We were hearing a call to service from scholars and activists – such as Anna Julia Cooper, Carter G. Woodson, Alaine Locke, W. E. B. Du Bois and others – whose work we were studying and whose shoulders we were standing on. This, in part, led to *Black Intellectual Thought in Education: The Missing Traditions* (Routledge, 2015). In 2015, we argued that the inclusion of Black Intellectual Thought, in considering American education serves three purposes:

1. it provides history and context for long-standing ideas in education, such as culture, race, knowledge and economic production and pedagogy;
2. it helps to correct inaccuracies, misrepresentations and omissions in the existing curriculum narratives and arguments of achieved and earned wealth;
3. and finally, we argued that Black Intellectual Thought helps to interrogate contemporary theories in education that situate African American students as sociological and psychological objects instead of as complex, complicated humans.

The argument we made has been my North Star and I followed it as I wrote *Du Bois and Education* (Routledge, 2017), *James Baldwin and The American Schoolhouse,*

(2021) and now as I write *Lorraine Hansberry, Don't Forget They are Young, Gifted and Black*. Personally, as I think about my recent publications and lectures, keeping in mind the African Americans I am writing about, I believe I am more "exercising a new voice" than decentering my scholarship in multicultural education. An education that is multicultural has a much better chance to become and to flourish if we know the thoughts and ideas of all people who make up the United States.

PREFACE

> It is your responsibility to change the society if you think of yourself as an educated person.
>
> *James Baldwin, 1963*

> A child cannot be taught be anyone who despises him, and a child cannot afford to be fooled.
>
> *James Baldwin, 1979*

James Arthur Baldwin is among the earliest proponents who argue what African American students should be taught, how they should be taught and why they should be taught. Baldwin argues for teaching African American students about life and about living life: problems, issues, challenges; good times, suffering and hopes that come with living life as an African American. Baldwin argues African American students should learn who they are, how they came to be enslaved; called colored, Negro, African American and worse. African American students, Baldwin posits should discover their history, be taught how to "dig it up" and learn how history impacts their life, their father's life, their mother's life and the lives of all of their brothers and sisters, other family members as well as the neighbor who lives across the hall or across the street.

Baldwin argues that teaching African American students should be with honesty and authenticity born out of a love, acceptance and appreciation of their humanity. Baldwin wants African American students to see their presence and identity throughout their education and for their academic learning to not be controlled by incentive-based measures.

Baldwin's writings and speeches about African American students in northern and western cities such as Harlem and San Francisco and in Southern spaces such as New Orleans, Atlanta and Durham, N.C. is prose of blunt reality about race and racism within a democracy that is failing to exercise freedom, equality and justice for African Americans. Baldwin's essays challenge the stereotypical racialized box into which schools place African American students and challenges the innocence and myths used to keep them "sunken." Baldwin's essays, talks and interviews teach that the American flag belongs to African American people equally as much as it belongs to European American people, that Crispus Attucks, a man of African, European and Native American identity and arguably a fugitive from slavery was the first person to make the ultimate sacrifice in the American Revolutionary War.

Baldwin's essays present intelligent African Americans with a heightened consciousness, proactive and hopeful and with family life grounded in values, rituals and relationships. Baldwin's essays rebel against African American student family life absent of tradition, sensibility and agency; they tell stories – speak truths – not told in teacher education programs and not imagined by most teacher educators.

Baldwin's writings are developed out of the death and deeds of African Americans during enslavement, WWI, WWII, the disrespect for African American soldiers in uniform returning home after fighting abroad, the lynching of Emmet Till and other African Americans, police violence, *Brown vs. the Board of Education*, the Civil Rights movement and mass incarceration; and out of his compelling desire for African American humanity and identity to be respected and accepted. Baldwin's writings about the education of African American children and youth is a different way of thinking about African American students in Schools of Education, much like W. E. B. DuBois' research of African Americans in Philadelphia (*The Philadelphia Negro*) was a new way of thinking, a new school of sociology.

James or "Jimmy" as he is called by friends was born, August 1, 1924, in Harlem Hospital, the son of Emma Berdis Jones. Emma works as a cleaning woman to support herself and her son. Jimmy never knew his biological father. When he was 3 years old, 1927, his mother marries David Baldwin, an evangelical preacher who demands strict religious behavior from the nine children he and Emma would parent. David and Emma struggle to put food on the table, clothes on the backs and a roof over the heads of their children and they move from one Harlem tenement to the next in order to survive.

Baldwin begins his journey to national fame as an essayist in 1955 writing about race as the civil rights movement is just getting underway – a year after *Brown* and the same year as the heinous lynching of Emmett Louis Till. During this time, Ralph Ellison's *Invisible Man* is "harmlessly ensconced" as Louis Armstrong sings "What did I do to be so black and blue?" On the other hand, the pathological and sadistic violence of Richard Wright's Bigger Thomas is vividly portrayed in *Native Son*. It is in this climate of systematic racism and unfettered white privilege that Baldwin publishes his first collection of essays, *Notes of a Native Son*, to instant acclaim. Alfred Kazin calls the publication "one of the one or two best books written about the Negro in America," and observes, Baldwin operates "with as much power in the essay form as I've ever seen." Baldwin's next two essay-volumes: *Nobody Knows My Name* in 1961 and *The Fire Next Time* in 1963 elicits even more enthusiastic praise that continues to this day.

James Baldwin and the American Schoolhouse draws upon Baldwin's in-depth understanding of being black in the U.S. and his moral, blunt and honest appeal to teachers who teach African American students to come out from behind myths and claims of willful ignorance or innocence, in the teaching of African American students. Baldwin's themes of identity, morals, reality, love and humanity challenge America's structural and personal racism, heteronormativity, imperialism and capitalism veiled in a guise of democracy and neoliberalism. Baldwin (1979) posits "A child cannot be taught be anyone who despises him, and a child cannot afford to be fooled" (p. 1).

Baldwin brings to schooling of African American students, ideas, actions and responsibilities rarely imagined before: black intellectual thought, critical and personal aims and purposes of education, an honest telling of African American history and culture and an authentic respect of African American humanity and language. Baldwin calls for acknowledgment of African students' consciousness, the complexities and humanness of their humanity, their contribution to America and civilization, and their service to America's fight to maintain liberty and freedom when they were enslaved, segregated and/or treated as second-class citizens. Further, Baldwin calls for discussions of the rights and responsibilities of African Americans such that they have the right to examine everything, make decisions based upon those examinations and accept the consequences (and to not simply obey policies and practices of any give administration or morality). Further, Baldwin is forthright and respectful when telling African American youth what he believes they need to hear.

Baldwin's writing about African Americans students do not position them as "victims" or "angry" or "smart" or "dumb." Rufus, the protagonist in *Another Country*, demonstrates Baldwin's unique ability to explain the complexities and complications of African American life and African Americans' responsibility and participation in their successes or failures; their suffering and hope without being caught up in the sentiments of an everyday African American person caught up in the web of systemic racism and white privilege. Yet, Baldwin also exposes the systemic racism and reason that control the limited freedom and opportunity African Americans have. Baldwin observes the following about Rufus: "He was in the novel because I don't think anyone had ever watched the disintegration of a black boy from that particular point of view" (*The Guardian*, 2001, p. 1). Similarly, in *Go Tell It on the Mountain*, Baldwin writes about an impoverished African American family in Harlem discussing how they fight against political and legal injustice and maintain agency and respect. Baldwin refuses to have his African American characters' futures controlled by white supremacy and white privilege. Similarly, in his speeches and

xviii Preface

writings for teachers, African American students have an enlightened consciousness and curiosity and are agents on their own behalf.

Baldwin's writings about African students, doesn't position the European American teacher's world as better than the world of African American students and their families; and European American teachers teaching African American students need such information. Baldwin posits:

> In the beginning, I thought that the white world was very different from the world I was moving out of and I turned out to be entirely wrong. It seemed different. It seemed safer—at least the white people seemed safer. It seemed cleaner, it seemed more polite, and, of course, it seemed much richer from the material point of view. But I didn't meet anyone in that world who didn't suffer from the same affliction that all the people I had fled from suffered from and that was that they didn't know who they were. They wanted to be someone that they were not.
>
> *(Baldwin, 1960, quoted in The Guardian, 2001, p. 1)*

James Baldwin and the American Schoolhouse employs Baldwin essays and speeches to discuss how the effect of race and racism enters the *soul* of African American students and becomes attached and difficult to dislodge. Yet, the same essays are full of comfort, courage and suggestions for how to identify and resist racism and develop an authentic self. Baldwin tells African American students to confront history (slavery, segregation, willful ignorance and whiteness), overcome it, develop their own identity and let nothing stand in the way of the pursuit of their dreams. Additionally, Baldwin argues that African American students should not foster American greatness but give attention to how to imagine the country anew.

More about this Book

James Baldwin and the American Schoolhouse is written for multiracial audiences, although it will convey different messages to African Americans and European Americans. European American teacher candidates who say the reason they want to teach is because they love children and because they want to help children will be academically and morally strengthened if their love is real. If their love is surface level, they will probably put the book down. African Americans and Latinx teacher candidates will quickly come to see that *James Baldwin and the American Schoolhouse* is a critical ally, the friend you want next to you when you are the only person of color in class or if you want to show how woke you are in classes with other students of color. Additionally, it is a resourceful companion when preparing lessons to meet the needs and interests of children.

In *James Baldwin and the American Schoolhouse* a statement by Baldwin may appear in more than one chapter. Baldwin didn't hesitate to use, reuse and refine statements and ideas again and again. What is good for the Teacher is good with me.

James Baldwin and the American Schoolhouse has five chapters: Chapter One "Welcome to America's Schoolhouse, James Arthur Baldwin." Within the "welcome" you learn how I first met Jimmy, you go with him to his new home: "Where Teachers Learn to Teach." You hear his remarks to European American teachers and then to African American teachers. Chapter Two, "The Teacher Within Him, James Arthur Baldwin" lets you know why I think Jimmy is already a teacher, a great one at that. Fanatic, I argue. Chapter Three, "Baldwin and Education: Purpose, Freedom, Defying Myth-making, Truth and Innocence" is in the reader's face. Not easy to read, perhaps more difficult to write, each of the sections are bluntly honest about race and teaching. Yep, some of the history is your mother's and father's history, but you are of them and teachers need historical contexts to understand and teach African American students. Additionally, teachers of African Americans need an accurate accounting of history; the real history. Chapter Four, "Go for Broke" is Jimmy at his best. Debate with William F. Buckley, renowned public intellectual and conservative author and commentator. Enjoy the read with your favorite morning beverage. "A Letter to My Nephew," requires you to turn your phone off, so you are not interrupted. Chapter Five: "Students be You": Developing Identity, Defying Place Taking Role" explains why it was necessary for Baldwin to leave America. Baldwin's self-discovery, identity formation, place and role in America are discussed and his motivation to return to the United States from Europe is explained. Baldwin's apprehension about his first trip South, along with meeting and observing and being awed by young civil rights workers is presented. "Living and Growing in a White World," Baldwin's speech at Castlemont High School to a predominantly all African American audience is highlighted. Finally, Pam and Ann discuss Baldwin's speech at Castlemont and Ann by chance "meets" Baldwin at a local coffee shop in Harlem.

There are many themes and topics in James Baldwin's oeuvre: African American History, Race/Racism, Human Rights, Art/Artists, Identity, Religion/Faith, Homosexuality, Exile and Education. In *James Baldwin and the American Schoolhouse* some themes of race/racism, identity, African American history, civil rights, African American students and education are distinctly visible and indivisible. Religion, self-worth, homosexuality, mythmaking and democracy are vivid threads.

Whereas *James Baldwin and the American Schoolhouse* takes full advantage of the full body of Baldwin's work – fiction, nonfiction, interviews, lectures, speeches, letters – its foundation is three speeches James Baldwin gives on the education of African American children and black–white race relations in the United States in the 1960s: Castlemont High School in Oakland, California, on May 8, 1963 xx Preface

("Living and Growing in a White World"); the Second Baptist Church in Los Angeles, California ("The Free and the Brave"); and in New York City, 1963 ("A Talk to Teachers" and "A Letter to My Nephew."

Awards

Throughout his life, James Arthur Baldwin was recognized not only for his achievements in literature but also for his work in the Civil Rights struggle and for his efforts to facilitate understanding and respect between all people. Private institutions, public organizations and government agencies all chose to honor him in their own ways:

1945: Eugene F. Saxon Fellowship
1948: Rosenwald Fellowship
1954: Guggenheim Fellowship and the MacDowell Colony Fellowship
1956: Partisan Review Fellowship and a grant from the National Institute of Arts and Letters
1959: Ford Foundation Grant
1961: Certificate of Recognition from the National Conference on Christians and Jews
1963: George Polk Memorial Award
1964: Honorary Degree from City University of New York
1965: Martin Luther King Memorial medal and an Honorary Degree from the University of Massachusetts
1981: Best Nonfiction Award from *Playboy* Magazine
1982: French Legion of Honor from François Mitterrand

Bibliography

Baldwin, J. (1963). *A Talk to Teachers*. pps.org/cms/lib010/MN01910242/Centricity/Domain/125/baldwin_atalktoteachers_1_2.pd. 10/9/2019.

Baldwin, J. (1968). James Baldwin: How to cool it. Interview. *Esquire magazine*.

Baldwin, J. (1965). James Baldwin debates William F. Buckley. "The American Dream and the American Negro". https://www.rimaregas.com/2015/06/07/transcript-james-baldwin-debates-william-f-buckley-1965-blog42/.

Baldwin, J. (1979). If black English isn't a language, then tell me what is? *New York Times*. https://archive.nytimes.com/www.nytimes.com/books/98/03/29/specials/baldwin-english.html?mcubz=3. 12/7/2019.

Baldwin, J. (2013). *The Price of the Ticket*. http://www.pbs.org/wnet/americanmasters/james-baldwin-about-the-author/59/. 10/9/2019.

Baldwin, J. (2018). *Quoted in*Araya Baker. What James Baldwin's activism can teach schools about social justice. https://educationpost.org/what-james-baldwins-activism-can-teach-schools-about-social-justice/. 11/21/2019.

Dewey, J. (1916). *Democracy and Education: An Introduction to the Philosophy of Education*. New York, NY: Macmillan.

Dunbar, P. L. (1896). *We Wear the Mask. The Complete Poems of Paul Laurence Dunbar.* New York, NY: Dodd, Mead and Company.

Glaude, E. (2019). James Baldwin and the moral crisis of American democracy. Washington University in St. Louis. https://diversity.wustl.edu/events/event/james-baldwin-and-the-moral-crisis-of-american-democracy/. 10/13/2019.

Govedar, D. (2015). The Online Mind. https://onlinemind.org/2015/12/02/the-role-of-the-television-in-the-1960s-us-civil-rights-movement/. 11/21/2019.

The Guardian. (2001). The Henry James of Harlem: James Baldwin's struggles. https://www.theguardian.com/books/2001/sep/14/jamesbaldwin. 10/12/2019.

Gyarkye, L. (2017). James Baldwin and the struggle to bear witness. *The New Republic.* https://newrepublic.com/article/140395/james-baldwin-struggle-bear-witness.

Huber, S. (2019). James Baldwin: Nonfiction of a native son. *ASSAY: A Journal of Nonfiction Studies.* Spring. https://www.assayjournal.com/sonya-huber-8203james-baldwin-nonfiction-of-a-native-son-31.html.

Paley Center for Media. (2019). The Civil Rights movement and television. https://www.paleycenter.org/the-civil-rights-movement-and-television. 11/21/2019.

1

WELCOME TO AMERICA'S SCHOOLHOUSE, JAMES ARTHUR BALDWIN

When any real progress is made, we unlearn and learn a new what we thought we knew before.

Henry David Thoreau, 1837

The price one pays for pursing any profession, or calling, is an intimate knowledge of its ugly side.

James Baldwin, 1961

I am first introduced to James Arthur Baldwin during the 1960s television and Civil Rights movement effort to inform and transform America. I am home early – 1 a.m. – on a Saturday night from partying. It has not been a fun evening and I am not sleepy. Hoping to find a diversion, I turn on *At Random*, hoping that Irv Kupcinet's (Kup) quests for the Show will be entertaining and informative. *At Random* is a Saturday late, late night talk show in Chicago, where I lived, and the conversations can be about most any and everything including the Vietnam War, antiwar activities, Broadway plays and civil rights. It is on this show that I first hear the words of James Baldwin that pique an interest and an excitement that will span a career in education that is, at that time, only getting started.

Out of the normal oratory from national and international intellectuals, political and social wannabes, truth-tellers and social changers on the show, I hear this *voice* and see a little man (5′ 6″) sitting on a sofa, with bug-eyes that remind me of the eyes of actor Bette Davis. He is the only African American sitting among a group of about eight European Americans. He holds a lit cigarette between his fingers and from it a bit of smoke rises up to his face, which he shoos away with his hand. His eyes are staring straight ahead, looking toward Kup, the host, but more into a TV camera behind Kup. He is relaxed and confident; shifting a bit,

2 Welcome to America's Schoolhouse

signaling to all that it is his time to speak. With an awareness and control of the moment, his bugged eyes take in the white faces seated around him and he begins to speak.

Good gracious, does he speak.

He speaks about the complexities of race and the evils and horrors of racism in America in illuminating ways. He addresses problems and issues of racism, myths that perpetuate white supremacy and white privilege directly and with a rhetorical ease that preserves the dignity and humanity of the European Americans in the studio and those watching the show at home. Baldwin's moral imagination of freedom in public and private life for African Americans and European Americans he contends is based upon love.

Baldwin discusses African American experiences, attitudes, actions and disappointments brought on by racism. He holds up the American narrative – democracy, equality, freedom and liberty – and asks, "What about African Americans? What does the failure to democratically address the American narrative do not only to African Americans but also to European Americans?" In his argument is an understanding that racism in America goes deeper than economic, politics and social equality, and although Baldwin speaks knowingly about poverty and the challenges of living (and dying) in decaying urban areas, his words cast a bright light on the darkness and evil in the consciousness and imagination of European Americans as they pretend innocence.

Baldwin speaks to educate – to teach – about historical and contemporary racism, the civil rights struggle, its complexities and controversies, the education of African American students and about how European Americans are fleeing from reality, refusing to embrace the challenge to make America democratic.

Baldwin tells African Americans young and old, they like their ancestors are beautiful and resilient. They daily meet and resist racist social conditions, turn aside from insults and repudiation of their humanity that includes 400 years of police violence, mass incarceration, unequal education, unemployment and/or underpaid employment, and much more. Baldwin points out to European Americans how the harsh realities of African American experiences are turned into labels and stereotypes of African Americans as destructive, academically unprepared, not involved with their children's schooling, and so forth. Baldwin argues, it is these myths that deny or limit African American progress. Baldwin commends African Americans who meet and resist racist social conditions and take action for civil rights.

Baldwin argues: we are responsible for the world in which we live because we are the only ones who can change it. Baldwin is not fiery. His voice didn't have the oratory cadence of Martin Luther King, Jr., nor did he have the presence or the outspokenness of Malcolm X. Baldwin isn't talking up or talking down to the studio guests and the television audience, he is just conversing with a compelling eloquence and honesty about race in the United States of America. Passion and urgency, studio guests or television viewers, may conclude is foundational to his delivery. His words convey the epigraph of Walt Whitman that he includes in *Giovanni's Room*: "I am the man, I suffered, I was there."

The observations Baldwin makes that night are illustrative of comments he makes at Hampshire College in 1984: straightforward, borrowed from *The Fire Next Time* (1962), Baldwin (1984) states:

> It's tragic, in a sense, because the bulk of white Americans treat and think of black people as though we came here yesterday—as though we are very different from and much less valuable than the bulk of white people—and do not realize what they're doing, what they think they're doing to black people, is what they're really doing to themselves.
>
> (p. 68)

"*Whoisthis brother and where does he come from?*" I ask myself. Recalling today, as if it was yesterday or only hours ago, I recall asking aloud again: "*Who is this MAN*, who powerfully and candidly speaks truths, offers honest compelling interpretations about ageless racism, oppression and power, who eloquently points a verbal fist at the white man, and who is openly personal, without concealment? Who is this man who defines 'truth as a devotion to the human being, his (sic) freedom and fulfillment' (Baldwin, 1965a, p. 11)?"

No one is saying it better, not even close – and they still are not: "I've been here 350 years, but you've never seen me … I represent sin, love, death, sex, hell, terror and other things too frightening for you to recognize" (Baldwin, 1962, p. 47). Baldwin's remarks are those that keep people listening, because you hope to hear more truth about race in America. Yes, you are tired of hearing about "race," but you have not heard about it like this. You are grateful that someone says aloud about African Americans, that their experience in America "testifies to nothing less than the perpetual achievement of the impossible".

Digging and Discovering

With a little digging and some luck, I discover, the answer to my "*who*" question. I find Baldwin's picture on the cover of *Time Magazine* (May 17, 1963), with an accompanying article that included the statement "in the U.S. today there is not another writer — white or black — who expresses with such poignancy and abrasiveness the dark realities of the racial ferment in north and south." I purchase his book, *The Fire Next Time*, at a North Michigan bookstore, up by Loyola University where I am attending graduate school. I also discover an article, "There's a bill due that has to be paid" about him in a *Life* magazine, (May 24, 1963) in my barbershop. The multiple page article in *Life*, written by Jane Howard helps me to understand why I don't know about Baldwin. *Life* describes him as "a celebrity overnight": For 10 years his novels sell well, although his first novel, titled at the time *In My Father's House* is rejected by two publishers; his

4 Welcome to America's Schoolhouse

essays are accorded respectful criticism, and Baldwin swam around fairly anonymously in the intellectual fishbowls of New York and Paris. The article in *Life* continues, giving texture and complexity to his rapid rise as a hero, mentor and everyman character.

> Then early this year (1963) a scarring essay he wrote for *The New Yorker* was combined with a gentle letter to one of his nephews and became a bestselling book called *The Fire Next Time*. So intuitively does it dissect the nation's explosive race problem that Baldwin *found himself a celebrity overnight* [my emphasis].

To this day, I find the photo essay in *Life* enlightening because it offers a snapshot-in-time of Baldwin's many interactions with people. Over several pages, there are photos of Baldwin that express a range of moods and emotions: empathy, when holding a little African American boy, who is abandoned by his parents; Baldwin, the teacher, lecturing to students at Xavier University, in New Orleans; Baldwin, the sage: talking with African American children on Dumaine Street; and Baldwin visiting with 7-year-old Emile Armstrong, who integrated his school. Other photos in *Life* include Baldwin in conversation at a party in Manhattan, New York, pointing a finger at actors Geraldine Page and Rip Torn and a picture of a black woman pointing her finger at Baldwin, with a citation that read: "You're not my spokesman, James Baldwin."

There are also excerpts from his writings and speeches in *Life*. Two of the excerpts make me expressively think of the students I am teaching in Chicago and my friends, and our struggle with European Americans to let go of their racist past and stop the willful ignorance:

> I know you didn't own a plantation or rape my grandmother, but I wasn't bought at auction either and you still treat me as if I had been.
>
> *(Baldwin, in Howard, 1963, p. 83)*

> We're taught from grammar school to accept segregation as a way of life. You lied to me because you never intended that I should be free, and I lied to you because I pretended that was all right. Small wonder our children are emotionally bankrupt and drifting toward disaster.
>
> *(Baldwin, in Howard, 1963, p. 84)*

With his "overnight celebrity" status, James Baldwin joins other leading spokespersons for civil rights including: Martin Luther King, Jr., Malcolm X, Roy Wilkins; and while each spokesperson has his own emphasis – Malcolm X, Black Muslim faith and outspokenly challenging mainstream civil rights efforts as not militant enough; Martin Luther King, Jr., civil and economic rights and eliminating racism – James Baldwin's emphasis addresses: African Americans' life in a country built on the

Welcome to America's Schoolhouse **5**

enslavement of Africans and African Americans and argued for close to 400 years European Americans are still desperately clinging to the myth of exceptionalism and supremacy. Baldwin's reverberating observations and relatable anecdotes (e.g., "Why was it necessary for America to invent the nigger?" bring compelling truth and honesty to U.S. race relations).

In novels, essays, speeches and lectures, while Baldwin addresses the social and psychological implications of racism and homophobia on both the oppressed and oppressor, he is nevertheless hopeful. Angry, frustrated, "yes," but Baldwin never drowns in pessimism. Baldwin counteracts racism with love: "transformative love." Baldwin argues transformative love, that is, love as a force can help European Americans to acquire the moral consciousness needed to eliminate their privilege and determination for supremacy.

After that first *At Random* encounter, whenever I would hear Baldwin or discover something he wrote, I would stop to listen or to read in order to learn. Baldwin teaches us African Americans about ourselves. Baldwin speaks bluntly and honestly about identity. The foundation and formation of the identity of African Americans as a people and individually are themes throughout his work. For Baldwin, African Americans' humanity is alive, complex, conscious and sacred and that he will say in many ways many times.

Baldwin describes the struggle and search by African Americans for their identity from childhood, through youth and as adults and he discusses African American identity development in spaces such as schools, the North, the South, and the West, in Europe and Africa and in other places; and importantly Baldwin discusses African American identity in American democracy. Baldwin wants African Americans to appreciate the wonders of their history and resiliency; their skin color and the diversity within their group. He calls out political correctness and African Americans who simplify what it means to be African American.

Baldwin's essays, interviews and books are teaching African Americans and European Americans and any others who will listen about how to help America live up to its democratic promise of equal justice for all. Baldwin, along with W. E. B. DuBois, Carter G. Woodson, Anna Julia Cooper and other black intellectuals and community activists, is my teacher about racism, power, white supremacy and America's need for structural transformation. The night I saw Baldwin on television, I was a Chicago schoolteacher in my fourth year of teaching African American children at Wadsworth Upper Grade Center. I immediately recognized Baldwin's words having meaning and ways to act not only for me, but also for my students, who are anxiously hoping the Civil Rights movement will bring a better life to them, their families and community.

Heightened and Continuous Interest

Baldwin is just as dynamic today as when I first heard him and read his work. My interest in his work continues to grow because of what it says to me as an African

6 Welcome to America's Schoolhouse

American and what it says to European American colleagues I work with and undergraduate and graduate students I teach. In a recent Baldwin class, a European American graduate student stated, "When it comes to racism, James Baldwin is clear about who the culprit is – white citizens who have not confronted their history." Baldwin's honesty and reason inspires African American women and men, girls and boys, and when given a chance, Baldwin's work does the same for European Americans.

Baldwin's work is also inspirational and significant because it is crafted through a lens of *hope* and a lens of *love* of African American students and their teachers. Most aspiring teacher candidates argue they want to teach because they are hopeful about their generation and future generations and they have a *love* of their students. Whereas much of Baldwin's work is grounded in human complexity, complication, economic and racial reality, *hope and love* are wellsprings. In *If Beale Street Could Talk*, the birth of an African American child counters severe racial oppression and gives an African American family including grandparents and other family members reasons to continue striving. Similarly, in "A Talk to Teachers," Baldwin invests "hope" in students who learn the purpose of education and teachers who stand tall during dangerous times and teach African American students the purpose of education.

Editing *James Baldwin and the American Schoolhouse* after receiving my editor's and reviewers' comments that have come at a time when "racial reckoning" is on the minds and hopefully in the hearts of many Americans of different racial groups who are angry and frustrated over the needless lynching of George Floyd, Breonna Taylor and Ahmaud Arbery and others, I am reminded of Baldwin's words at another time of crisis in America – in *The Fire Next Time*:

> Everything now, we must assume, is in our hands; we have no right to assume otherwise. If we – and now I mean the relatively conscious whites and the relatively conscious blacks, who must, like lovers, insist on, or create, the consciousness of the others – do not falter in our duty now, we may be able, handful that we are, to end the racial nightmare, and achieve our country, and change the history of the world. If we do not now dare everything, the fulfilment of that prophecy, re-created from the Bible in song by a slave, is upon us: God gave Noah the rainbow sign, No more water, the fire next time!

The pertinence and power of Baldwin's eloquences inform us that George Floyd's – "I can't breathe … I can't move … Momma! Momma! … Please, sir. Please" – America, is James Baldwin's America; an America he loves, but complains of its racism. In his last speech at U.C. Berkeley in 1979 Baldwin made a statement to the audience that speaks to our moment of racial and COVID-19 crises today: "When you try to slaughter a people and leave them with nothing to lose, you create somebody with nothing to lose. If I ain't got nothing to lose, what you gonna do to me?" Powerfully prophetic and literally real – on May 25, 2020, a white police officer in Minneapolis is captured on video using his knee to pin George Floyd, a 46-year-old Black American man, to the ground for more than eight minutes as Floyd dies uttering: "I can't breathe anymore" more than 20 times along with calls to his mother. Days later, carrying signs "I can't breathe" and many wearing facial covering, thousands of protesters demonstrated in marches across the country ... starting, perhaps, the fire that Jimmy foretold.

Not of a small matter, to you the reader, Baldwin while blunt, candid and commanding is not harsh or authoritative. Toni Morrison describes Baldwin's communication with others best when she recalls upon his death:

> I never heard a single command from you, yet the demands you made on me, the challenges you issued to me, were nevertheless unmistakable, even if unenforced: that I work and think at the top of my form, that I stand on moral ground but know that ground must be shored up by mercy, that "the world is before [me] and [I] need not take it or leave it as it was when [I] came in."

Over the past decade, I am discovering Baldwin's speeches, articles and novels increasingly on syllabi in classes in colleges of education. When Baldwin's name comes up in conversations among teacher educators and others in the School of Education, it is greeted with: "Which of his works are you using, and how?" and, "Are the European American teacher candidates able to deal with his blunt honesty?" In other words, professors of education are inquiring about how to include Baldwin, because they are learning if they wish to go to the historical and social core of the African American, an educator who is African American at a predominately European American research-one university, who teaches courses in the School of Education, I find Baldwin's exploration and interrogation of race in education in both an in-school and out-of-school context (e.g., "A Talk to Teachers," "Take This Hammer") as relevant from an ideological, pedagogical and pedagogical content knowledge perspective today as the day they were published. Today, as decades and centuries ago, schools do not offer curriculum nor instruction to teach African American students the purpose of education as it would equally benefit the student and society, nor do they provide their European American students with culturally relevant ways, and ways that are ideologically respectful of African American students. Baldwin's articles and videos therefore go a long away to help undergraduate and graduate students to better understand race and education in America, yesterday, today, into tomorrow. It is for that reason, that I argue James Baldwin's work is needed in America's houses of education. Below I welcome Jimmy into colleges of education. He next talks to European American teachers and this discussion is followed by his discussion with African American teachers.

Welcome to Where Teachers Learn to Teach, Jimmy

> The paradox of education is precisely this – that as one begins to become conscious one begins to examine the society in which he is being educated.
>
> *James Baldwin, 1963a*

The position of *James Baldwin and the American Schoolhouse* is that James Baldwin's works (e.g., essays, speeches and books) are in need in colleges or schools of education as much, if not more than in colleges of humanities. Baldwin's writings and ideas are needed more – or equally as much – in the colleges of education where teachers are educated, professors of education prepared and in middle and high school classrooms where teachers teach than in the colleges of humanity, where academics discuss, compare and critique literature, because Baldwin does an outstanding job of making clear the purpose of education for African American children and all children. For Baldwin, education is not about making money or climbing the status ladder. Baldwin (1963a) contends,

> the purpose of education is to create in a person the ability to look at the world for himself, to make his own decisions, to say to himself this is black or this is white, to decide for himself whether there is a God in heaven or not. To ask questions of the universe, and then learn to live with those questions is the way he achieves his own identity.
>
> *(p. 2)*

Baldwin argues education is to make the world a more humane place and education is to help conquer the confusion within oneself. Baldwin is needed in colleges of education because in his writings, he does not pass along information as a conduit passes along an electrical current, or a history text passes along battles, generals and dates. In his writing, Baldwin examines attitudes, goes beneath the surface to tap the source (Baldwin, 1984 p. 2). Baldwin argues, to become educated it is about developing a conscience and assuming the responsibility of changing society.

Colleges of education reading and discussing Baldwin's essays and other of his works will move closer to having their graduates graduate with an understanding of what is required to acquire the ability to make one's own decision. Teacher candidates will receive their teacher's license understanding the paradox that confronts them as teachers; "that the whole process of education occurs within a social framework and is designed to perpetuate the aims of society" and that as they begin to become conscious they begin to examine the society in which they are being educated.

Colleges of education reading and discussing Baldwin's essays will discover his writings bring attention to the oppressor and the oppressed and in his writings he celebrates and rejoices in the humanity of each and every person. Baldwin doesn't promote conflict and is not trapped in the bitterness found in African American and European American relationships. Baldwin (1955) argues "this bitterness is folly" (p. 1) and to acquiesce to this bitterness is to acquiesce to one's own destruction. Instead, Baldwin argues it is important to hold on to things that matter

Colleges of education reading and discussing Baldwin's essays, especially those that deal with his student–teacher relationship with Orilla Miller (whom he called Bill), a European American woman who grew up on an Illinois farm and attended Antioch College, will receive an answer to the question asked by many European American teacher candidates: "Can I successfully teach Students of Color, particularly African American students; and especially African American male students?" Also, reading Baldwin's essays will help teacher candidates of color and progressive European American teacher candidates to understand that the teacher education curriculum is not dedicated to preparing them mainly for schools who are concerned with testing, accountability and deportment.

Colleges of education reading and discussing Baldwin's essays will learn that the African American students, that they perceive as a problem to their teacher candidates – the alleged Black problem – is not, in fact, an African American problem, but a European American problem. Reading Baldwin informs European American teacher candidates, that not only did their ancestors create the conditions for making being African American problematic, but also "a complex syndrome of deprivation, exploitation, fear and guilt has made racist European Americans a problem to themselves and to society" (Jones, 1966).

Colleges of education reading and discussing Baldwin's essays will give undergraduate teacher candidates and graduate students a way to rethink the content they learned in their history and literature classes, and give them reasons for doing so, especially when teaching students of color. Baldwin's essay "Stranger in the Village," – a case in point – makes the argument that the most illiterate person of European heritage, has a relationship with "Dante, Shakespeare, Michelangelo, Aeschylus, Da Vinci, Rembrandt, and Racine; the cathedral at Chartres" that he and others non-European of African heritage, including African Americans do not have. Furthermore, people of color are not beating up on themselves for not having the relationship. Baldwin explains in "Stranger in the Village" to European American teacher candidates, why, as brilliant as Dante, Shakespeare and others, and the best of the best European literary and artistic work is, African American students don't fall all over themselves about it. Baldwin, as Bill Miller learned when he was a youth, is more interested in his own culture and in a 1964 interview Baldwin argues "I can't accept Western values because they don't accept me" (Baldwin 1964, p. 1).

Colleges of education reading and discussing Baldwin will be informed that one of the reason African American students have difficulty accepting school policy and practices is because schools are constructed on Western European values that don't accept them. Baldwin argues an African Americans born in the U.S. spends a great deal of time trying to be accepted, trying to find a way to

10 Welcome to America's Schoolhouse

operate within a culture and not to be made to suffer so much by it, but nothing they do works. No matter how many showers they take, no matter what they do, these Western values absolutely resist and reject you. So that, inevitably, you turn away from them or you re-examine them.

Baldwin's essays and speeches will place students in colleges of education face to face with African American students' racial reality. They discuss problems and issues African Americans students and their families confront each school day: the absence of African Americans in curriculum, the ostracizing of African American students, the difficulty of European American teachers teaching African American students and the failure of American democracy to accept African American people. Baldwin explains in a prose European Americans don't turn away from how African American people – men, women, youth and children – are personally and collectively denigrated, excluded from ordinary American life in schools, at work, seeking employment and searching for food and shelter. Simply put, Baldwin makes clear through historical and contemporary examples how and why African Americans are excluded from the American dream and the opportunity to achieve a middle-class life; and are denied resources necessary to become a part of mainstream institutions.

Reading Baldwin lets teacher candidates know they should be bluntly honest with African American students. Baldwin (1963a) told New York teachers that they should let African American students know "that those streets, those houses, those dangers, those agonies by which they are surrounded, are criminal" [and that] "these things are the results of a criminal conspiracy to destroy them" (p. 2). That if an individual African American student "intends to get to be a man or woman, they must at once decide that they are stronger than this conspiracy and that they must never make peace with it" (p. 2). That "there are currently very few standards in this country which are worth a man's respect" [and] "it is up to them to begin to change these standards for the sake of the life and the health of the country" (p. 3).

Reading Baldwin tells teacher candidates that the study of history is necessary and honest presentations of history are in need. Future teachers of African American students need to know what African American students learn about the same time they are learning to eat at the kitchen table without assistance,

> that slavery was not an accident, it was not an act of God, it was not done by well-meaning people muddling into something which they didn't understand. It was a deliberate policy hammered into place in order to make money from black flesh.
>
> *(Baldwin, 1963a, p. 2)*

Colleges of education studying and discussing Baldwin will be informed about the progress, or lack thereof, U.S. institutions including schools have made against racism over the past 75 years. Stereotypes (e.g., the absence of African American fathers, overwhelmed mothers and African Americans as a people who refuse to grit it out) about African Americans that teacher candidates arrive on campus believing are debunked with logic and reason. Similarly, African American families are discussed in context to themes that crisscross in Baldwin's writing and speeches: rampant poverty in urban communities, police violence toward African American youth, inferior education of African American students, voter suppression, poor housing and living conditions, minimal respect of African American people; and the power teachers have to make a difference.

Baldwin's essays are a mirror for European American educators. They ask European American teachers to look at themselves; to shine a bright light in the dark corners of their minds. "Whatever white people do not know about Negroes reveals, precisely and inexorably, what they do not know about themselves" (Baldwin, 1962b, p. 4). Baldwin argues implicitly and explicitly that European American teachers should know the true history of America, and the role of African Americans in that history. They should have an imagination powerful and fair enough to see African American students successfully fulfilling their dreams and learning to dream dreams they have never dreamt before. Dreams can and should include much, much more than excelling in sports and entertainment. COVID-19 uncovered numerous people of color serving as doctors, nurses and teachers, contributing to society in important ways.

Baldwin's essays have a knowledge of life in and out of school walls that help teachers to develop an understanding of why African American students select the actions they do and the norms they choose to adhere to. In simple words, Baldwin's essays help African American students to know who they are, what they are and that there are no roles that they cannot and should not aspire to.

Baldwin brings to teachers the realization that a lesson designed to meet state standards does not have to be in opposition to lessons that are culturally relevant to African American students. *The Odyssey*, Odysseus' personal goals, both long-term and short-term can be related to African American students' goals to escape and/or make better their poor, crowded and dangerous conditions. Baldwin explains, "I would try to teach them—I would try to make them know, that those streets, those houses, those dangers, those agonies by which they are surrounded, are criminal" (Baldwin, 1963 p. 5).

On the other hand, Sonya Huber (2019) contends, Baldwin is not in the classroom because teachers are more interested in dealing with practicality and ease, than engaging in conflict, in spaces where conflict should be confronted and examined. About such lack of action, Huber (2019) quotes Baldwin: "the sum of these individual abdications menaces life all over the world" (p. 1). Huber argues that, in high schools, the opportunities to read Baldwin are not good because national curriculum reform doesn't and hasn't included Baldwin and because teaching "an essay outside a pre-vetted anthology can be dicey because teachers are under intense scrutiny." Huber (2019) posits:

12 Welcome to America's Schoolhouse

> Rather than seeing urban America as beset with a host of challenges described so eloquently by Baldwin himself, our entire debate about race, segregation, and poverty has been reduced to the code phrase "failing schools." The curriculum in many of these schools are limited by standardized test, and many teachers feel they can't teach whole books by selected authors because there simply isn't time.
>
> *(p. 2)*

James Baldwin and the American Schoolhouse agrees with Huber, and contends that Baldwin is not included in the curriculum because teacher educators and educators have not *studied* Baldwin; they have not engaged with his words and connected his work to their work. Teachers have not been tasked to study Baldwin, for to engage in such a task is to commit to an equal and equitable education for African American students thereby pushing back on willful ignorance and promoting African Americans' ability to lead, govern and achieve

Of most importance to teaching African American students, Baldwin argues, is honesty, sincere regard and a belief in their ability to learn. Baldwin (1955) posits:

> When I was around nine or ten I wrote a play which was directed by a young white schoolteacher, a woman, who then took an interest in me, and gave me books to read, and, in order to corroborate my theatrical bent, decided to take me to see what she somewhat tactlessly referred to as "real" plays.
>
> *(p. 67)*

Ultimately, as a result of Baldwin's interaction with an European American teacher, he believes European American teachers can teach African American students.

Today, the activism of organizations such as Black Lives Matter, and the efforts of protestors that developed out of the lynching of George Floyd continues to be directed toward many of the same problems and issues and, at almost the same level of severity that Baldwin wrote and spoke. Reading Baldwin, teacher candidates and graduate students will learn about the history of white supremacy from someone who experienced its brutality, studied it, debated about it and writes about it; and how it continues to affect African American children today. You discover as Erin Overbey (2019), archive editor of *The New Yorker* observes, that "Baldwin's work is notable for its insistence that we resist the mythology of our history and openly face the stories and factual accounts that make us uncomfortable" (p. 8).

Baldwin points out that African American children continue to be treated unjustly in school and viewed as the *problem*, a problem created in his terms by his European American "countrymen." Though Baldwin is not a teacher in the traditional sense, Baldwin is a teacher, especially of African American children, because his work teaches that although schools are places where they spend much of their time, they are not sites of racial healing but are a microcosm of the racist world in which they live. Baldwin explains how and why America is an unequal society and remains an unequal society by design and willfulness. Baldwin argues that American racism is expansive and goes deeper than political, social and economic inequalities outlined in civil right efforts and congressional rollbacks. The problem of racism, Baldwin contends, is grounded deep in American consciousness and imagination. Money, Baldwin argues, is not adequate to explain the deeds of Europeans and European Americans during the time of slavery and during the years of segregation and today as both racial micro and macroaggressions take place.

Baldwin learns about systems of power (e.g., police power, parental power and governmental power) early in life and he wants African American students to know about "power"; about how it inheres and manifests in social conditions (e.g., poverty, segregation) rather than in discrete identity categories. Baldwin (1962b) wants African American students to know that "The *power* of the white world is threatened whenever a black man refuses to accept the white world's definitions" and "The relationship of morality and power is a very subtle one. Because ultimately power without morality is no longer power" (p. 7). Discussion of power flows throughout Baldwin's work as he chronicled and advocated for the aims of the Civil Rights movement, protested the Vietnam War and the Algerian War through an anticolonial lens and discusses life in America and Europe for a gay African American man.

Baldwin thinks deeply about African American children and their education, and he gives serious attention to teachers of African American students. These thoughts have high currency value today. Baldwin argues that teachers of African American students must reject the false pretense of being apolitical servants of the system, but rather, be professional and truthful about the system in which they live and work. That it is designed to teach European American students that they are achievers, leaders, in other words they are superior and to teach African American students they are underachievers, can't lead, in other words they are losers. Rigid adherence to "teaching to the test" is not in the best interest of children in general and is of low interest to African American students because the curriculum taught is predominately Eurocentric, that is, it miseducates African American students. Baldwin urges teachers of African American children to confront their teaching selves, school policies, curriculum and practices that shape – "mis educate" (Woodson, 1933) – African American students' lives (Smith, 2017). Also, Baldwin (1963) charges teachers to teach African American children that

> America belongs to them as much as anybody else and that they do not have to be bound by the expediencies of any given administration, any given policy, any given morality, that [they have] the right to question and examine everything.

> *(p. 27)*

14 Welcome to America's Schoolhouse

Baldwin tells teachers of African American children that their teaching responsibility is about empowerment and revolution.

James Baldwin and the American Schoolhouse contends that teachers would be smart to accept Baldwin as an instructional coach when teaching African American children. Baldwin's suggestions to teachers about teaching is consistent to his charge to artists: to have integrity, be responsible, bear witness (e.g., give evidence/testify), demonstrate your respect and appreciation of humanity. To Baldwin, the artist's struggle for integrity is universal, daily, and a metaphor for the struggle of all people to become human beings. This request to artists coincides with the request Baldwin made to teachers of African American students: to examine their conscience and engage in struggle for their own professional integrity and to validate their craft through antiracist teaching.

James Baldwin and the American Schoolhouse argues, Baldwin is *desperately* needed throughout colleges of education (e.g., teacher education programs, superintendent and principal licensing programs, education policy programs, and so forth) and in middle and high schools because Baldwin connects to educators and students by speaking truth, delivering honest social criticism about race and democracy in America, and pragmatically pointing out that when it comes to race and self, no one can do for you what only you can do. Baldwin is a must in colleges of education because he addresses education/school "miseducation" for African American students from an African American's perspective –oppression as the day-to-day African American life – and he discusses African American students' consciousness and perceptions of in school and out of school reality. Baldwin's essays challenge the stereotypical racialized box in which schools place African American students. They present African American family life grounded in tradition, values, rituals and relationships; they argued against African American student family life absent of tradition and sensibility; and they tell stories from African American history and culture – not told in teacher education programs. Also, Baldwin brings into the schooling of African American children ideas, concepts, possibilities that were not there before: an honest telling of struggles, suffering, hopes, achievements; discussions of the aspirations and dreams of African American people and African American students. In addition, Baldwin has the unique ability to explain – make real – the complexities and complication of African American life and an African American person's responsibility and participation in his/her successes or failures. Finally, Baldwin's essays and speeches discuss how the effect of race/racism enters the *soul* of African American students, becomes attached and difficult to dislodge; yet, the same essays are filled with comfort, courage and suggestions for how to resist racism and fight back.

Jimmy's Words to European American Teachers

Education is indoctrination if you're white – subjugation if you're black.
James Baldwin, 1972

From all that I have read and from all of the videos I have reviewed, Jimmy Baldwin enters spaces to talk to European American teachers in order to do his very best to help them successfully teach African American students. For 45–60 minutes, perhaps longer, Jimmy is there to give 110% percent of himself. He is not there, for the speaking fee, or to promote his latest publication; but because of his high regard for African American and European American humanity.

Out of respect to his audience's humanity and his love of America, Baldwin is also bluntly honest with European American teachers. Baldwin tells European American teachers that whiteness is a dangerous concept – it's not about skin color, and not even about race, but about willful blindness, ignorance and innocence to justify and keep in place white supremacy. Whiteness is about using moral rhetoric to maintain position atop social hierarchies (e.g. using the Bible to justify the dehumanizing treatment of enslaved people, it – "whiteness" – is a deficit discourse to teach down to African American students). Baldwin wants European American teachers of African American children to know that the African American students they teach will not be the "Negro" that white supremacists imagine and a racist school system encourages through policy and practice; a person incapable of love and dignity and short on brains and humanity. Instead, Baldwin wants European American teachers to look closely and deeply into themselves and ask why they treat African American students differently than European American students. Baldwin is direct and specific, the way your grandmothers fought for women's rights. Gloria Steinem (1971) would say a few years later:

> The first problem for all of us, men and women, *is not to learn, but to unlearn* [author's emphasis]. We are filled with the popular wisdom of several centuries just past, and we are terrified to give it up. Patriotism means obedience, age means wisdom, woman means submission, black means inferior: these are pre conceptions imbedded so deeply in our thinking that we honestly may not know that they are there.
>
> *(p. 1)*

Baldwin's writing and speeches are accessible to all audiences and he is helpful to any and all who enter and do any work in colleges of education, a predominately white institution –all encompassing. Baldwin is candid and direct when speaking to a European American audience, for he has personally seen and felt the lash of white supremacy and lived under the conditions of white oppression. Nevertheless, his love of America motivates him to speak to European Americans in a humble and respectful manner with the hope of helping them gain a critical consciousness of love and justice for all people.

Baldwin, European American teachers should know, is not vindictive; his purpose in not to scold but to enlighten. Baldwin advocates that European Americans must be accepted with love – a love that encompasses "a state of being or a state of grace" across the color line (Harris 2014, p. 56). Baldwin, (1962a) in

16 Welcome to America's Schoolhouse

a letter to his 14-year-old nephew, offers him a way to consider European American teachers at his school. Baldwin (1962a) tells his nephew, "you must accept them, and I mean that very seriously. You must accept them and accept them with love" (p. 1). Baldwin, addressing race relations like Martin Luther King, Jr., advocates "love" over "hate." King (1957) states in "Loving Your Enemies": "Darkness cannot drive out darkness; only light can do that. Hate cannot drive out hate: only love can do that. I have decided to stick to love. Hate is too great a burden to bear" (p. 3). The "love" that Baldwin is addressing, however, is not a love of passion or sentiment. Instead, Baldwin is discussing love as a "transformative project," dedicated to helping European Americans become free from the "trap" of history, free from their self-delusion of supremacy and free from their self-basing need for the "negro" (Maguire, 2018). Lina Martin Alcoff (1998) offers an example of a "transformative project" in the article "What Should White People Do?" Drawing on the movie *Dances with Wolves*, Alcoff (1998) explains:

> In the movie *Dances with Wolves* (1991), Kevin Costner plays a white Union soldier stationed on the Indian frontier who undergoes a political transformation. He comes to realize that the native peoples his militia intends to kill are not the uncivilized heathens they were portrayed to be, and in fact have a rich civilization in many ways superior to his. Thus, he realizes that he is fighting on the wrong side. The remainder of the movie chronicles his struggle to figure out what this realization means *for him*.
>
> *(p. 2)*

Next, Alcoff (1998) posits: "I believe that this narrative represents a collective, semiconscious undercurrent of psychic and political struggle occurring now in the United States among significant numbers of white Anglos" (p. 1). It is the "psychic and political struggle" – "transformative project" – that Baldwin identifies and that Alcoff recognizes, in which European American people must engage. However, as Baldwin discusses and Alcoff (1998) reports, the transformation project for European Americans is challenging. Efforts to implement antiracism are often flawed, filled with white supremacist pretensions, refusal to let go of privilege and colonizer's myths and a deep dive into white fragility (Di Angelo, 2011). Thus, as Baldwin (1963a) argues in *The Fire Next Time*, white people should disconnect from whiteness so they can join in the "suffering and dancing" around them.

Below I continue discussing how studying James Baldwin can be valuable to European American teachers. In doing so, first I tell European American teachers to get ready for "truth and bluntness" about whiteness; next I discuss Orilla Miller – "Bill," Baldwin's European American teacher – and her life-long impact on him; interracial solidarity, follows and a discussion of the N-word concludes the section.

"Layer by Layer" with Cool Logic

European American teachers reading Baldwin's novels, plays and essays will be taken by the way he explores the psychological and political implications of racism on both African American and European American people and the way he, according to Orde Coombs (1976) removes "layer by layer, the hardened skin with which Americans shield themselves from their country" (p. 1). European American teacher candidates who have grown up in the era of Black Lives Matter, the death of George Floyd, and are witness to the racial reckoning movement but who continue to struggle with questions of race and African American children will come to appreciate Baldwin's essays as they offer honesty, realism, and deep understanding to questions of black and white humanity that textbooks don't cover, most teacher education programs don't teach, the country has yet to face and news accounts don't explore in depth. European American teacher candidates who are searching for or trying to establish their positionality as they hear voices advocating for social justice and voices advocating to Keep America Great will find Baldwin explains the results from both choices.

Baldwin told Jane Howard (1963) of *Life* magazine "His role is to make you realize the doom and glory of knowing who you are and what you are". Understanding of self and developing personal identity, European American teacher candidates will by reading Baldwin, discover is of utmost importance in order to have a fulfilling life and a satisfying professional career. Bigsby (1969) argues,

> Baldwin's central theme to European American teachers is to accept reality as a necessary foundation for individual identity and as a logical prerequisite for the kind of saving love in which he places his whole faith. For some, this reality is one's racial or sexual nature, for others it is the ineluctable fact of death.
>
> *(p. 10)*

David Levin (1964) writing about Baldwin's efforts to reach out to European Americans, argues:

> for "white" Americans, the eloquent, indignant prophet of an oppressed people, a voice speaking … in an all but desperate, final effort to bring us out of what he calls our innocence before it is (if it is not already) too late.
>
> *(Quoted in McWilliams, 2017, p. 250)*

Levin continues,

> This voice calls us to our immediate duty for the sake of our own humanity as well as our own safety. It demands that we stop regarding African Americans as an abstraction, an invisible person, and that we begin to recognize each African American in his/her "full weight and complexity" as a human being;

18 Welcome to America's Schoolhouse

that we face the horrible reality of our past and present treatment of African Americans—a reality we do not know and do not want to know.

(McWilliams, 2017 p. 251)

Baldwin, argues the *Poetry Foundation* (2019), explains European Americans to themselves and at the same time voices protest against African Americans' role in a socially unjust society. And, Baldwin, as Cunningham (2015) argues, is the earnest pragmatic exceptionalist, who contends

If we—and now I mean the relatively conscious whites and the relatively conscious blacks, who must, like lovers insist on, or create, the consciousness of the other—do not falter in our duty now, we may be able, handful that we are, to end the racial nightmare, and achieve our country, and change the history of the world.

(Baldwin, 1963a, p.105)

Baldwin's discussion of race in varying formats and settings – books, movies, essays, employment and elected offices – can help European American teachers discover that historically, and pretty much today within the dominant society, there is very little information available that addresses the silence of racism other than somebody's – usually a government official – declaration: "We need to have a conversation on race." Much, much more is needed than a "conversation" that is never began with enough determination to see it resulting in substantive change. As we – American society – wait for the conversation on race to take place. Racism, Baldwin argues, continues to poison the mind causing a person to become a monster. Baldwin (1955) posits:

It is only now beginning to be borne in on us — very faintly, it must be admitted, very slowly, and very much against our will — that this [racist] vision of the world is dangerously inaccurate, and perfectly useless. For it protects our moral high-mindedness at the terrible expense of weakening our grasp of reality. People who shut their eyes to reality simply invite their own destruction, and anyone who insists on remaining in a state of innocence long after that innocence is dead turns himself into a monster.

(pp. 174–175)

European American teachers reading Baldwin should be aware, as Williams (1987) argues, that Baldwin drops "truth so it explodes like ripe fruit being thrown against a concrete sidewalk" (p. 2).

Channeling Bill: Orilla Miller

Baldwin is an excellent resource to European American teachers because he addresses teachers as educated people who can create social change through their power in the classroom, and he respects the effects a non-racist caring, European American teacher can have on African American students. Baldwin's belief is based upon his relationship with Orilla Miller (whom he referred to as Bill), a teacher who accepts and appreciates his humanity when he is a young student at P. S. 124 and who lays the foundation for his belief in the power of art and political action (Leeming, 2007). Baldwin describes Bill as "a young white school teacher, a beautiful woman, very important to me" who "I loved … absolutely, with a child love" (Leeming, 1994, p. 14).

Arguably, when Baldwin writes or speaks to European American teachers of African American students, it is with thoughts of Bill, about whom he states: "It is certainly partly because of her, who arrived in my terrifying life so soon that I never really managed to hate white people" (Baldwin, 1976, p. 13). Baldwin validates for Bill her belief in the humanity of people as people, especially people who are poor and oppressed. Bill validates for Baldwin that there are good European American people and such people, Baldwin learns, can facilitate opportunity for African American students' intellectual potential to grow. David Leeming (1994), Baldwin's biographer, notes, "Baldwin would often say that his association with Bill Miller gave intellectual support to his instinctive resistance to the oppression he already knew firsthand" (p. 16). Baldwin and Bill would discuss books by Dickens, attend movies and plays, and discuss national and international politics. Leeming (1994) contends that from Bill, her husband, Evan, and her sister, Henrietta, Baldwin begins to suspect that "white people did not act as they did because they were white, but for some other reason" (p. 17). What Baldwin learns from Bill and Evan Miller, and from his experiences growing up in Harlem along with traveling abroad is why *James Baldwin and the American Schoolhouse* believes he can forthrightly tell teachers about their responsibility and duty as teachers of African American students.

Baldwin explains to European American teacher educators and teachers that it is the parent's duty to civilize the child and the teacher's duty to create in the student the ability to make good decisions, ask critical questions, live with those questions, and from that achieve one's identity. Baldwin contends the paradox of education is that as African American children become conscious, they begin to examine the society in which they are being educated. Baldwin and Bill engaged in discussions about the rise of Nazism, police brutality in Harlem, poverty, and other local, national and international issues. Today's teachers reading about Baldwin and Bill will take away that Bill visited Baldwin's home, met his parents and siblings, and got to know him as a person. Baldwin's appeal to teachers of African American students has as much relevance today as when he first made it: to teach truth and not the sugar-coated version of American history, understand their present-day life realities and explain to African American children the "criminal conspiracy" devised by systemic racism to keep them in a "sunken" place.

Baldwin wants public school teachers in Harlem to explain to students how systematic racism traps them in the void between uptown and downtown New

20 Welcome to America's Schoolhouse

York, causing them to have to take the A train downtown in order to escape poverty for a few hours, and observe in real time the difference between privilege and poverty. Baldwin implores teachers to encourage African American students to develop a sense of ownership of action, to realize that each one should be his/her own self and to understand that they do not have to listen and blindly obey unjust administrative policies and procedures. Bill models this behavior for Baldwin and shows him she is someone he can trust. Additionally, Bill models for European American teachers that they, too do not need to obey, implement and enforce unjust administrative policies and practices that harm African American children. Leeming (1994) explains how Bill's trust and agency is demonstrated when she stands up to a hostile police officer: "There was supposed to be ice cream handed out at a police station, but the police were not expecting 'colored kids.' Baldwin, Leeming says, proudly tells the story as follows:

> I don't remember anything Bill said. I just remember her face as she stared at the cop, clearing intending to stand there until the ice cream all over the world melted or until the earth's surface froze, and she got us our ice cream, saying, "Thank You!" I remembered as we left.
>
> *(Leeming, 1994, p. 17)*

One can argue that Bill's actions on behalf of Baldwin and his fellow African American classmates is simply a teacher standing up for her class, assuring that a promise made by a governmental institution is kept for African American children the same as for European American children. Of significance is that Baldwin long remembers someone – a European American teacher – who stands up for him.

Teachers, Baldwin contends, must foster in African American students qualities that help them gain confidence as educated people and to believe in their agency to commence positive societal change. Baldwin urges teachers to use education as a weapon against ignorance in order to incite change in society. Baldwin contends he had qualities, such as the importance of becoming educated ingrained in him along with the importance of fostering societal change during his time with Bill. Leeming (1994), writing about Bill and Baldwin's movie-going time, describes how *A Tale of Two Cities* is among their favorite. Baldwin explains to Leeming that when he and Bill would go to see the film, she (Bill) wants him to discover in the movie "something of the inevitable human ferment which explodes into what is called a revolution" (p. 18). However, Baldwin's critical insight into the film goes deeper than discovering how revolutions evolve; instead, the film leads him to wonder where the black proletariats are, not in the French Revolution, but in the American Revolution? Baldwin knows African Americans have been in the country since the 16th century. Therefore, why are they erased, except for Crispus Attucks, a man of African and Native American descent and the first person killed in the Boston Massacre? Where are other African Americans? For there to be only one African American is strange.

Baldwin wants Harlem teachers to teach African American students that during the Revolutionary War, both freed and enslaved African Americans served as soldiers, spies, cooks, gunners and sailors. In other words, African American men and women do what European American men and women do, fighting in the war against England, and often at the resistance of some European American people who rebel against their service. According to Edward Ayres (n.d.), "In 1774 Abigail Adams wrote, "it always appeared a most iniquitous scheme to me to fight ourselves for what we are daily robbing and plundering from those who have as good a right to freedom as we have" (p. 1). Abigail Adams' characterization of an "iniquitous scheme" is well-stated and describes the insidiousness and longevity of American racism. In addition, Adams' statement brings to mind U.S. soldiers of color, since the Civil War up through current battles today, being denied the rights the Revolutionary War was fought over: freedom and liberty.

Baldwin is important for European American teachers because he addresses their internalized white superiority, their lack of racial accountability and many (if not most) of the contradictions they face in schools teaching African American students, and he suggests how they can accept their responsibility of teaching African American students. Baldwin, advocates of the white fragility thesis will learn, takes European American teachers to the historical depth of and early beginning of white supremacy, a necessary journey to put white supremacy away for good. Baldwin (1962b) tell his European American readership:

America became white—the people who, as they claim, "settled" the country became white—because of the necessity of denying the Black presence and justifying the Black subjugation. No community can be based on such a principle—or, in other words, no community can be established on so genocidal a lie. White men—from Norway, for example, where they were Norwegians—became white: by slaughtering the cattle, poisoning the wells, torching the houses, massacring Native Americans, raping Black women.

Baldwin's remarks to today's European American teachers, especially those who are engaging in "white fragility" discourse, is that eliminating racism requires much more than "consciousness raising" or having more "racial stamina." "White Fragility," as Roediger (2018) observes at best provides evidence that America is mired in racism; it does not "imagine anything redemptive about whiteness" (p. 1) nor does it hope for so-called white people to become "less white" (p. 2). Baldwin explains to today's European American teachers why the school's athletic department are either relieved or embittered by the presence of an African American male youth as quarterback of the football team or when more than one African American female is on the cheer squad at a multiracial high school or college. Baldwin explains the struggle against white superiority by African American youth (and their families) to occupy status positions and argues that many European Americans continue to only want to see European American youth in those positions. Baldwin (1984) states:

22 Welcome to America's Schoolhouse

I do not know if they remember how long and hard they fought to keep him or her off it. I know that they do not dare have any notion of the price Black people (mothers and fathers) paid and pay. They do not want to know the meaning, or face the shame, of what they compelled—out of what they took as the necessity of being white—Joe Louis or Jackie Robinson or Cassius Clay (aka Muhammad Ali). I know that they, themselves, would not have liked to pay it.

(p. 92)

Juan Williams (December 2, 1987) writing in *The Washington Post* the day after Baldwin's death argues: "White people reading Baldwin sensed his truth about the lives of black people and the sins of a racist nation" (p. 1). "His accuracy was the key," Williams asserts: "In his works, the reader could resonate to the sounds of the street corner, as drawn by Baldwin, could feel the anger of black Americans so long denied a role in American life as Baldwin wrote about that anger" (p. 2). Baldwin offers European American teachers artifacts of historical and contemporary origins to understand racism in its different forms and formats. Reading Baldwin, for example, can help European American teachers to understand if they are born and bred in racial segregation and argue they have not lost anything of value, although the U.S. Constitution starts with: "We the people"; they are more than likely internalizing white superiority. Baldwin, as Therman B. O'Daniel (1977) contends, is a writer who is not afraid to search into the dark corners of white America's social consciences and to force out into public view the hidden, sordid skeletons of American society.

Interracial Solidarity

Most students in colleges of education and in America teaching corps are European American. According to Myers (2016), "On average, 75 out of 100 full-time faculty members at four-year colleges are white. Five are African American and even fewer are Hispanic". According to Loewus (2017), public school teachers tend to be white, female, 42 years of age and have 14 years of teaching experience.

Baldwin is helpful for European American teacher educators and teachers because, as Beard (2016) and others note, Baldwin speaks to European Americans in powerful ways that are important in the present time. Baldwin's message to European American teacher educators and teachers of African American children is that white racial identity forecloses interracial solidarity (Hooker, 2009, quoted in Beard, 2016, p. 8). White identity is not invisible, it is visible, although European Americans have not been forced or required – until recently – to think about their identity.

Colleges of education, perhaps more so than other colleges on a university campus, should reflect racial diversity and interracial solidarity because teacher candidates are being prepared to teach in a multicultural United States and they are being prepared to prepare the future leaders of America's democratic project. It is a myth to pretend that colleges of education, with predominately European American faculties who have received little, if any, formal multicultural education, who themselves struggle with interracial solidarity, and who are teaching a predominately Eurocentric curriculum and methods courses that characterize African American students as at-risk or absent of culture, can prepare teacher candidates to teach African American students. White racial identity and a lack of engagement in interracial solidarity by faculty at most colleges of education makes it extremely difficult for them to prepare European American teacher candidates to teach African American students.

Baldwin, colleges of education will discover, is a strong believer in interracial solidarity. He is forever hopeful that Africans Americans and European Americans will figure out how to collectively work for the well-being of America. Baldwin argues the future of America depends on interracial solidarity. Baldwin's ideas on racial solidarity called for equal respect between African Americans and European Americans. "Equal respect," according to Baldwin demands that European American teachers cast aside false notions that African American students are "less than," that they or their families are a "problem," or that colleges of education and European American teachers are saving African American students. Interracial solidarity and capitalizing on racial diversity, from a Baldwinian perspective, calls for "boundness" – the idea that people's lives are co-constituted, and their freedom (and education to maintain freedom) are bound together across racial lines. Beard (2016) argues that, Baldwin uses boundness as a political strategy to resist historical amnesia and to compel European Americans to see their own responsibility for ending racism.

In speaking to European Americans on the topic of racism, Baldwin is straightforward and honest. Baldwin told Dick Cavett, a late-night television host: "I don't know what most white people in this country feel, I can only conclude what they feel from the state of their institutions." Baldwin argues the most segregated hour in the United States is at high noon on Sunday and he asserts the real estate lobby keeps African Americans in the ghetto, and living in America is a real social danger for African American people. The COVID-19 crisis illuminates Baldwin's observation. Numbers from the Centers for Disease Control and Prevention show 23% of COVID-19 deaths are African Americans even though black people make up 13% of the U.S. population. Doctor Tiffany Green at the University of Wisconsin-Madison argues the reason black people are more likely exposed to COVID-19 is because of structural racism. Green states: "We have a long history of black people being shuffled into occupations that are less likely to have insurance, safe working conditions; and ... black people are much less likely to be able to work at home, they are the essential workers" (Interview with Karley Marotta, June 18, 2020). Next, Baldwin tells Cavett how America's claims of racial equality are a false ideal. "You want me to make an act of faith—risking myself, my wife, my woman, my sister, my children—on some idealism which you assure me exists in America, which I have never seen" (Baldwin, 1969).

24 Welcome to America's Schoolhouse

In these remarks, Baldwin is calling for solidarity and arguing that dealing with racism is intimate and political. McWilliam, drawing on Alicia Garza's (2014) essay, "A Herstory of the #BlackLivesMatter Movement" addresses – in a Baldwinian framing – both the intimate and political struggle with race when she discusses how Garza invokes solidarity. Garza illuminates the "intimate and political" as she argues "our collective futures" depend on white people's active "unwavering" solidarities with black people "in defense of our humanity" and asserts that black people's freedom is and will be transformation for everyone: that "when Black people get free, everyone gets free" (p. 3).

Baldwin's straightforwardness when speaking to European Americans and the challenge it brings to interracial solidarity is also exemplified in 1963 when, at the request of Attorney General Robert F. Kennedy, he set up a meeting with civil rights leaders, academics and artists at Kennedy's father's home in New York. The now famous meeting becomes contentious and "active and unwavering" solidarity is threatened when Kennedy's and Baldwin's groups disagree over the efforts of the Kennedy administration on advancement of African American civil rights. Lena Horne, an African American actor and singer, who is ostracized in Hollywood because of her racial activism and one of Baldwin's invited guests, makes a statement that is both political and intimate. Horne tells Kennedy that his brother's administration has not done enough to bring about racial justice. Horn and other guests argue, Freedom Riders, an integrated group of college students, organized by the Congress of Racial Equality (CORE) who ride buses into the segregated South in 1961 to protest against segregated bus terminals, "white-only" rest rooms and lunch counters in bus stations, in Alabama, South Carolina and other southern states, initially receive little help from the Kennedy administration, as the Kennedy Brothers are indifferent and preoccupied with the Cold War and Russian leader Nikita Khrushchev.

In response, Robert Kennedy tries to reconnect with the activists, noting the discrimination his family suffers and stating that he thinks that in 40 years an African American would be president (Tye, 2016). Instead of re-establishing rapport with the group, Kennedy's comment shows a shocking unawareness of racism in America. The comment is a put down on African Americans and demonstrates the important and timely need to confront the evil power of racism with the power of federal government. Michael Eric Dyson (2018) writes in *What Truth Sounds Like*, the Baldwin group wants the Kennedy brothers to understand the moral dimension of race not the political ones. When the Baldwin group asks, "Why doesn't your brother [President Kennedy] commit to a powerful symbolic gesture, like escorting black students to school in the face of George Wallace?" Kennedy balks and argues such action would be pure theater, a ridiculous stunt and that the Kennedy administration is working behind the scenes to promote change. Dyson (2018) argues: "And that is exactly the problem, whereas it is about politics; it is also intimate; about the morality and dignity, of African Americans. It is about taking a symbolic stand in front of the entire country". Kennedy, as Dyson (2018) notes, didn't get it. "He kept insisting that change was hard and slow" (p. 10).

Jerome Smith, a young activist at the meeting states,

> Mr. Kennedy, I want you to understand I don't care anything about you and your brother ... I don't know what I'm doing here, listening to all this cocktail party patter. The real threat to white America isn't Black Muslims, it is when nonviolence advocates like me lose hope.
>
> *(Tye, 2016)*

Smith adds that if the police come at him with more guns, dogs and hoses, he will answer with a weapon of his own: "When I pull a trigger," he says, "kiss it goodbye" (Tye, 2016). Next, Lorraine Hansberry, author of *A Raisin in the Sun*, says to Kennedy, "You've got a great many very, very accomplished people in this room, Mr. Attorney General. But the only man who you should be listening to is that man over there" (p. 216), Hansberry says, pointing to Smith. A comment from Baldwin follows. Baldwin tells Kennedy, "That boy, after all, in some sense, represented to everybody in this room our hope. Our honor. Our dignity. But, above all, our hope" (Tye, 2016, p. 1).

The Baldwin and Kennedy confrontation is not isolated to a swanky apartment in New York or to yesteryear. In colleges of education across the country, when the local African American community is invited to the campus or African American scholars come to campuses to discuss the education of African American children, or the preparation of teachers to teach African American students, rhetoric abounds more so than action plans, including putting people in place who can do the job. European Americans continue to believe they know best about educating all America's students. However, their ideas are more often in European American interest than visionary in all American students' interests. In addition, on college faculties, there are only a token number of African Americans, Latinx, Asian Americans, and American Indians; and fewer people of color are in governing positions (Deans, Chairs of Departments, Chancellors) of power. More than likely, one meets several nonteaching staff members or administration assistants of color; caring people, but people with little power. Baldwin, and increasingly activists today, call into question the social system in which African Americans live and their children are educated, and the institutions that prepare teachers to teach their children.

The N-word

McWhorter (2019) argues "the N- word" has "one of the richest, nastiest, and most complex ranges of meaning in the English language" (p. 1). The N-word, *James Baldwin and the American Schoolhouse* contends, is an awful word; the First Amendment should never attempt to rescue it, and it cannot be washed clean with all the bottles of Clorox and Dawn detergent made by the manufacturer. I do understand that some African Americans use the N-word and for generations some have used it as a term of endearment with one another, thereby complicating "to use or not to use" among African Americans. But, when European Americans ask if they may use the N-word or why can't they use the N-word, after I say "No!" I wonder about the origin of the question. I hope that the question comes from a good place; it is honest and sincere and not disingenuous. But, I wonder, if it is not a kind of "white performative wokeness" (McWhorter, 2019, p. 2).

Teacher candidates, wondering what to do when they hear it in common areas or in schools, bring the use of the N-word to me. Used most often by African American students talking with one another and in classrooms when it is directed at an African American teacher by a European American student, and so forth. It is the use of the N-word by a European American student toward an African American teacher that got me involved in a summer faculty and staff project as the "intellectual leader." It is too early to report any meaningful preliminary observations from the six planned sessions that included 25 people: teachers, school administrators, three university faculty and two graduate students, a union president and two school district staff. However, Baldwin's (1963a) "A Talk to Teachers" that I will discuss in greater detail in Chapter 2, is read and discussed by the group; and "go for broke" a phrase in the article Baldwin (1963a) argues teachers of African American students should exercise, is roundly adopted by the group.

Baldwin uniquely addresses the N-word in his work. He is candid and informative. The N-word, with its derogatory labeling of African American students and its broader use in society, continues to demand attention as part of the informal curriculum of schools. According to *Education Week* and ProPublica (August, 2018) who conducted a three-year study on how hate, intolerance and bias affect school climate and impact students and the school staff, the N-word and other racist rhetoric (e.g., "build the wall," "go back to [insert foreign country name here]), are frequently-used hate speech heard in schools. *Education Week* cautions that, although the 2016 election of President Trump is to blame for some of the rise in hate speech, the U.S. Department of Justice in 2015 reports that 25% of students polled indicated seeing hate-related graffiti in their schools.

Baldwin, addressing the N-word, tells European Americans that "what you say about somebody else … reveals you. What I think of you as a human being is dictated by my own necessities, my own psychology and my own fears and desires" (Baldwin in Moore, 1963, p. 1). Baldwin argues in the United States, "we've got something called a nigger" (Baldwin in Moore, 1963, p. 2). Baldwin explains that the N-word, since its conception, is detached and unpaired from African Americans' bodies. The word floats disembodied as an idea and invention, a problem to African Americans and European Americans together. Baldwin

(1963a) asserts, "I have always known that I am not a nigger; and if it's true that your invention reveals you, then who is the nigger?" (*Take This Hammer*, Video). Baldwin, as Beard (2016) explains, challenges European Americans' investment in the N – word and refuses to hold European Americans' problem for them. Baldwin continues: "You still think the 'n' is necessary. Well, he's unnecessary to me; so, he must be necessary to you. So, I give you your problem back. You're the n★★★★★, baby, it isn't me" (Baldwin in Beard, 2016, p.12). As Beard (2016) argues, Baldwin's return of the N-word and its meaning to European Americans exposes their obsession with power, violence and denial.

Baldwin's historical, ideological, psychological and social analysis of the N-word is useful when teachers search out why a word that is considered off limits is used with ease on school grounds. "Black-ish," a popular television show, opened the 2015 season using the N-word in the premier episode. Black-ish did not take a stand on how to use the word, leaving that up to the viewers. If Clorox and Dawn can't clean-up the word, move on; find another subject for the premier episode. Baldwin contends that only when European Americans own everything they have projected onto African Americans and European Americans consent, in effect, to become black then they can be free. Baldwin believes European Americans are redeemable and are not a "different people" from African Americans. However, Baldwin argues that European American identity is not redeemable; and he warns against narratives of separated histories and future (Baldwin, 1963a, p. 83, as cited in Beard, 2016, p.8).

Jimmy's Words to African American Teachers

> The question of who I was had at last become a personal question, and the answer was to be found in me.
>
> *James Baldwin, 1965b*

James Baldwin had a good deal to say to African Americans about being African American in America that African American teachers of African American children will find useful. Toni Morrison argues Baldwin, or Jimmy, as she called him, "gave us ourselves to think about, to cherish" (p. 1). Morrison (1987) also notes three other gifts that Baldwin gives to African Americans: speaking first-person singular, Morrison says: (1) "You gave me a language to dwell in, a gift so perfect it seems my own invention"; (2) "Courage … to go as a stranger in the village and transform the distance between people into intimacy with the whole world; courage to understand that experience made it a personal

Most of the teaching material in teacher education is prepared for European American teacher candidates and graduate students. This section is prepared for African American teachers and teacher candidates and other teachers of color, as I "bear witness" to Toni Morrison's statement: "I'm writing for black people … I don't have to apologize."

28 Welcome to America's Schoolhouse

revelation for each of us … [and] the courage to appropriate an alien, hostile, all-white geography because you had discovered that 'this world [meaning history] is white no longer and will never be white again.'"

Saying more about "courage" that today's abolitionist, culturally relevant and multicultural social justice African American teachers will identify with, Morrison states: "Yours was the courage to live life in and from its belly as well as beyond its edges, and to see and say what it was, to recognize and identify evil but never fear or stand in awe" (p. 2). Morrison (1987) asserts, Jimmy gives me a

> Tenderness so delicate I thought it could not last, but it did and develop me it did …. Something almost as hard to catch as a whisper in a crowded place, as light as definite as a spider's web, strikes below my ribs, stunning and astonishing my heart … the baby, turning for the first time in its incredible veil of water, announces its presence and claims me; tell me, in that instant, that what can get worse can get better … in the meantime—forever—it is entirely up to me.
>
> *(p. 2)*

Baldwin gives African American teachers his deep inner thoughts about being African American and its connection to the larger U.S. society and the world. His thoughts in his writings and speeches speak of African Americans from enslavement (e.g., "I picked the cotton," "I built the ships") to the present day (e.g., "I am not your negro") into the future (e.g., "*the fire next time*"). Baldwin's prose changes the way many African Americans see the world; he challenges any prescribed place for African Americans in the world, he is concerned about African Americans' role in the world, especially in the U.S. People of Baldwin's generation argue and African American students today similarly argue, Baldwin helps them to see that "race is a sickness that devoured both the racist and racism's victims" (Casmier, 2017, p. 1). Baldwin's message to African American teachers is to teach African American students that they must resist any peripheral role that seems their social fate, and he tells them, know that the primary agent of this resistance is their imagination. Imagination or the ability to see themselves in an alternative world, is a vision that African American teachers can especially model for African American students.

Candid and Relevant: Whispers of Courage in the Ear

Baldwin is candid and relevant with his African American brothers and sisters and he is particularly candid, relevant and heartfelt when speaking to African American youth for he knows their journey into American society is filled with obstacles and universality is denied to them because of the color of their skin. Baldwin wants African Americans to know that equal rights efforts are not about the integration of African Americans into European American society, but about changing European American society by forcing it to accept what it has done to African Americans (Pfeffer, 1998). Baldwin (1962) posits:

> Please try to be clear … about the reality which lies behind the word's acceptance and integration. There is no reason for you to try to become like white people and there is no basis whatever for their impertinent assumption that they must accept you.
>
> *(p. 8)*

Baldwin and Malcolm X as Pfeffer (1998) argues "were not trying to break down the door of white society so they could be let in; they were breaking down the door so they could get out" (p. 2).

Baldwin is candid and relevant with African American teacher educators and teachers as he discusses the psychological challenges (e.g., distress, coping, self-estrangement) that many African American students face. Baldwin explains to African American students how his self-discovery took place and he explains his reconciliation with his racial heritage and how he came to accept himself. Baldwin, African American teacher educators and teachers will appreciate how he addresses the anger and bitterness of growing in poor, European American controlled, African American communities and discusses the significances of African American youth activism (e.g., protest, electoral action) against the problems (e.g., racism) causing the problem. Baldwin's witness-bearing words afford a realistic transition into today's current political context.

Baldwin is candid and relevant as he points out the complexities of African American–European American relations in different contexts, for example: white privilege and the "Black problem." Baldwin informs students that American racism is an evil that activism and congressional legislations cannot quickly change because it [racism] is deep in American consciousness. Baldwin describes how European Americans' positive statements about African American ability and equality, or their calls for equity and fairness often ring hollow, for they are structured within a context where white privilege remains in place and European Americans don't imagine or have in their consciousness African American equality. Policies and practices implemented supposedly to improve the education of African American students often, when closely examined, reveal European American interest directing the show. Policies and practices are underwritten, or European American interest is centered because European Americans do not easily accept African Americans as equal. Baldwin argues much of what is defined as the "Black problem" in American education (e.g., the curriculum – academic or agricultural – African Americans should receive after Emancipation; the "need" for *Brown*; the need for Headstart programs; the placement of students into special education classes, and so forth) is a problem brought on because of white supremacy and it demands that European Americans look at the damage they have done and their role in the miseducation of African Americans.

30 Welcome to America's Schoolhouse

African American teachers can point out to African American students that Baldwin is an advocate of racial solidity with European Americans. But his advocation, is not because Baldwin is naive, about European Americans and the racial misdeeds they orchestrate, far from it. "I know that what I am asking is impossible" (Baldwin, 1962a, p. 104). Baldwin is not delusional about how deeply racism is anchored in the United States or the force needed to dislodge it. However, Baldwin believes that it is his duty to address possibilities of better race relations between African Americans and European Americans. Baldwin (1962a) states:

> But in our time, as in every time, the impossible is the least that one can demand – and one is, after, emboldened by the spectacle of human history in general, and American Negro History in particular, for it testifies to nothing less than the perpetual achievement of the possible.
>
> *(p. 104)*

Baldwin tells African Americans that in America, the races all must live together, not as African American and European American, but as human beings. In his 1963 film *The Price of the Ticket* Baldwin argues, "From my point of view – no label, no slogan, no party, no skin color, and indeed, no religion is more important than the human being."

African American teachers can point out to African American students that Baldwin speaks and writes about African Americans positively, as complex, complicated human beings. He does not describe them as one-dimensional characters popularized in movies of the 1930s–1970s or as the tokens, the first character killed off that continues in movies today. Searching for a change of pace in this area of COVID-19 between teaching my classes, attending Zoom meetings and working on this book, I begin watching *Homeland* – the reviews argued it was excellent TV. However, after spending morning into the evening reading and rereading Baldwin as I work on this book and then watching *Homeland* as my relief, I become annoyed because examples of what I have been reading earlier in the day pass before me as I watch TV. How easy African Americans are written out of the telling of U.S. history although they were not only involved, but were highly involved. African Americans learned spy craft during the Civil War. When Baldwin speaks of the lack of American consciousness and imagination, he is including artists (e.g., writers) who have the imagination to capture a nation's attention on Sunday evening, but do not have the imagination to include – in a meaningful way – African American characters.

African American teachers can point out to African American students the realism – the differences, similarities and complexities of Baldwin's characters. Baldwin's characters do not show African Americans as monoliths, quite the opposite. Bigsby (1979) argues, Baldwin's characters are highly self-conscious, reflecting not only upon their social situation but on the nature of their consciousness itself (p. 328). In *If Beale Street Could Talk*, a film based upon Baldwin's book of the same name, and one many students may have seen, Tish, the 19-year-old protagonist, who falls in love with Fonny, a sculptor and father of her child, shows a range of human emotions: sadness, joy, anger, love and mature intelligence; is highly self-conscious and takes action to achieve social justice. Baldwin's description of African Americans in his writings and speeches are vividly human, so clearly based in reality that they come across as timeless.

African American teachers can point out to African American students that their skin color is beautiful, their hair, a prideful blessing and their facial features proud, attractive humanity. From Toni Morrison, Baldwin's good friend, African American teachers will find a wonderful story and a rich resource in her *God Help the Child*. Morrison's protagonist, Bride is a beautiful dark-skinned young woman who tries to shield herself from her own past with surface beautification. Morrison, in an interview with Hermione Hoby (2015) about the book, offers two Baldwinian observations that African American teachers will appreciate: (1) "I'm writing for black people in the same way that Tolstoy was not writing for me, a 14-year-old colored girl from Lorain, Ohio. I don't have to apologize or consider myself limited because I don't [write about white people] – which is not absolutely true, there are lots of white people in my books" (Hoby, 2015, p, 2). (2) About black skin, Morrison tells Hoby (2015) "it just a color," (p. 2).

African American teachers can point out to African American students that Baldwin is a person, who refuses to be trapped by his skin color. Baldwin argues, his skin color is simply a projection of his racial inheritance, a symbol of oppression or resistance that he does not allow to stand as an expression of his self. Baldwin (1993) contends that the question of who he is, is a personal question to be found within himself.

African American teachers can point out to African American students that Baldwin's rich and beautiful description of African American people, as Morrison's Bride, is of the ordinary person, the African American he meets riding the train, passes on the street, or meets at a grocery store. Whereas Baldwin knows, and hangs out with Hollywood stars and world-renowned athletes, the characters in his books are ordinary people. Particularly, young African American children should hear that Baldwin supports and celebrates their humanity, their everyday language (Ebonics), and admires the way they "recognize and navigate obstacles in their lives" (Lodge, 2017). For Baldwin (1979 language is experience and language is powe and Baldwin's *Little Man, Little Man*, a picture book about African American children, models this point for African American students. The book is about 4-year-old TJ, coming of age as a "Little Man" with big dreams, playing with his good friends WT, age 7 and Blinky, age 8. Set in Harlem in the 1970s and playing on the block where they live, TJ encounters adult adventures and realities. The storyline explores and celebrates childhood joy despite the challenges of systemic oppression.

African American teachers of young African American children will find *Little Man, Little Man* timely, refreshingly engaging and different from most literature

32 Welcome to America's Schoolhouse

they receive in school. African American students, especially those living in urban areas can see how Baldwin takes their everyday experiences and writes about them in such a beautiful way and that words have power. Baldwin, according to his niece Aisha Karefa-Smart states: *Little Man, Little Man* is "a celebration of the self-esteem of Black children" (the consciouskid.org, 2018, p. 1).

African American teachers should inform African American students that the realistic attention given to police violence and white supremacy; and the positive characterizations of African Americans in American literary culture is grounded in Baldwin's novels, essays and speeches. Juan Williams (1987) observes that Baldwin "became a standard of literary realism …. Given the messy nature of racial hatred, of the half-truths, blasphemies and lies that make up American life, Baldwin's accuracy in reproducing that world stands as a remarkable achievement" (p. 2). African Americans reading Baldwin know he writes truth and he will not accept willful ignorance from European Americans. European Americans reading Baldwin know he speaks truth about the lives of African Americans and the original sins of a racist nation (Poetry Foundation, 2019).

African American educators can use Baldwin's analysis of racism in schools to argue for curriculum and instruction that centers African American children. Baldwin (e.g., "A Talk to Teachers") in the hands of African American educators supports their argument to curriculum officials that African American students need a culturally relevant curriculum – a curriculum that is honest and provides authentic school experiences and events for African American children.

Baldwin is important for African American teachers because he sees himself as a "disturber of the peace" and "he mirrors African Americans' aspirations, disappointments, and coping strategies in a hostile society" (Poetry Foundation, 2019, p. 1). Here, I am reminded of a school where the student population was all European American that rapidly became a school where the population is all African American. The European American school administrators continued at the school during the racial demographic change and they continued to adhere to the superiority of whiteness. They keep in place in the many common locations throughout the school pictures of European American heroes, alumna and former athletes. Pictures of African American heroes, scholars and noted civil rights leaders are not given space on the school walls. In addition, the school graduation of all African American students, with an auditorium filled with African American parents, family members and friends maintained a Eurocentric celebration (e.g., songs sang, poetry read). Denied was room for African American cultural symbols in music, poetry reading or speeches; but needed was Baldwinian activism: "disturber of the peace" (Poetry Foundation, 2019, p. 1).

Baldwin is also patient with African American youth, he encourages them to not settle with a first attempt but to take a second look, if they don't get it or see it first time around. Baldwin learns the importance of the taking a second look lesson from his mentor and friend, artist Beuford Delaney. The way the story goes, or the lesson is taught, according to Baldwin, happens when he is a youth.

He is asked by his mentor to peer down into a street gutter and tell what he sees. Baldwin stares down into the gutter looking into the mixture of oil and water and other debris and tells Delaney he sees nothing. Delaney asks Baldwin to look again; with the second look, Baldwin sees the reflections of buildings in the gutter's oil and water. Delaney's lesson, powerful but simple, says to Baldwin that you may see something the second time you look that you miss the first time you look. Such is the case as I read and re-read "A Talk to Teachers" and other Baldwin books and essays. You see so much more the second time around.

Finally, African American teachers of African American children may use Baldwin to inform their students that they carry their history (e.g., enslavement, Reconstruction, Civil Rights movement, Black Lives Matter movement, George Floyd death, living with COVID-19) with them, and as they accept their history – a history they cannot escape from – they, Baldwin argues, will learn to handle both history and their current positionality. Baldwin (1984 posits: "I am the grandson of a slave, and I am a writer. I must deal with both" (p. 2). African American teachers will discover passages from Baldwin's books (e.g., *Go Tell It on the Mountain*; Baldwin, 1953) give students an honest view of the intersection of racism and poverty in the North and South as well as make realistic and relevant a Charles Dickens situation: "best of times; worst of times" in the lives of African American people.

Baldwin Matters in the Moment

John Grimes, the protagonist in *Go Tell It on the Mountain* awakes on *his* Saturday morning, fourteenth birthday, ready for fun and games and sadly discovers no one in his family remembers this is his big day. His mother, Elizabeth, prepares the same ol' breakfast; he is told to do the same ol' Saturday chores, sweep the living room. John reeks with disappointment as he obeys his mother. However, his unhappiness is short-lived. Elizabeth, John's mother of course knows it's John's big day and gives him some money and tells him to buy something he likes. After a few hours of fun and reflection on his life, including musing over his inability to deal with his stepfather and the racist society into which he was born, John returns home.

Baldwin, through his characters, describes significant aspects of life in America, including its contradictions and seductions; and the push and pulls of love and hate that so many feel towards the country. *Go Tell It on the Mountain* based on Baldwin's life story has three parts: John's discovery that his career goal is outside of career expectations previously imagined by his family, especially his father; the impact of racial oppression in the north and south on the lives of his mother and father as they grow up; and John's acceptance of religion as a way to escape the oppression that surrounded him. Looking back on what many consider his greatest novel, *Go Tell It on the Mountain*, decades later, in 1984, Baldwin tells *The Paris Review* what he was trying to say in the novel about all of us and about his own life:

34 Welcome to America's Schoolhouse

> [Writing *Go Tell It on the Mountain*] was an attempt to exorcise something, to find out what happened to my father, what happened to all of us, what had happened to me and how we were to move from one place to another.
>
> *(Elgrably, 1984)*

African American teachers of African American children may challenge them with the following: James Baldwin refuses to align himself with the Black Arts Movement; instead, Baldwin sees himself not as a "black writer," but as an "American writer." What do they think of Baldwin's position? If they were a writer, would they want to be considered a "black writer" or an "American writer?"

African American teachers can use Baldwin's statement, "To be a Negro in this country and to be relatively conscious is to be in a rage almost all the time" to discuss "inconvenient presence" incidents, that are happening increasingly to many African Americans. Nic Stone, author of the *New York Times* bestseller *Dear Martin*, in a HuffPost article describes how such rage comes about. Stone (2018) describes how she and a girlfriend are policed by a white manager of a bookstore as they are making decisions over which books to purchase. According to Stone (2018), although they politely comply with the manager's statement that they may no longer sit at a back table in the bookstore to decide upon the book they want to purchase and need to relocate to tables or benches on the other side of the store, the manager continues to hover over them and follow them about the store until they checked out. Stone, looking back on the incident argues:

> To be black and #woke is to be aware that it's a short journey from being seen as an inconvenient presence in a bookstore or a public park to being gunned down in the street by a cop who sees you as a "demon" instead of as a human being. It is to be constantly bombarded with evidence that you live in a country where, on sight alone, it's assumed that you're less civilized. Less capable. More dangerous. Less valuable.
>
> *(Stone, 2018)*

African American teachers can impress on African American youth that Baldwin is relentless in his efforts to imbue black bodies with humanity, to call out racism, and to encourage African American people, especially African American youth, to be optimistic about life. Baldwin, African American teachers can convey to their students, is not down on life. Baldwin states in a 1968 appearance on the Dick Cavett show,

> I am not a pessimist because I am alive. To be a pessimist, it means that you have agreed that human life is an academic matter. So, I am forced to be an optimist. I'm forced to believe that we can survive whatever we must survive.

Baldwin (*I Am Not Your Negro*, 2017) asserts the "Future of life is precisely as bright or as dark as the future of the country. It is entirely up to the American people and our representatives [...] whether or not they will deal with and embrace the stranger they have maligned for so long."

African American teachers can tell African American youth that, according to Toni Morrison (1987), Baldwin made American English honest – genuinely international. "[He] expose its secrets and reshaped it until it was truly modern, dialogic, representative, humane .... In [his] hands language was handsome again" (p. 2). And, "The root function of language is to control the universe by describing it" (Baldwin, 1965a, p. 141). When I read the debate over the statement "Black Lives Matter" (*vs* All Lives Matter) it gives meaning to Baldwin's statement; in that African Americans have said – controlled – what they wanted said and how they wanted it stated.

Baldwin, as Coombs (1976) recalls from reading Baldwin during his undergraduate days, seemed "so sure-footed, then, so certain in his vision of this country, that his lacerating words were like balm to the Black students who were on a whirligig in search of their identities" (p. 1). It is because Baldwin existed that, Coombs (1976) argues,

> [w]e felt that the racial miasma that swirled around us would not consume us, and it is not too much to say that this man saved our lives, or at least gave us what we knew would continue to be a hostile and condescending world.
>
> *(p. 1)*

Coombs (1976) continues recalling how Baldwin's words and thoughts stay with friends after college days' reading and discussion.

> [O]ne of the group, a man employed by a large Wall Street firm, and making his way with assurance up the greasy pole, returns to "the fire next time" after some special corporate praise, in order to cleanse his mind of superficial cant and to anchor himself, again, in what he calls "the real reality of America."
>
> *(p. 1)*

Baldwin is excellent for teacher candidates of color, who contend with their white peers' willful ignorance or their avoidance of reality when discussing the education of African American children. Teacher candidates of color will discover in Baldwin's illuminating explorations of white innocence and willful ignorance, two behaviors used by their peers in student teaching seminars. Baldwin (1963b) teacher candidates of color will learn, believed that "It is not permissible that the authors of devastation should also be innocent. It is the innocence which constitutes the crime" (p. 1). Woubshet (2019) adds "To author devastation – that is, to enslave, maim, lynch, and disenfranchise a group of people – entails one type of power. And, as Baldwin delineated, it takes yet another kind to disavow those violent act" (p. 2).

36 Welcome to America's Schoolhouse

Baldwin offers realism about a society that is confounded in half-truths, lies and racial prejudice that makes up America. His analysis and description of racism provides a language to expound on African American humanity. Baldwin inspires African Americans to resist the meaning European American give to them: "To be a Negro meant, precisely, that one was never looked at but was simply at the mercy of the reflexes the color of one's skin caused in other people" (Balfour, 2001, p. 70). Baldwin is an essential read by All because, as Amiri Baraka (2007) noted in his eulogy of Baldwin, "Jimmy was the creator of contemporary American speech that is needed in order for people to talk to another," and Cornell West (2017) reflecting on "Why James Baldwin Matters More Than Ever" argues Baldwin exemplifies eloquence at its highest level: "'wisdom speaking' that's rooted in a courage that refuses to sell out" (p. 1).

Bibliography

Acham, C. (2004). *Revolution Televised: Prime Time and the Struggle for Black Power*. Minneapolis, MI: University of Minnesota Press. p. 6.

Alcoff, L. M. (1998). What should white people do? History is a weapon. https://www.historyisaweapon.com/defcon1/alcoffwhitepeople.html. 6/16/2019.

Ayers, E. (n.d.) African Americans and the American Revolution. Jamestown & American Revolution. Museum at Yorktown. https://www.historyisfun.org/learn/learning-center/colonial-america-american-revolution-learning-resources/american-revolution-essays-timelines-images/african-americans-and-the-american-revolution/. 6/24/2019.

Baldwin, J. (1953). *Go Tell It on the Mountain*. New York, NY: Knopf.

Baldwin, J. (1955). *Notes of a Native Son*. Bristol, Mass.: Beacon Press.

Baldwin, J. (1959/1985). Nobody knows my name. In *The Price of the Ticket*. New York, NY: St. Martin's Press.

Baldwin, J. (1961). The black boy, looks at the white boy. *Esquire*, May.

Baldwin, J. (1962a). A letter to my nephew. *The Progressive*. https://progressive.org/magazine/letter-nephew/. 6/15/ 2019.

Baldwin, J. (1962b). The creative process. In *The Price of the Ticket*. New York, NY: St. Martin's Press.

Baldwin J. (1963a). My dungeon shook. History is a weapon. https://www.historyisaweapon.com/defcon1/baldwindungeonshook.html.

Baldwin, J. (1963b). *The Price of the Ticket*. Film. https://www.huffpost.com/entry/11-james-baldwin-quotes-on-race-that-resonate-now-more-than-ever_n_58936929e4b06f344e40664c. 8/8/2019.

Baldwin, J. (1964). I can't accept Western values because they don't accept me. Interview by Robert Penn Warren. New Press. Literary Hub (lithub.com). 12/3/2020.

Baldwin, J. (1965a). Quoted in Dwight McBride (1999). *James Baldwin Now*. New York, NY: New York University Press.

Baldwin, J. (1965b). *Going to Meet the Man*. New York, NY: Dial Press.

Baldwin, J. (1969). James Baldwin talks racism on "The Dick Cavett Show." Mental Floss.

Baldwin, J. (1972). *No Name in the Street*. New York, NY: Dell.

Baldwin, J. (1976). *The Devil Finds Work*. New York, NY: Vintage.

Baldwin, J. (1976/2018). *Little Man, Little Man*. Durham, NC: Duke University Press.

Baldwin, J. (1979). If black English isn't a language, what is? *The New York Times Book Review*. July 29. https://www.nytimes.com/2010/09/26/opinion/eq-baldwin.html. 6/11/2019.

Baldwin, J. (1984). On being "White" and other lies. *Essence*. April.

Baldwin, J. (1984). Interview with Julius Lester. *The New York Times Book Review*. James Baldwin, eloquent writer in behalf of civil rights, is dead. The New York Times. (nytimes.com)

Baldwin, J. (1993). *Nobody Knows My Name: More Notes of a Native Son*. New York, NY: Vintage Books.

Balfour, L. (2001). *Evidence of Things Not Said. James Baldwin and the Promise of American Democracy*. Ithaca, NY: Cornell University Press.

Baraka, A. (2007). Our man Jimmy. Amiri Baraka on James Baldwin. *Pen America*. 12/3/2020.

Beard, L. A. (2016). 'Flesh of their flesh, bone of their bone': James Baldwin's racial politics of boundness. *Contemporary Political Theory*. https://www.academia.edu/28698985/Flesh_of_their_flesh_bone_of_their_bone_James_Baldwins_racial_politics_of_boundness. 6/12/19.

Bigsby, C. W. E. (1969). Editor. *The Black American Writer, Volume 2: Poetry and Drama*. Northampton, MA: Everett/Edwards.

Bigsby, C. W. E. (1979). The divided mind of James Baldwin. *Journal of American Studies*, 13, 3, 325–342.

Casmier, S. (2017, February 5). Did I get James Baldwin wrong? NPR, Code Switch. https://www.npr.org/sections/codeswitch/2017/02/05/513144736/did-i-get-jam. 6/25/2019.

Coombs, O. (1976, May 2). The devil finds work. *The New York Times Book Review*. http://movies2.nytimes.com/books/98/03/29/specials/baldwin-devil.html. June 9, 2019.

Cunningham, V. (2015). Why Ta-Nehisi Coates isn't our James Baldwin. *The Intelligencer*. August 15. 12/10/2020.

Di Angelo, R. (2011). White fragility. *International Journal of Critical Pedagogy*, 3, 3, 54–70.

Dyson, M. E. (2018). *What Truth Sounds Like*. New York, NY: St. Martin's Press.

Edelman, M. W. (1992). *The Measure of Our Success: A letter to My Children & Yours*. Boston, Mass.: Beacon Press.

Education Week (2018). Hate in school. August 6. https://www.edweek.org/ew/projects/hate-in-schools.html. 6/12/19.

Elgrably, J. *(1984). James Baldwin, the art of fiction no. 78. The Paris Review* 91, Spring.

Harris, F. (2014). James Baldwin, 1963, and the house that race built. *Transition*. Bloomington, IN: Indiana University Press.

Hoby, H. (2015). Toni Morrison: "I'm writing for black people … I don't have to apologize". Interview. *Guardian Weekly*. https://www.theguardian.com/books/2015/apr/25/toni-morrison-books-interview-god-help-the-child. 9/27/2019.

Howard, J. (1963). Telling talk from a Negro writer. *Life*. May 24, 81–93.

Huber, S. James Baldwin: Nonfiction of a native son. *ASSAY: A Journal of Nonfiction Studies*. https://www.assayjournal.com/sonya-huber-8203james-baldwin-nonfiction-of-a-native-son-31.html. 3/30/2019.

Hughes, L. (1958). Notes of a native son. Baldwin, J. Reviewed by Langston Hughes. *New York Times Book Review*.

Jones, B. F. (1966). James Baldwin: The struggle for identity. *The British Journal of Sociology*, 17, 2, 107–121.

King, M. L., Jr. (1957). Loving your enemies. Sermon. Dexter Avenue Baptist Church. The Martin Luther King, Jr., Research and Education Institute (stanford.edu). 12/3/2020.

38 Welcome to America's Schoolhouse

Leeming, D. (1994). *James Baldwin: A Biography*. New York, NY: Arcade.

Leeming, D. (2007). The White problem. Pen America. https://pen.org/the-white-problem/. 4/30/2020.

Levin, D. (1964). (James) Baldwin's autobiographical essays. The problem of Negro identity. *The Massachusetts Review*, V, Winter, 239–247.

Lodge, S. (2017). James Baldwin's sole children's book come back into print. *Publishers Weekly*. (publishersweekly.com). 12/3/2020.

Loewus, L. (2017). The nation's teaching force is still mostly White and female. Education Week. April. https://www.edweek.org/ew/articles/2017/08/15/the-nations-teaching-force-is-still-mostly.html. 12/3/2020.

McWhorter, J. (2019). The idea that Whites can't refer to the N-word." *The Atlantic*. April. https://www.theatlantic.com/ideas/archive/2019/08/whites-refer-to-the-n-word/ 596872/. 5/1/20.

McWilliams, S. J. (2017). Editor. *A Political Companion to James Baldwin*. Lexington, KY: The University Press of Kentucky.

Moore, R. O. (1963/2013). Director, "Take this hammer". In Rachel Brahinsky *Tell Him I'm Gone*. Susan J. McWilliams (2017), Editor, *A Political Companion to James Baldwin*. Lexington, KY: The University Press of Kentucky.

Morrison, T. (1987). James Baldwin: His voice remembered; Life in his language. *The New York TimesBook Review*. http://movies2.nytimes.com/books/98/03/29/specials/baldwin-morrison.html. 1/2/2019.

Myers, B. (2016). Where are the minority professors? *The Chronicle of Higher Education*. February 14. https://www.chronicle.com/interactives/where-are-the-minority-professors. 6/15/2019.

O'Daniel, T. B. (1977). *James Baldwin: A Critical Evaluation*. Washington, D.C.: Howard University Press.

Overbey, E. (2019). James Baldwin's Letter from a region in my mind. *The New Yorker*. <newyorker@newsletter.newyorker.com. 12/12/2019.

Pfeffer, R. (1998). The Fire This Time: James Baldwin and the Civil Rights movement. https://leo.stcloudstate.edu/kaleidoscope/volume4/fire.html. 6/19/2019.

Poetry Foundation. (2019). James Baldwin. 12/3/2020.

Roediger, D. (2018). On the defensive: Navigating White advantage and White fragility. *Los Angeles Review of Books*. September 6. https://lareviewofbooks.org/article/on-the-defensive-navigating-white-advantage-and-white-fragility/#. 8/82019.

Schomburg, A. A. (2010). Racial integrity: A plea for the establishment of a chair of Negro history in our schools and colleges. In Miriam Jiménez Román and Juan Flores (Eds), *History and Culture in the United States*. Durham, N.C.: Duke University Press.

Smith, C. (2017). James Baldwin's lesson for teachers in a time of turmoil. *The New Yorker*. September 23. https://www.newyorker.com/books/page-turner/james-baldwins-lesson-for-teachers-in-a-time-of-turmoil. 4/10/2019.

Steinem, G. (1971). The new egalitarian life style. *The New York Times*. https://www.nytimes.com/1971/08/26/archives/a-new-egalitarian-life-style.html.

Stone, N. (2018). To be black and #woke is to be in a rage all the time. HuffPost. August 8. https://www.huffpost.com/entry/opinion-mike-brown-rage-racism_n_5b6992cee 4b0de86f4a52959?guccounter=. 6/16/2019.

The conscious kid. An interview with Aisha Karefa-Smart on James Baldwin's Little Man, Little Man: A Story of Childhood. https://www.theconsciouskid.org/littlemanlittleman. 9/27/2019.

Thoreau, H. D. (1837). Henry David Thoreau's Journal. https://hdt.typepad.com/henrys_blog/1837/. 8/16/20.

Tye, L. (2016). The most trusted white man in blackAmerica. *Politico Magazine*. July 7. https://www.politico.com/magazine/story/2016/07/robert-f-kennedy-race-relations-martin-luther-king-assassination-214021. 6/14/2019.

West, C. (2017). Cornell West on why James Baldwin matters more than ever. In conversation with Christoper Lydon. Literary Hub (lithub.com). 12/3/2020.

Williams, J. (1987). Quoted in James Baldwin. Poetry Foundation. 12/3/2020.

Woodson, C. (1933). *The Mis-Education of the Negro*. Chicago, IL: African American Images.

Woubshet, D. (2019). How James Baldwin's writings about love evolved. *The Atlantic*. January. 12/3/2020.

2

THE TEACHER WITHIN HIM, JAMES ARTHUR BALDWIN

> For those of us who teach, this is one of our responsibilities; we are–or could be–in the business of empowerment and revolution.
>
> *James Baldwin, 1963a*

Baldwin is a teacher, not of the "ordinary branches of school education." Baldwin is a teacher of truth and he is devoted to the human being; their humanity, freedom and fulfilment. Baldwin is a teacher who teaches African American students that they are stronger than the conspiracy manufactured to control them and they must never make peace with it.

Baldwin is a teacher who teaches students to examine the world. Baldwin rejects the false pretense of being apolitical or supporting the thesis, that education is neutral. Instead, Baldwin confronts the problems in students live. Baldwin, the teacher, would want African American students to discover why the rate of COVID-19 infections are three or four times more in African American communities than other communities and to take actions to stop it.

Baldwin is a teacher who teaches African American students that the media they view, the newspapers and magazines they read – the press – is not as free as it says it is. Baldwin is a teacher that wants African American students to know that they are not "bound by the expediencies of any given administration, any give policy, and any given morality; that [they have] the right and the necessity to examine everything" (Baldwin, 1963a, p. 4). Baldwin is a teacher who teaches African American students that they can and should be heroes and heroines of stories and in films. Baldwin would support Jonathan Majors' (who plays Atticus Freeman, a veteran of the Korean War returning "home" to a hostile America in *Lovecraft Country*) thesis that "Heroes now can come in any shape and form … [t]here can be a Black James Bond, a female James Bond. Atticus Freeman exists. We have

The Teacher Within Him **41**

taken something that is so iconically White and male and pushed the scope" (Andrews-Dyer, 2010).

Baldwin is a teacher of African American students who teaches them that they are not "n......" and he teaches them people who call them by that epithet and believe that they are that epithet, are in actuality saying something about themselves; about a fault in their humanity. Additionally, Baldwin is a teacher who teaches African American students they are none of the stereotypes (e.g. lazy, destructive) invented by European Americans about African American people. Baldwin (1963a) argues when he was young, he realized he was none of the things he was told he was; those things (stereotypes) are invented by White people ... "I came to understand, that whatever White people invent, whatever they project is them" (p. 2).

Baldwin is a teacher pointing out a problem upsetting the U.S. The problem, Baldwin contends, is the U.S. sense of its own identity. Chants that make America the home of only one racial group of people and legislation or executive actions that crackdown on immigrants from Latin America and Mexico are frustrations grounded in racism about the country's identity. The U.S. is no longer majority European American, "white." Baldwin is a teacher who points out that what passes for identity in America are myths and lies. Lies that begin with Columbus, myths about people on the Mayflower and myths about the "settling" of the west.

Baldwin is a teacher about life in times of turmoil (e.g., COVID-19, police violence, voter suppression, racial reckoning) and he offers a framework for teachers who want to teach students more so than teach to the test. Baldwin teaches that the individual – their voting rights, the right not to be hassled because they are African American – is much more than an image of a race and that one's individual reality is outside of their availability as a public symbol (Bigsby, 1969).

Baldwin is a teacher that instructs that the reality and lives of African Americans are primary and universal; and he is a teacher, along with Toni Morrison (1992) and others that questions: "When does racial unconsciousness or awareness of race enrich literary thought or telling of history, when it impoverishes it?" (p. iii).

Baldwin is a teacher of history and the historical process. Baldwin wants African American students to know that they are the totality of all of the forces that produced them and that America is not innocent of its history. Baldwin (1963a) teaches African American students to know that slavery

> was not an accident, it was not an act of God, it was not done by well-meaning people muddling into something which they didn't understand. It was a deliberate policy hammered into place in order to make money from black flesh.
>
> *(p. 3)*

Now, in the second decade of the 21st century, because we have never faced this fact, racial unrest remains a problem.

42 The Teacher Within Him

Baldwin is a teacher of the continuing African American struggle to acquire full and complete democracy and American identity. Baldwin explains economic, social and political oppression of African Americans through a frame of educational justice with candor that has no room for political appeasement. Baldwin teaches that schools are major sites of struggle for social justice: "It is almost impossible for any Negro child to discover anything about his actual history," (Baldwin, 1963a, p. 2); therefore, Baldwin argues an accurate accounting of history is needed. Elaborating on what schooling is doing to African American children, Baldwin argues that schools destroy their self-concept leading them to believe they have a backward culture and that their future is dark and gloomy. However, Baldwin (1974) contends: "Those kids aren't dumb. But the people who run these schools want to make sure they don't get smart: they are really teaching the kids to be slaves" (p. 39).

Baldwin is a teacher like the ones bell hooks (1994) describes in *Teaching to Transgress: Education as the Practice of Freedom*. Hooks describes having African American teachers who explained to her the bias and racism she would face as an African American female and used engaged pedagogy to encourage students to become involved in classroom activities. In a speech at Goucher College in Baltimore, hooks (2003) argues Baldwin sees the "world as classroom." Baldwin's curriculum scope and sequence includes critical discussions of race, gender, class, sexuality, home, family, nation, economics, imperialism, capitalism and democracy.

Baldwin's teaching is both revolutionary for the time and relevant to the current educational crisis that continues to be bogged down in racism. I am aware that Baldwin (1963a) in "A Talk to Teachers," declares: "I am not a teacher myself." Baldwin defines himself as a person, an artist who: "bears witness." Socrates made a similar denial. Socrates vehemently denied that he was a teacher and argues, "If you have heard from anyone that I attempt to educate human beings and make money from it, that is not true" (quoted in Mintz, 2014, p. 735). However, claiming one is not a teacher doesn't make it so, especially if your work and actions suggests otherwise, as Plato, his student, and the teacher of Alexander the Great, lamented. Avi I. Mintz (2014) argues, "Teachers have christened their pedagogical methods 'Socratic' precisely because they take Socrates to be such an inspiring model of a teacher" (p. 736). Staying with the Baldwin–Socrates analogy a bit longer, both Socratic and Baldwin questions, cajole, challenge, encourage and chastise their interlocutors to educate them; and both educate not by transferring information or serving as a conduit, but by heightening critical consciousness and speaking truth. Schlosser (2013) argues that Baldwin continues the Socratic practices of self-examination and social criticism while also shifting his Socratic undertaking to examine the horrible effects of slavery and racism on African American people.

Baldwin is a teacher who attended to one of the more important characteristics of being a teacher: he is constantly striving to know himself so he will grow as a professional. He works at developing beliefs and attitudes important to not

The Teacher Within Him **43**

succumbing to myths and stereotypes. Truth and honesty to self about self and others, Baldwin discovers, are foundational to his speeches and writing; and it is honesty with self that Baldwin contends saved him from going to jail or being killed. Baldwin posits in 1948 that he left Harlem and went to Paris to save himself after his friend Eugen Worth leaped off the George Washington Bridge to his death. In an interview with *The Paris Review* in 1984, Baldwin states: "My luck was running out. I was going to go to jail, I was going to kill somebody or be killed."

Being an African American male in racist America had become too much. In Paris, although arriving with only $40 in his pocket, Baldwin develops his bearing witness skills and his artist/teacher voice and discovers what it means to be an American; better yet, what it means to be human and to be treated as a human. Baldwin becomes more openminded and understanding as he lives in different parts of the city and develops friendships with different people, including pimps and prostitutes in Pigalle and Egyptian bankers in Neuilly. Baldwin also comes to understand that he doesn't hate America. In *Notes of a Native Son*, Baldwin (1955) writes: "I love America more than any other country in this world, and, exactly for this reason, I insist on the right to criticize her perpetually" (p. 9).

In 1959 in an essay "The Discovery of What It Means to be An American," Baldwin states "The very word 'America,' remains a new, almost completely undefined and extremely controversial proper noun. No one in the world seems to know exactly what it describes, not even we motley millions who call our-selves Americans" (p. 17). In 2014, Damien Cave, a *New York Times* reporter, travels the length of highway I-35, which runs south to north through the middle of the United States, for his "The Way North" project. Along the way, he asks people, "What does it mean to be American?" Based upon Cave's sample, Bald-win is correct – the word is undefined, a controversial proper noun and no one seems to know exactly what it describes.

Ironically, in the 1950s, the time Baldwin is gaining national attention, a pro-fessor at Columbia University – not many city blocks from where Baldwin grew up – Arthur T. Jersild, is gaining national attention and the two have common interests: children, understanding self and teachers. Jersild's books, *In Search of Self* (1952) and *When Teachers Face Themselves* (1955), I believe, Baldwin would have found informative and validating. Jersild, like Baldwin, has a high regard for children. Jersild's research centers on the importance of thoughts, feelings, and "self" in the inner life of the developing child, along with the subjective dimen-sions of human existence and his key thesis is: a teacher must strive to know self in order to help others because understanding of others and understanding self are closely interwoven. Jersild (1952) argues, "The little child knows what it is to have his feelings hurt, to be sad, to be disappointed" (p. 9). Baldwin's "Little Man, Little Man: A Story of Childhood" a tale of 4-year old TJ, Baldwin's nephew, that I discuss above, also demonstrates that African American children understand the life importance of joy and have agency as they resist the systemic oppression that surrounds them.

Calling up Memories of Great Teachers and Teaching

When I argue that Baldwin is a teacher, I am thinking of some of the African American teachers (and a few European American teachers) I had in school and adults in my life who speak truth about the life and experiences of African American people and the "sins" of a racist country; who discuss with dignity the humanity and culture of African Americans as complex and complicated; who shine light into the dark corners of my mind, to make me more consciously aware of others who are different from me; who encourage excellence, hold me to high expectations; challenge white supremacy, black inferiority and defeatism; and who never hold their tongue when advocating for African American agency and achievement. Baldwin is such a teacher when he works as a professor, lecturer and speaks to teachers and students.

Baldwin more than meets the demands of the African American scholarly and intellectual community for African American teachers to be activists and have social intelligence. He possesses a broad understanding of African American history and a "keen insight" into the social, racial, economic and political problems of American society (Fultz, 1995). Baldwin understands history and he explains to both, African Americans and European Americans how it acts upon them. Baldwin (1965a), as previously noted, argues that history is not something to be only read, or something that refers mainly to the past. Instead, Baldwin contends, "we carry [history] within us, and are unconsciously controlled by it in many ways; and history is literally present in all that we do" (McBride, 1999, p. 343). Baldwin (1965a) wants African Americans, especially students and their teachers, to know "it is to history that we owe our frames of reference, our identities, and our aspirations. And it is with great pain and terror that one begins to realize this" (p. 1). Baldwin's writings and speeches are replete with historical references to slavery, state-sanctioned segregation, the Civil Rights movement, his childhood, and so forth, and he integrates the burden of these histories he carries throughout his writing. Children who are growing up in the Black Lives Matter movement era, the death of Breonna Taylor and COVID-19 will carry with them throughout their life what they learn, what they saw, how they felt in 2013 when George Zimmerman was acquitted for the shooting death of Trayvon Martin, when Chicago police officer Jason Van Dyke was found guilty of murder for shooting Laquan McDonald 16 times and when they saw the video of George Floyd being lynched, crying out: "I can't breathe." In his first novel, *Go Tell It on the Mountain*, Baldwin's history, the one he carries with him, is beautifully told as he tells about his pain as a gay, black 14-year old living in Harlem in the 1930s experiencing a religious awaking and dealing with his embittered stepfather.

Baldwin's essays, speeches and novels can be used as professional development for teacher educators who come to their position unclear of their role as an educator, with a naive understanding of race in America; lacking a critical consciousness about their self and the power and privileges they command; underestimating

The Teacher Within Him **45**

their role in maintaining a racist society; and/or needing to know more about race in America to teach teacher candidates and graduate students how to be educators in multicultural America. Baldwin's writings will help teacher educators who are serious about their craft, ready to learn, and unafraid to teach to the needs and interests of the students who sit before them.

No! To Willful Ignorance; "Living while Black"

Baldwin demands that teachers not engage in willful ignorance, "The practice or act of intentional and blatant avoidance, disregard or disagreement with facts, empirical evidence and well-found arguments because they oppose or contradict your own existing personal beliefs" (Urban Diction, n.d.). For Baldwin "willful ignorance is resistance to facing the horrors of the American past and present and their implications for the future" (Balfour, 2001, p. 27). In other words, Baldwin contends the idea of innocence is a denial of the reality of others and a dis-claiming of this refusal (Schulman, 2008, p. 134).

In this present era of horrific difficulty, as fearmongering fuels consecutive years of hate growth toward African Americans (SPLC, 2019), also known as "Living while Black," Baldwin's writings are as relevant as the day they were published. Baldwin's words, analysis, discourses on the African American experience beg to be retold today because they address the racism seen in Charlotte, Baton Rouge, Ferguson and Baltimore and the rise in hate crimes in cities like Los Angeles where LGBTQ and African Americans are the most targeted. According to Richard Winton (2019) of the *Los Angeles Times*, hate crimes are in the hundreds and rising. Winston states: "Last year, [2018] L.A. tallied 289 hate crimes, com-pared with 256 in 2017 [and] Members of the LGBTQ community, African Americans and those of Jewish faith were the most frequently targeted" (p. 2). Ironically, a report in *The Texas Tribune* by Lillianna Byington, Brittany Brown and Andrew Capps (2018) contends that hate crimes have not received urgent attention from federal prosecutors from January 2010 to July 2018 (the time of the article). Byington, Brown and Capps state

> [J]ust 100 hate crimes — including 10 in Texas — have been pursued by federal prosecutors between January 2010 and July 2018 … Half of those cases across the country — and half of those in Texas — involved racially motivated violence against black Americans, more than any other group.
>
> *(p. 1)*

The Urgency of Reading … Baldwin

The current racial and economic problems in America – that are directly con-nected – demands an urgency for teachers to confront the problems that shape their students' lives by teaching them how to do so. In a 1963 interview with

46 The Teacher Within Him

Jane Howard, Baldwin speaks to the importance of reading to learn about people; to better understand oppression and why people do the things they do. Baldwin (Howard, 1963) states:

> You think that your pain and your heartbreak are unprecedented in the history of the world, but then you read. It was books that taught me that the things that tormented me most were the very things that connected me with all the people who were alive, or who had ever been alive.
>
> *(p. 89)*

Three of Baldwin's books: *Go Tell It on the Mountain* (1953), *Notes of a Native Son* (1955) and *The Fire Next Time* (1953) can connect teacher educators with African Americans who serve as a foundation of the professional development curriculum. The books discuss African American life in the United States, issues of race, interracial relationships, sexuality, social inequality, oppression, economics, capitalism and democracy. Writing about *Notes of a Native Son*, Sonya Huber (2019) offers the following observation that I believe holds true for much of Baldwin's work:

> [F]or a white readership, it is accessible. With its muted somber voice and lasering gaze, Baldwin allows the reader completely into the heart of a nonintimidating presence as it experiences the entire gamut of emotions in waking up to the effects of racism. It has the potential to transform a reader and expose the inner workings of racism by allowing the reader to go along this emotional journey with Baldwin.

Baldwin purposely writes to allow European Americans to enter his work and to appreciate the experiences he discovers (Stein/Gevinson, 1986). Baldwin, throughout his essays and other writings, readers of *James Baldwin and the American Schoolhouse* will discover, wants people to be able "to see the place and people" he is writing about (Stein/Gevinson, 1986). He adopts an authorial voice that assumes a connection with the reader regardless of race (Gevinson, 1986). Baldwin does not complain about being a poor African American man in a country controlled by European Americans, nor does he proclaim hatred of European Americans; instead, he pragmatically explains the effects of racism on African Americans and European Americans. Baldwin, as Granville Hicks argues, has the "ability to find words that astonish the reader with their boldness even as they overwhelm him with their rightness" (Hicks/Gevinson, 1986, p. 7). Baldwin, speaking about his positionality in *Notes of a Native Son* states: "I shifted the point of view to 'we.' Who is the 'we'? I'm talking about we, the American people."

In *Go Tell It on the Mountain* (1953), that I introduce above, Baldwin describes the brutality of systemic racism and gives readers a picture of the dehumanization of African Americans after Emancipation as he discusses the physical, social and psychological circumstances of different characters' lives. *Go Tell It on the Mountain* is not the typical book found on teacher educators' syllabi; it has been banned and challenged by some parents for violence, profanity and explicit homosexuality (John masturbates in a bathroom while thinking of other boys, noting that he "watched in himself a transformation of which he could never dare to speak"; p.13). Nevertheless, the book takes teacher educators into a space they have not ventured into before and allows them to explore the complexity and humanity of an African American family, particularly an African American boy growing up in poverty, overwhelmed by racism and having to live in human misery he does not understand. *Go Tell It on the Mountain* will help teacher educators to appreciate the reasoning, for example, of African American students who sit with their hat and coat on in the classroom because they cannot afford to lose them, or fear that if they are stolen, there is no more money for coats and hats in the family budget. Teacher educators who stereotype African American families and argue they don't do things because they are lazy will discover how parents are haunted by their circumstances, limited choices, and fear of what is happening (structural racism) to their children.

Go Tell It on the Mountain establishes the author's signature characteristic of speaking truth to power and common people and doing it at the expense of being killed or harassed. Baldwin's goal is to break free of racism and oppression as he speaks difficult truths as an act of love, act of protest and act of transformation (*The Inquirer*, 2019). Baldwin's first book has a special significance for teacher candidates or first year teachers who are striving to meet the needs of their students but feel the pressure from the principal's office to teach to the test. Baldwin centers "role" over "place" and tells teachers that their role is to educate students for life in a democracy. Baldwin too was feeling pressure – pressure from within himself and pressure from a society that constructs African Americans in stereotypes; anti-theoretical to democratic life. About *Go Tell It on the Mountain*, Baldwin said, "*Mountain* is the book I had to write if I was ever going to write anything else. I had to deal with what hurt me most. I had to deal, above all, with my father" (Baldwin, interviewed by Leslie Bennetts, 1985, January 10, p. 1).

Baldwin's (1953) advice: "to know who you are" to teachers teaching African American children is pertinent:

> Go back to where you started, or as far back as you can, examine all of it, travel your road again and tell the truth about it. Sing or shout or testify or keep it to yourself: but know whence you came.
>
> *(Baldwin 1953, quoted in* Glassland*, 2016)*

Notes of a Native Son (1955) is a collection of ten autobiographical essays. The essays offer a perspective of African American life and thought on American society after WWII and the Double V social activism campaign led by African American soldiers and citizens to promote a fight for democracy both in the United States and in Europe on the eve of the Civil Rights movement, within a year of *Brown v. Board of Education* (1954) and the soon to be lynching of Emmett Till. *Notes of a Native Son* are Baldwin's recollections of his life experiences that include his contested relationship with his stepfather, discussion of anti-black policies and practices at the time when strange fruit hung on trees in the South and African Americans are paid lower wages and victimized by police in the North. Also, it is a time when racism set in place the poverty, poor housing conditions, depressed community resources that causes COVID-19 to kill so many African American people.

Notes of a Native Son addresses the mystification, depersonalization and stereotyping of African Americans, and it lays bare what it means to be African American in America, the ongoing struggle for voice and food; and it, to borrow from Henry Louis Gates, Jr.: "named for me the things you feel but couldn't utter ... articulated for the first time to European Americans what it meant to be American and an African American at the same time (*Notes of a Native Son*, 2012/1955, back cover).

The ten essays include Baldwin's critique of "Carmen Jones," "Everybody's Protest Novel" and "Many Thousands Gone." The critiques of the misrepresentation of African Americans and the denial that "Black Is Beautiful," ("Carmen Jones"); the failure to interrogate people's actions and a simplistic portrayal of African American humanity ("Everybody's Protest Novel") and the invisibility, negativity, along with false characterizing of African American life as well as the reification of racial stereotypes and taking-up of the cloak of willful innocence in the case of Richard Wright's (1940 character, Bigger Thomas.

Baldwin's analysis and critique of these American cultural artifacts provide teachers with lens and strategies to analyze the instructional materials that cross their desk. Baldwin (1964) speaks clearly about the role of the artist ... and his role when he states, "The role of the artist is exactly the same as the role of the lover. If I love you, I have to make you conscious of the things you don't see" (Dick Cavett Show). The teacher's role, because they love their students, is to make the textbook publishers, curriculum committees responsible for ordering textbooks, and other curriculum materials, as well as the students they teach, aware of the racism, sexism and poverty they are not seeing and, in so doing, refuse to use them.

In addition, the essays in *Notes of a Native Son* point out the feelings of African Americans who suppress their emotions in a European American dominated society. Baldwin's story of not being served in a diner, being ignored, and his humanity not prized is illustrative of what African American parents and students experience in U.S. schools. The African American parent entering the school to "talk" to teachers and administrators about their son or daughter enters feeling much more than a bit anxious, because this is not a moment of celebration, but a time when they will be scolded in some form or fashion or have to deal with a white gaze. The African American parent also enters carrying history of the education system's failure to make schools meaningful to her (including her mother and other female family members) and blaming her 100% for the problem. Schools, as important as they are to her child's life success, are not places of

The Teacher Within Him   **49**

working together, where the adults in the room come together to work out what is best for children and youth, given their needs and interests. African American students are ignored, marginalized or considered deficit when it serves the white interest of school policy and practices.

Teacher educators reading *Notes of a Native Son* will have their white fragility and willful innocence challenged and will be encouraged to accept "The story of the Negro in America is the story of America – or, more precisely, it is the story of Americans" (Baldwin 1955/2012, p, 23). Teacher educators reading *Notes of a Native Son* will learn ways African Americans affects American psychology are betrayed in our popular culture and in our morality; and in our estrangement from African Americans is the depth of our estrangement from ourselves (Baldwin, 1955/2012). Baldwin continues with a question that demands so much more than for African Americans and European Americans to talk about race; what is demanded is to honestly put one's feelings on the line. Baldwin posits

> We cannot ask: what do we really feel about him [African Americans] – such a question merely opens the gates on chaos. What we really feel about him is involved with all that we feel about everything, about everyone, about ourselves.
>
> *(p. 24)*

In *Notes of a Native Son* teachers and teacher candidates will learn of African Americans' deep frustration with European Americans "not getting it"; that is, not understanding how racism governs and influences African Americans' lives. Dan Wakefield (1988), a friend of Baldwin writes about "how white folks not getting it" turned his relationship with Jimmy sour. Wakefield describes a time when Baldwin was fearful that his ambitious and talented 16-year-old sister, who wants to become a fashion designer is in pain because of the effects of racism on her at her fashion show. Wakefield sets the scene, by describing how a French-woman friend at the show describes the "pain" of Jimmy's sister as pain that comes with being a 16-year-old girl: "But, Jimmy, all 16-year-old girls are in pain!" said the Frenchwoman. Wakefield posits, he jumped into the discussion on the side of the Frenchwoman arguing with passion: "Even all 16-year-old boys suffer, no matter what color they are!" Wakefield, next reports: Upon hearing these remarks, Jimmy's enormous eyes grew wider, his brows raised in shock, as he turned on me and said, simply, "You don't understand." Jimmy argued, Wakefield states, "that we didn't understand, that his sister's suffering was of a different order, a more tragic one, because of her being a Negro."

Years later, Wakefield continues, he remained haunted by the incident and therefore decided to discuss the experience in an introduction to a book: *Between the Lines* (1966). Wakefield posits "I quoted from *Baldwin's own* 'Letters From a Journey'," *where he wrote*, "I have said for years color does not matter." Followed by: "I am now beginning to feel that it does not matter at all, that it masks something else which does matter; but this suspicion changes for me, the entire nature of reality."

Wakefield then says, I added my own reprise: "When each of us is able to entertain that suspicion, we will have no choice but to move ahead, out of the easy poses of public rhetoric and into more difficult interior territory."

In this "more difficult territory," Wakefield concludes: "All of us then, black and white, will be forced to grapple with the far more important calculation of what Henry James so eloquently called 'the terrible algebra of your own existence.'" Finally, Wakefield explains, he continued to feel unsatisfied with his attempt to justify himself, or his view, and that it was something that had come back to him over the years. It was one of those troubling loose ends that tickle and disturb one's consciousness, and conscience, in the night. It was not, posited Wakefield until he sat down and wrote out again a copy of his own words, that he understood Jimmy's point *"What I understand several decades (and lifetimes, it seems) later is that part of the very 'algebra' of one's existence is the factor of color—as real in the equation as is a factor in mathematics—which in this society may still, quite literally, kill you* [author's emphasis]."

In reading *Notes of a Native Son*, teacher educators bear witness to Baldwin's – or African Americans' – thoughts and actions toward social, cultural and political issues in America. *Notes of a Native Son*, in this time of Black Lives Matter and activists for LGBTQ rights, teacher educators will discover, is as relevant and powerful as when it was written. For, although black representation in movies, literature and in settings such as the Super Bowl and NBA All Star Games have improved in recent years and African Americans "protest novels" and movies such as "Get Out" and "Us" are popular, Baldwin argues, they do not bring about real social change, but instead foster a false sense of understanding and identification that still maintains "otherness" (Nemeth, 2013).

Teacher educators will also see European Americans as supportive and not as hapless missionaries. Baldwin is never out to malign European Americans, but to help them realize they are the problem, they are impairing the American democratic project. Willful ignorance, flawed understanding of U.S. history, refusal to investigate one's life experience, including schooling experiences related to African Americans, obstruct the American democratic project. Teacher educators who don't have a factual account of U.S. history can't challenge the historical omissions and inaccuracies teacher candidates bring to their class. In addition, teacher educators who have not recently examined the social theory they learned in college to instruct teacher candidates about teaching African American students are inadequately serving both teacher candidates and the students they will teach.

Reading *The Fire Next Time* published in 1963 at the height of the Civil Rights movement when race relations were nearing a boiling point will provide teacher educators with a picture of U.S. European American–African American relations at a critical time in U.S. history and the questions of racial gains debated today. Many African Americans today argue that the Civil Rights movement did

The Teacher Within Him **51**

not produce much improvement for the average African American person. Though there are no snarling attack dogs or young African American women being soaked by a fireman's hose to break up racial protest demonstrations, there remains an America where African American women mysteriously die in jail, or are murdered as they lay sleeping in their bed by police, and an African American man is choked to death by a police officer on the suspicion of selling single cigarettes, and where American institutions do not treat non-white people with the same degree of respect as they treat European Americans. In *The Fire Next Time,* Baldwin is arguing that if African Americans and European Americans don't put aside their anger and work things out, a "fire" will come. Baldwin, as Henry Louis Gates, Jr. contends in "The Fire Last Time" is arguing that our private neuroses are shaped by public ones, the questions of self, lead not to an escape from racial drama, but a rediscovery of it. Gates notes that Baldwin (1955) dismissed the non-racial self, instead observing:

> There are few things on earth more attractive than the idea of the unspeakable liberty which is allowed the unredeemed. When, beneath the black mask, a human being begins to make himself felt one cannot escape a certain awful wonder as to what kind of human being it is. What one's imagination makes of other people is dictated, of course, by the laws of one's own personality and it is one of the ironies of black-white relations that, by means of what the white man imagines the black man to be, the black man is enabled to know who the white man is
>
> *(Gates, 1992)*

The Fire Next Time has two parts: "Down at the Cross: Letter from a Region in My Mind" is the second essay and "My Dungeon Shook: Letter to My Nephew on the One Hundredth Anniversary of the Emancipation" is the first essay, which I will return to in Chapter 3, "Teachers 'Go for Broke.'" In the book, Baldwin evaluates African American progress a century after the Emancipation Proclamation, which supposedly gave African Americans their freedom. He describes the challenges and barriers to African American life, especially young African American male life in "Letter to My Nephew." Baldwin is candid about the everyday dangers and degradations African Americans face and he is angry about European American complacency and apathy. Baldwin, teacher educators will learn, believes that for African American students to be free in America, teachers need to decenter whiteness in their classrooms. While European American teachers may not be able to eliminate institutional white supremacy and the privileges that come with white skin color, on an individual level, they can work to undercut white supremacy in their teaching practice. Baldwin argues that schools must educate African American children to accept and appreciate their culture and prepare them so they have the knowledge and skills to pursue their dreams of choice.

52 The Teacher Within Him

Teacher educators will learn that Baldwin is not down on African American people. He knows that African American undergraduate and graduate students are a proud thoughtful group. They know that "Black is beautiful" is found within them and not according to European Americans' measuring stick. Baldwin explains the hate European Americans have of African Americans is self-hatred and guilt that they project onto African Americans. Baldwin (1962a) argues,

> The only way he the white man can be released from the Negro's tyrannical power over him is to consent, in effect, to become black himself, to become part of that suffering and dancing country that he now watches wistfully from the heights of his lonely power and, armed with spiritual traveler's checks, visits surreptitiously after dark.
>
> *(p. 4)*

Baldwin would say in an *Esquire* (1968) interview, "White ... is not a color – it's an attitude. You're as white as you think you are, it's your choice" (p. 2).

"Letter to My Nephew" takes European American teacher educators into guarded space and no-nonsense moments in the life of African American young males and increasingly, African American young females; when an adult in the family or community speaks directly, eyeball to eyeball, about life outside of the front door: on the sidewalk, in the streets and alleys where African American children travel ... in the innocence, they are denied. Baldwin (1962a) explains,

> This innocent country set you down in a ghetto in which, in fact, it intended that you should perish. Let me spell out precisely what I mean by that for the heart of the matter is here and the crux of my dispute with my country. You were born where you were born and faced the future that you faced because you were black and for no other reason.
>
> *(p. 7)*

Teacher educators reading "Letter to My Nephew" will note in Baldwin's first paragraph he tells his nephew that the cause of any lack of success on his part will be due to his being sucked into whites' lies about him: "believing that you really are what the white world call a nigger" (p. 4). Teacher educators will also discover that the birth of an African American child is a time to rejoice and celebrate and that African American parents reject discourses that describe them as lazy or not wanting to go all out to help their children succeed. Baldwin (1962a) states:

> Well, you were born, here you came, something like fifteen years ago; and though your father and mother and grandmother, looking about the streets through which they were carrying you, staring at the walls into which they brought you, had every reason to be heavyhearted, yet they were not. For

The Teacher Within Him **53**

here you were, Big James, named for me—you were a big baby, I was not—
here you were: to be loved.

(p. 6)

In addition, teacher educators will discover why African American students may
hesitate to believe or trust them. They have been disappointed and lied to by their
previous teachers' misconceptions or denials of their ability and worth because they
are African American. In "Letter to My Nephew," Baldwin (1962a) warns his
nephew, James about his uncertain future because of his skin color, and for no
other reason. He explains to James that his race, perhaps, unknown to him, was the
cause of some of his rejections and determines how others viewed his worth.

Similarly, in "Letter from a Region in My Mind" Baldwin (1962b) posits:

In any case, white people, who had robbed black people of their liberty and
who profited by this theft every hour that they lived, had no moral ground
on which to stand. They had the judges, the juries, the shotguns, the law—
in a word, power. But it was a criminal power, to be feared but not respected, and to be outwitted in any way whatever. And those virtues preached
but not practiced by the white world were merely another means of holding
Negroes in subjection.

(p. 23)

Some European American teacher educators reading Baldwin will ask, "Am I the
problem?" Reading Baldwin demands honest self-reflection and responsibility,
otherwise the time spent reading is wasted. Baldwin argues that everyone,
including teacher educators, must understand their past and present reality and
must act on that understanding. Baldwin (1968) posits: "All that can save you
now is our confrontation with your own history – which is not your past, but
your present" (*Esquire*, p. 2).

Other Baldwin books, such as *Nobody Knows My Name: More Notes from a Native
Son* (1961), teacher educators working to find their teaching identity, striving to
establish their role in the field and seeking to help teacher candidates find their
teaching identity, will discover useful. Baldwin does not allow himself to be defined
by others (e.g., Norman Mailer), he stands up to friends and colleagues (e.g., Richard
Wright), is introspective about being African American in America, and is simply
outstanding when describing racism in America (e.g., Buckley). Baldwin speaks rea-
listically about what it means to struggle for recognition of African American
humanity in a world in which one's existence – in and of itself – is a form of resistance. In 1961, J. Michael Crichton, reviewing *Nobody Knows My Name* for *The
Harvard Crimson* wrote at the conclusion of his review:

The result is a series of essays which push, gently—and often, not so gently—
toward a single theme: the idea that Negroes want to be treated like men,

54 The Teacher Within Him

that they will no longer allow white men to put them in their "place", and that the United States must be prepared to accept the Negro in the North, in the South, and in all the world. It is an important idea in a turbulent world, and few men have been able to discuss it in so eloquent and honest a fashion.

In 2013, Ta-Nehisi Coates's article in *The Atlantic* asked: Is James Baldwin America's Greatest Essayist? Coates closed the first paragraph of the article: "Some people who are important to us as young people, wither under our gaze as older adults. And then other people who we know as genius somehow just increase in our estimation." Coates open the second paragraph: "Baldwin is among those people for me." Baldwin's essays on contemporary culture address being black and white in America, politics, movies, literature, education, schools and other topics, fearlessly and honestly. Natasha Balwit (2016) states Baldwin, besides being the greatest American essayist in history, is also a sharp examiner of the urban environment. Balwit (2016) contends that Baldwin's writings about Paris, New York, and especially Harlem are "marked by vividness and specificity ... that grounded his explorations of black life and human experience" (p. 1). Balwit (2016) marvels at Baldwin's ability to capture the rhythms of city life, the characters and habits and various circumstances of their inhabitants, as well as the broader character of cultures, populations and institutions. In addition, Balwit calls Baldwin's essays "bouncy, free-ranging, ebullient, conversational juggling of current events" (p. 2). Such discerning observations about African American humanity and life is informative to teacher educators and teachers who are dedicated to learning how to teach African American students; that Baldwin's work is "free-ranging" and welcoming of readers should be a call to teacher educators and teachers to encourage their students to read James Baldwin. Baldwin's books and essays are at home in cultural studies and black queer studies programs on university campuses; and his works, while up to now sparingly used in schools of education (except "A Talk to Teachers"), can bring historical and current insights and discoveries to the schools' overt and hidden curriculum and school policies and procedures.

James Baldwin as Genuine and Jeanes Teacher

Baldwin as teacher meets the yardstick of my colleague and historian of African American education, Michael Fultz's (1995) idea of the "genuine teacher." The genuine teachers were African American teachers in the South in the first half of the 1900s. These teachers knew that their duty was not bound by the four walls of the classroom and that teaching African American children and community members about social conditions, the changing society, along with upholding the mental, moral, religious and physical status of African Americans were equally important. Fultz (1995), drawing on the education literature written about African American teachers, describes the characteristics of the "genuine teacher" that

Baldwin reflects: one who provides selfless service to the race, one whose integrity and racial commitment is beyond question, one who is a social critic about racism, oppression and how it affects African American children, and one who does not shy away from being the messenger for hope and expectations of the race.

Baldwin also embodies characteristics of the celebrated Jeanes Teachers, who were supervisors of teachers in the South from 1908 to 1968. Jeanes Teachers were dedicated "to make life better for poor black people" (Williams and NASC Interim History Writing Committee, 1979, p. 94) and they understood that power is created by those who make it. Baldwin, like Jeanes Teachers, advocates a curriculum that challenges white supremacy and addresses illiteracy and poverty in African American communities (Littlefield, n.d.). Treuhaft-Ali (2017), speaking about Jeanes Teachers, argues,

> These African-American women were originally hired to implement a curriculum designed to instill black students with an acceptance of the white supremacist racial hierarchy. Instead, they transformed the curriculum into one that stressed African American community development, economic self-determination, and one that visualized African American children as future citizens and leaders.

Baldwin too, when he writes or speaks, transforms white supremacists' racial design. Baldwin debunks America's claim of racial innocence and race blindness and discourses of sincere efforts to bring about equality for all as myth.

James Baldwin: Reflective Teaching

Baldwin also is a reflective teacher and he practices critical reflection (Schon, 1983) to address issues of race, inequality, sexuality, violence, family and personal transformation. Baldwin identifies and examines how African Americans are erased. He points out the power at play and the forces at work. Baldwin uses critical reflection to unearth hypocrisies and ironies in American culture. Baldwin's criticism of American life and history exemplifies the kind and quality of work reflective teachers using critical reflection do.

Let me be more specific about my meaning of reflective teacher and critical reflection and how I arrived at my thinking about the concept. In the early 1980s, I was invited by Allyn & Bacon publishers to edit an anthology of readings to help European American teachers better teach and connect with a student population that was rapidly becoming Latinx and African American. The result was *Preparing for Reflective Teaching* (1984). Ironically, at the time public education was being declared in crisis because America was losing its preeminence in the world and American students' reading and math scores were below many other developed nations. *A Nation at Risk: The Imperative for Educational Reform*, a report commissioned by President Ronald Reagan's National Commission on Excellence in Education described the quality of education in the United States as a "rising tide of mediocrity" and demanded *excellence* and *equity*. In response to the *Nation at Risk*, the Holmes Groups, a consortium of 96 institutions of higher education, proposed to make the education of teachers intellectually more solid and create standards of entry and The Carnegie Forum on Education and the Economy proposed to restructure schools to strengthen the role of teachers and the creation of the National Board for Professional Teaching Standards. Also helping to establish *excellence*, but ignoring *equity* at the time was Allan Bloom's (1987) *The Closing of the American Mind*, E. D. Hirsch, Jr.'s *Cultural Literacy* and Arthur Schlesinger, Jr.'s *The Disuniting of America*. The three books dismissed *equity*, ignored the efforts of the Civil Rights movement, and challenged the arrival of multicultural education (including a culturally relevant curriculum), a growing multiracial population and rock music. Bloom (1987), a fierce advocate for the Western canon and "high" art (e.g., Wagner's operas), asked in an article titled "Is Rock Music Rotting Our Kids' Minds?" concluded the article, asserting "[A]s long as they [young people] have the Walkman on, they cannot hear what the great tradition has to say. And, after its prolonged use, when they take it off, they find they are deaf." For Bloom, popular culture, to use the analysis of Vogel (2018), author of *James Baldwin and the 1980s*, is "not only absurd but also dangerous" (p. 3).

In this complex educational moment: changing demographics, China and other countries rising up and America, slipping back, reading and math scores of students in the U.S. dismal, and people of color expecting racial progress from the Civil Rights movement, Allyn and Bacon (A&B) wanted a book that would take these problems and issues into account. A&B didn't want a formal hardcover textbook, but a text that would appeal to European American teacher educators, mostly men, responsible for the selection of texts for their Methods, Foundation, and Introduction to Education courses. Additionally, the publisher wanted a text that would engage and be informative to European American female teacher candidates who knew they would soon be teaching African American and Latinx students. The publishers knew most of these teacher candidates knew very little about their future students, and some were fearful – or their parents were fearful – of them teaching African American students in urban neighborhoods. My mission, which I accepted, was to edit such a text. "Reflective teaching" was a cutting theme in the academic community at the time and had a deep connection to John Dewey, one of America's foremost philosophers and educators. Furthermore, and important to those who this project would ultimately affect (i.e., African American and Latinx students), Dewey's philosophy and pedagogical practices didn't view African American students as inferior or only capable of a vocational education.

Dewey had earned creds in the African American education and political community. Dewey was one of the founding members of the National Association for the Advancement of Colored People (NAACP). Also, Dewey's remarks on the Negro brain at the National Negro Conference in New York in 1909 included "there is no inferior race," and the members of any race should each have the same opportunities of social environment and personality as those of a more favored race. Such beliefs, to me, were a necessity for developing a text.

The first chapter, "On Becoming a Reflective Teacher," authored by my good friend and colleague, Kenneth M. Zeichner, and me, addresses how teachers should teach African American and Latinx students, and students in general. Ken and I borrowed from the work of John Dewey about teachers and argue that in teaching, there is an important distinction between human actions that are *reflective* and *routine*. Dewey contended that routine action is behavior guided by impulse, tradition and authority.

As I think about Baldwin as a teacher, I know that his work is not guided by impulse, tradition or authority. Baldwin's work is deliberate – it questioned tradition, it is critical, it holds up the third finger to European American authority, and it challenges European Americans to examine themselves and their leaders. Baldwin (1963) told European American activists to critically reflect, for:

> [T]hey had not realized, how cheaply, after all, the rulers of the republic held their white lives to be. Coming to the defense of the rejected and destitute, they were confronted with the extent of their own alienation, and the unimaginable dimensions of their own poverty. They were privileged and secure only so long as they did, in effect, what they were told: but they had been raised to believe that they were free.

Baldwin's actions are reflective. In *The Fire Next Time*, Baldwin (1963) states, "Privately, we cannot stand our lives and dare not examine them" (p. 89). Like the renowned teacher Anna Julia Cooper, and principals, of M Street High School in Washington, D.C., Baldwin told young people not to let America define who you are, and like Cooper, Baldwin is resolute when addressing the humanity of African Americans. Cooper (1892) unswervingly challenges the ways and means African Americans are systematically and structurally dehumanized and located below European American models of humanity. Baldwin, too, rebels against discourses that negatively describe African Americans and throughout his fiction and nonfiction argues against African Americans having to reinvent or justify their humanity over and over again, in every generation.

Baldwin exhibits three critical attitudes, along with moral reasoning that Dewey defines as prerequisites for reflective teaching. First, *openmindedness* refers to an active desire to listen to more than one side, to consider multiple perspectives and to be willing to change when facts support change. Baldwin demonstrates openmindedness, as I discuss above, during his stay in Paris as he willingly engages with different people and comes to understand that he loves America. *Openmindedness*, ironically, Baldwin also demonstrates, as he thinks about African

58 The Teacher Within Him

Americans, not the way European Americans want him to think about African Americans; or with fear; that is, how family members, including parents are pressured to only think about African Americans. In "Letter from a Region in My Mind," Baldwin (1962) demonstrates his openmindedness. A mind not shackled by racist ideology and structures to keep African Americans in "their" place. Baldwin (1962) states:

> The fear that I heard in my father's voice, for example, when he realized that I really *believed* I could do anything a white boy could do, and had every intention of proving it, was not at all like the fear I heard when one of us was ill or had fallen down the stairs or strayed too far from the house. It was another fear, a fear that the child, in challenging the white world's assumptions, was putting himself in the path of destruction.
>
> *(p. 26)*

Baldwin's openmindedness allows him to think outside of the box constructed by racism and wrapped in traditions of power and privilege.

Second, an attitude of *responsibility* involves careful consideration of the consequences to which an action leads. Throughout Baldwin's work, he shows an attitude of responsibility and addresses the consequences of the black–white racial struggle. Baldwin (1962) accepts his responsibility in the struggle when he argues one "must never cease warring with his society, for its sake and for his own" (p. 317). Baldwin (1962) contends that much more than politics, much more than the political theater of the March on Washington, is needed to put down the ugly moral problem of racism in American hearts and mind. Baldwin (1962) accepts his responsibility when he argues,

> the conquest of the physical world is not man's only duty. He is also enjoined to conquer the great wilderness of himself. The precise role of the artist, then, is to illuminate that darkness, blaze roads through that vast forest, so that we will not, in all our doing, lose sight of its purpose, which is, after all, to make the world a more human dwelling place.
>
> *(p. 1)*

Third, Baldwin fully engaged in an attitude of *wholeheartness* throughout his life, and especially so, with his critical forthright discussions of racism and bluntly pointing out that African Americans stand outside the promise of democracy. Baldwin is wholehearted in his attack on America's racial innocence and developing a race consciousness. Baldwin (1959) posits that "Any honest examination of the national life proves how far we are from the standard of human freedom with which we began. The recovery of this standard demands of everyone who loves this country a hard look at himself" (p. 170). Baldwin argues that European Americans adopt an ignorance about race/racism; they refuse to deeply examine

The Teacher Within Him **59**

racial injustice as they protect beliefs about the character of American society from countervailing evidence of American history. Baldwin acknowledges the expansion of formal equality (e.g., *Brown*) and the rise of middle-class African Americans to positions of power (e.g., big-city mayors); nevertheless, he argues that a line between "white" and "black" Americans persists. The persistence is evident in income levels, residential patterns, incarceration rates, life expectancy, and a variety of other empirical measures that suggest ways the link between the color line and racial injustice exist. Such persistence argues that European Americans are unwilling – wholeheartedly – to confront the ongoing significance of the color line.

In *James Baldwin: A Biography* by David Leeming (1994), the author gives an account of Baldwin, the *reflective teacher* demonstrating the moral attitudes of *openmindness, responsibility*, and *wholeheartness*. Leeming (1994) describes Baldwin, as he would rail against racism and oppression of Americans, especially those who were poor, gay and African American or Latinx at Thursday night meetings held to discuss literary magazine projects. Here Baldwin – the *reflective teacher* – would give his European American friends an assignment to rewrite the Gettysburg Address to reflect critically the reality of America. Leeming (1994) describes:

> The guru [Baldwin] handed out assignments to what the group thought of as his "informal army." Once he told them to rewrite the Gettysburg Address to reflect the reality of America. They did, and Claire Burch in 1989 was still rewriting it…. The scenes in the Burches' living room would be reenacted in hundreds of white living rooms in which James Baldwin felt compelled to preach – *teach* – during the forty-two years following the Gettysburg Address assignments.
>
> *(Leeming, 1994, p. 48)*

Throughout Baldwin's essays and as you listen to him speak, he is teaching; he is a *reflective teacher: openmindedness, responsibility* and *wholeheartness* are fundamental to his pedagogical creed and practice of critical reflection. Teacher educators, teachers and teacher candidates should emulate James Baldwin's openmindedness, responsibility and wholeheartness as they teach.

Bibliography

Acham, C. (2004). *Revolution Televised: Prime Time and the Struggle for Black Power.* Minneapolis, MI: University of Minnesota Press. p. 6.

Alcoff, L. M. (1998). What should white people do? History is a weapon. https://www.historyisaweapon.com/defcon1/alcoffwhitepeople.html. 6/16/2019.

Alicke, M. (2017). Willful ignorance and self-deception. *Psychology Today.* https://www.psychologytoday.com/us/blog/why-we-blame/201709/willful-ignorance-and-self-deception. 6/21/2019.

60 The Teacher Within Him

Andrews-Dyer, H. (2010). Jonathan Majors is your new American hero. *The Washington Post.* August 13. https://www.washingtonpost.com/entertainment/jonathan-majors-profile-lovecraft-country/2020/08/12/8b64de9a-dc0a-11ea-b205-ff838e15a9a6_story.html?hpid=hp_sundayarts-panel-8-12_majors-1210pm%3Ahomepage%2Fstory-ans. 8/13/20.

Baldwin, J. (1953). *Go Tell It on the Mountain.* New York, NY: Knopf.

Baldwin, J. (1953/2016). Quoted in *Glassland*, 2016. https://www.kickstarter.com/projects/1555843610/glassland. 8/8/2019.

Baldwin, J. (1955). *Notes of a Native Son.* New York, NY: Beacon Press.

Baldwin, J. (1959/1985). Nobody knows my name. In *The Price of the Ticket.* New York, NY: St. Martin's Press.

Baldwin, J. (1962a). A letter to my nephew. *The Progressive.* https://progressive.org/magazine/letter-nephew/. 6/15/ 2019.

Baldwin, J. (1962b). The creative process. In *The Price of the Ticket.* New York, NY: St. Martin's Press.

Baldwin J. (1963a). My dungeon shook. History is a weapon. https://www.historyisaweapon.com/defcon1/baldwindungeonshook.html.

Baldwin, J. (1963b). *The Price of the Ticket.* Film. https://www.huffpost.com/entry/11-james-baldwin-quotes-on-race-that-resonate-now-more-than-ever_n_58936929e4b06f344e40664c. 8/8/2019.

Baldwin, J. (1964). Values because they don't accept me. Interview with Robert Penn Warren. Literary Hub. https://lithub.com/james-baldwin-i-cant-accept-western-values-because-they-dont-accept-me/. 4/23/2020.

Baldwin, J. (1965a). Quoted in Dwight McBride (1999). *James Baldwin Now.* New York, NY: New York University Press.

Baldwin, J. (1965b). *Going to Meet the Man.* New York, NY: Dial Press.

Baldwin, J. (1968). Interview James Baldwin: How to cool it. *Esquire.* July.

Baldwin, J (1974). *If Beale Street Could Talk.* New York, NY: Dial Press.

Baldwin, J. (1976). *The Devil Finds Work.* New York, NY: Vintage.

Baldwin, J. (1979). If black English isn't a language, what is? *The New York Times.* July 29. https://www.nytimes.com/2010/09/26/opinion/eq-baldwin.html. 6/11/2019.

Baldwin, J. (1984). On being "white" and other lies. *Essence.* April.

Baldwin, J. (1985). James Baldwin reflects on "Go Tell it" PBS Film. Interview by Leslie Bennetts. *The New York Times.* https://www.nytimes.com/1985/01/10/books/james-baldwin-reflects-on-go-tell-it-pbs-film.html. 6/22/2019.

Balwit, N. (2016). James Baldwin's cities. Bloomberg CityLab. https://www.bloomberg.com/news/articles/2016-08-02/james-baldwin-s-essays-on-cities-are-as. 12/4/2020.

Baldwin, J. (1993). *Nobody Knows My Name: More Notes of a Native Son.* New York, NY: Vintage Books.

Baldwin, J. (1998). On being "white" … and others lies. In Editor David R. Roediger. *Black on White: Black Writer on What it Means to be White.* New York, NY: Schocken Books. https://bannekerinstitute.fas.harvard.edu/files/bannekerinstitute/files/on_being_white.and_other_lies_bald. 6/11/2019.

Baldwin, J. (2016). *I Am Not Your Negro.* Film.

Balfour, L. (2001). *Evidence of Things Not Said: James Baldwin and the Promise of American Democracy.* Ithaca, NY: Cornell University Press. p. 27.

Balto, S. E. (2012). James Baldwin's America and the paradox of race. *The Progressive.* https://progressive.org/magazine/james-baldwin-s-america-paradox-race/. 12/10/2018.

The Teacher Within Him **61**

Beard, L. A. (2016). "Flesh of their flesh, bone of their bone": James Baldwin's racial politics of boundness. *Contemporary Political Theory*. https://www.academia.edu/28698985/Flesh_of_their_flesh_bone_of_their_bone_James_Baldwins_racial_politics_of_boundness. 6/12/19.

Bigsby, C. W. E. (1969). Editor. *The Black American Writer, Volume 2: Poetry and Drama*. Northampton, MA: Everett/Edwards.

Bloom, A. (1987). Is rock music rotting our kids' minds? *The Washington Post*. https://www.washingtonpost.com/archive/opinions/1987/06/0. 12/18/2018.

Bone, R. (1965). James Baldwin. In *The Negro Novel in America*. rev. ed. New Haven: Yale University Press. pp. 215–239.

Byington, L., Brown, B. and Capps, A. (2018). Black Americans are still victims of hate crimes more than any other group. *The Texas Tribune*. August, 16. https://www.texastribune.org/2018/08/16/african-americans/. 6/22/2019.

CNN Live Update. (4/27/2020). Coronavirus pandemic: Updates from around the world. https://www.cnn.com/world/live-news/coronavirus-pandemic-04-27-20-intl/index.html. 4/27/2020.

Coates, T. (2013). Is James Baldwin America's greatest essayist? *The Atlantic*. September 26. 12/4/2020.

Cohan, A. and Howlett, C. F. (2017). John Dewey and his evolving perceptions of race issues in American democracy. *Faculty Works: Education*, 24. http://digitalcommons.molloy.edu/edu_fac/24.

Conrad, J. (1897). *The Nigger of the "Narcissus": A Tale of the Sea*. Harvard University.

Crichton, J. M. (1961). Book of essays describes state of Negro race. *The Harvard Crimson*. https://www.thecrimson.com/article/1961/11/10/book-of-essays-describes-state-of/. 4/6/2019.

Cunningham, V. (2015). Why Ta-Nehisi Coates isn't our James Baldwin. *The Intelligencer*. August 5. http://nymag.com/intelligencer/2015/08/why-ta-nehisi-coates-isnt-our-james-baldwin.html. 6/20/ 2019.

Dewey, J. (1909). Address to National Negro Conference. *Proceedings of the National Negro Conference*. New York, May 31 and June 1. http://moses.law.umn.edu/darrow/documents/Proceedings%20of%20the%20National%20Negro%20C. 12/18/2018.

Dewey, J. (1916). *Democracy and Education*. New York, NY: Macmillan & Co.

Dunbar, P. (1896). We wear the mask. Poems by Paul Laurence Dunbar. (poets.org). 12/4/2020.

Dyson, M. E. (2015). Between the world and me: Baldwin's heir. *The Atlantic*. https://www.theatlantic.com/politics/archive/2015/07/james-baldwin-tanehisi-coates/399413/. 1/ 3/2019.

Freedmen's Record, April1865. https://www.americanantiquarian.org/Freedmen/Intros/freedteachers.html. 12/6/2018.

Fultz, M. (1995). African American teachers in the South, 1890–1940: Powerless and the ironies of expectations and protest. *History of Education Quarterly*, 35, 4, 401–422. https://www-jstor-org.ezproxy.library.wisc.edu/stable/369578?sid=primo&origin=crossref&seq=11#metadata_info_tab_contents. 12/6/2018.

Garrett, D. (2002). The inner life and the social world in the work of James Baldwin. Book review." *Identity Theory*. http://www.identitytheory.com/life-social-world-work-james-baldwin/. 3/27/2019.

Gates, H. L., Jr. (1992). The fire last time. *The New Republic*. June 1. https://newrepublic.com/article/114134/fire-last-time. 3/29/2019.

Gevinson, A. (1986). James Baldwin at the National Press Club. December 10. https://www.loc.gov/rr/record/pressclub/pdf/JamesBaldwin.pdf. 3/28/2019.

Gilliam, D. (1980). Public education in the '80s: A sense of deepening crisis. *The Washington Post.* https://www.washingtonpost.com/archive/local/1980/01/07/p. 12/13/2018.

Govedar, D. (2015). The role of the television in the 1960s US Civil Rights Movement. https://onlinemind.org/2015/12/02/the-r
ole-of-the-television-in-the-1960s-us-civil-rights-movement/.

Green, T. (2020). Interviewed by Karley Marotta. Local experts weigh in on black communities disproportionate share of COVID-19 deaths. June 18. 27 abc. WKOW.com. https://wkow.com/2020/06/18/local-experts-weigh-in-on-black-communities-disproportionate-share-of-covid-19-deaths/. 8/6/2020.

Gyarkye, L. (2017). James Baldwin and the struggle to bear witness. *The New Republic.* https://newrepublic.com/article/140395/james-baldwin-struggle-bear-witness. 3. 27/2019.

Hedges, C. (2017). James Baldwin and the meaning of whiteness. February 20. Common Dreams. https://www.commondreams.org/views/2017/02/20/james-baldwin-and-meaning. 6/15/2019.

hooks, b. (1994). *Teaching to Transgress: Education as the Practice of Freedom.* New York, NY: Routledge.

hooks, b. (2003). James Baldwin conference keynote address. C-Span.org. 12/4/2020.

Howard, J. (1963). Telling talk from a Negro writer. *Life,* 54, 21, May 24, 81–93.

Hughes, L. (1958). Notes of a Native Son. Baldwin, J. Reviewed by Langston Hughes. *The New York Times Book Review.*

Huber, S.James Baldwin: Nonfiction of a native son. *ASSAY: A Journal of Nonfiction Studies.* https://www.assayjournal.com/sonya-huber-8203james-baldwin-nonfiction-of-a-native-son-31.html. 3/30/2019.

Index Magazine, Harvard Museum. (2018). Scenes from James Baldwin's world. https://www.harvardartmuseums.org/article/scenes-from-james-baldwin-s-world.

Jensen, A. R. (1969). How much can we boost IQ and scholastic achievement? *Harvard Educational Review,* 39, 1–123.

Jersild, A. T. (1952). *In Search of Self; An Explanation of the Role of the School in Promoting Self-understanding.* New York, NY: Teachers College Press.

Jersild, A. T. (1955). *When Teachers Face Themselves.* New York, NY: Teachers College Press.

Jones, B. F. (1966). James Baldwin: The struggle for identity. *The British Journal of Sociology,* 17, 2, 107–121.

Kazin, A. (1961). The open form: Essays for our time. New York, NY: Harcourt.

Kennedy, J. (1963). Radio and television report to the American people on Civil Rights, June 11. https://www.jfklibrary.org/archives/other-resources/john-f-kennedy-speeches/civil-rights-radio-and-television-report-19630611. 6/22/2019.

King, M. L K., Jr. (1957/2010). *Strength to Love.* Minneapolis, MN: Fortress Press.

Leeming, D. (1994). *James Baldwin: A Biography.* New York, NY: Arcade.

Leeming, D. (2007). the white problem. Pen America. https://pen.org/the-white-problem/. 4/30/2020.

Levin, D. (1964). Quoted in Susan J. McWilliam (2017). Editor. *A Political Companion to James Baldwin.* Lexington, KY: University of Kentucky Press.

Levin, D. (1964). Baldwin's autobiographical essays: The problem of Negro identity. *The Massachusetts Review,* 5, 2, 239–247. JSTOR. 12/4/2020.

The Teacher Within Him   **63**

Littlefield, V. (n. d.). Jeanes teachers—History, goals, and duties, the Homemakers Clubs Rosenwald Schools, health care, contribution. http://education.stateuniversity.com/pages/2135/Jeanes-Teachers.html. 12/10/2018.

Lodge, S. (2017). James Baldwin's sole children's book comes back into print. December 7. https://www.publishersweekly.com/pw/by-topic/childrens/childrens-book-news/article/75551-james-baldwin-s. 6/20/2019.

Lydon, C. (2017). Cornel West on why James Baldwin matters more than ever. Literary Hub, Radio Open Source. March 2. https://lithub.com/cornel-west-on-why-james-baldwin-matters-more-than-ever/.

Maguire, L. (2018). James Baldwin and racial justice. Philosophy Talk. 12 February. https://www.philosophytalk.org/blog/james-baldwin-and-racial-justice. 6/15/2019.

McBride, D. (1999). *James Baldwin Now.* New York, NY: New York University Press.

McWhorter, J. (2019). The idea that whites can't refer to the N-word. *The Atlantic.* April. https://www.theatlantic.com/ideas/archive/2019/08/whites-refer-to-the-n-word/596872/. 5/1/20.

McWilliams, S. J. (2017). Editor. *A Political Companion to James Baldwin.* Lexington, KY: University of Kentucky Press.

Mintz, A. I. (2014). Why did Socrates deny that he was a teacher? Locating Socrates among the new educators and the traditional education in Plato's Apology of Socrates. *Educational Philosophy and Theory,* 46, 7, 735–747. https://www.tandfonline.com/doi/full/10.1080/00131857.2013.787586. 12/18/2018.

Morrison, T. (1987). James Baldwin: His voice remembered; Life in his language. *The New York Times Book Review.* http://movies2.nytimes.com/books/98/03/29/specials/baldwin-morrison.html. 1/2/2019.

Morrison, T. (1992). *Playing in the Dark: Whiteness and the Literary Imagination.* Boston, Mass.: Harvard University Press.

Murphy, B. M. (2015). Black, child, hood: From Vince Staples to James Baldwin. *Kenyon Review.* July 21. https://www.kenyonreview.org/2015/07/black-child-hood-from-vince-staples-to-james-baldwin/. 6/11/2019.

Myers, B. (2016). Where are the minority professors? *The Chronicle of Higher Education.* February 14. https://www.chronicle.com/interactives/where-are-the-minority-professors. 6/15/2019.

Nemeth, M. (2013). Notes of a Native Son. Review. February 1. https://www.goodreads.com/book/show/410810.Notes_of_a_Native_Son. 3/29/2019.

Norman, B. (2015). James Baldwin and the question of privacy: A roundtable conversation at the 2014 American Studies Convention. 1,1. September. https://www.manchesteropenhive.com/view/journals/jbr/1/1/article-p207.xml.

O' Daniel, T. B. (1977). *James Baldwin, A Critical Evaluation.* College Language Association. Washington: Howard University Press.

Paris Review (1984). Jordan Elgrably, Interviewer. *James Baldwin, the art of fiction, No. 78.* 91, Spring. https://www.theparisreview.org/interviews/2994/james-baldwin-the-art-of-fiction-no-78-james-baldwin. 9/28/2019.

Pfeffer, R. (1998). The fire this time: James Baldwin and the Civil Rights Movement. https://leo.stcloudstate.edu/kaleidoscope/volume4/fire.html. 6/19/2019.

Pratt, L. H. (1978). James Baldwin. *Twayne's United States Authors Series.* N.Y: Twayne.

Schlosser, J. A. (2013). Socrates in a different key: James Baldwin and race in America. *Political Research Quarterly,* 66, 3, 487–499.

Schon, D. A. (1983). *The Reflective Practitioner.* New York, NY: Basic Books.

64 The Teacher Within Him

Schulman, G. (2008). *American Prophecy: Race and Redemption in American Political Culture.* Minneapolis, MN: University of Minnesota Press. p. 134.

Scott, E. (2020). 4 reasons coronavirus is hitting black communities so hard. *The Washington Post.* April 10. https://www.washingtonpost.com/politics/2020/04/10/4-reasons-coronavirus-is-hitting-black-communities-so-hard/. 4/27/2020.

Smith, C. (2017). James Baldwin's lesson for teachers in a time of turmoil. *The New Yorker.* September 23. https://www.newyorker.com/books/page-turner/james-baldwins-lesson-for-teachers-in-a-time-of-turmoil. 4/10/2019.

Southern Poverty Law Center (SPLC). (2019). The year in hate and violence. Spring. 12/4/2020.

Stone, N. (2018). To be black and #woke is to be in a rage all the time. HuffPost. August 8. https://www.huffpost.com/entry/opinion-mike-brown-rage-racism_n_5b6992cee4b0de86f4a52959?guccounter=. 6/16/2019.

The conscious kid. An interview with Aisha Kardra-Smart on James Baldwin's "Little Man, Little Man: A Story of Childhood". https://www.theconsciouskid.org/littlemanlittleman. 9/27/2019.

Treuhaft-Ali, L. (2017). The rich implications of everyday things. The Jeanes Teachers and Jim Crow, 1908–1968. Yale University. http://educationstudies.yale.edu/sites/default/files/files/Treuhaft-Ali%20Layla_Historythesis_2017. 12/4/2020.

Inquirer Staff. (2019). Living black history: 4 African American leaders to learn from this month. *Inquirer,* Daily News. February 1. philly.com. https://www.philly.com/opinion/commentary/black-history-month-philadelphia-ida-b-wells-james-baldwin-20190201.html. 4/2/2019.

Urban Dictionary. (2005). Cronosis. April 21. https://www.urbandictionary.com/define.php?term=willful%20ignorance. 6/21/2019.

Vogel, J. (2018). *James Baldwin and the 1980s.* Urbana/Chicago/Springfield: University of Illinois Press.

Wakefield, D. (2017,). James Baldwin was an honest man and a good writer. The Stacks. https://thestacks.deadspin.com/james-baldwin-was-an-honest-man-and-a-good-writer-1793599858. 3/28/2019.

Wilkerson, I. (2016). The long-lasting legacy of the great migration. Smithsonian.com. September. https://www.smithsonianmag.com/history/long-lasting-legacy-great-migration-180960118/. 3/31/2019.

William, J. (1987). Baldwin the witness testament. *The Washington Post.* https://www.washingtonpost.com/archive/lifestyle/1987/1. 6/9/2018.

Williams, M. M. and NASC Interim History Writing Committee (1979). *The Jeanes Story: A Chapter in the History of American Education, 1908–1968.* Atlanta: Southern Education Foundation.

Winton, R. (2019). Hate crimes in L.A. highest in 10 years, with LGBTQ and African Americans most targeted. *Los Angeles Times.* January 31. https://www.latimes.com/local/lanow/la-me-ln-hate-crime-la-big-cities-20190131-story.html. 6/22/2019.

Wouubshet, D. (2018). How James Baldwin's writings about love evolved. *The Atlantic.* January 9. https://www.theatlantic.com/entertainment/archive/2019/01/james-baldwin-idea-of-love-fire-next-time-if-beale-street-could-talk/579829/. 6/20/2019.

Wright, R. (1940). *Native Son.* New York, NY: Harper Collins.

3

BALDWIN AND EDUCATION

Purpose, Freedom, Defying Myth-making, Truth and Innocence

> He who opens a school door, closes a prison.
>
> *Victor Hugo, 1862*

James Baldwin believes that educators and educated people are obligated to change society and he spends his life acting on this belief. Baldwin (1963) states that the commitment to change society should be energetic and passionate and that any and all who consider themselves responsible, especially those who work with children must be relentless in their efforts to bring about change. This vigorous effort Baldwin describes as "going for broke." "I know a good teacher is rare" writes Baldwin who quickly adds, "I also know that they are not as rare as all of that – I am a survivor" (p. 4). Baldwin speaks of the effort to change society as "at war with your society" and Baldwin argues that teachers who are successful teaching African American students are at war with society. They have to be, argues Baldwin, because racism and intolerance in society remain strong and, some say, are growing stronger. It is because of racism and the need to "go for broke" against white supremacy and oppression that educators seek out the ideas of James Baldwin. *James Baldwin and the American Schoolhouse*, too, argues that educators must "go for broke" to change society in order to make it equal and fair for the present and following generations of students.

Although much of his work, especially the writings and speeches on education are written in the 1950s and 1960s their relevance today is without question. William J. Maxwell (2017) in "Reading James Baldwin in the Black Lives Matter Era," quotes Yale Professor Eddie Glaude, Jr.'s observation "Jimmy is everywhere" and then adds "in the advocacy and self-scrutiny of the young activists who bravely transformed the killings of Trayvon Martin, Michael Brown, Natasha McKenna, and far too many others into a sweeping national movement against police brutality

66 Baldwin and Education

and campus racism" (p. 1). Not only does Jimmy show up everywhere, he is centered; not relegated to footnotes or an oblique reference. His words on race and class, the Civil Rights movements and America's racial legacy are highlighted and situated in today's context. The nation's leading newspapers and magazines cite Baldwin's observations on democracy, race relations in America and police actions. Blogs are written by people discovering him and asking, "Why didn't I learn about James Baldwin in school?" Academic publishers and conferences are showcasing his work.

Although cumbersome as a chapter title: "Baldwin and Education: Purpose, Freedom, Defying Myth-making, Truth and Innocence" brings together Baldwin's observations on education. I start with a talk he has with teachers in New York City about the African American children they are teaching, Additionally, I draw from two other talks: "The Free and Brave" that Baldwin delivers at Second Baptist Church in Los Angeles, CA in April 1963 and "Living and Growing in a White World" that he delivers at Castlemont High School in Oakland, CA, May 1963.

A good teacher is rare ... [but] ... they are not as rare as all of that.

On that autumn day in New York, October 16, 1963, when James Baldwin speaks to teachers of his city, he most likely wants to be somewhere else, and with some other people. Having a good time with family or friends would be much more pleasant than trying to keep the attention of teachers who are tired and ready to go home after a busy teaching day. It isn't that he is not dedicated, but he too is tired; both physically and mentally drained. He has been traveling and speaking for civil rights on behalf of CORE (Congress of Racial Equality) for much of the year; and with his increased fame, including his picture on the cover of *Time*, invitations to speak are overwhelming. Also, observing African American children of a similar age as his brothers and sister protest in the South without regard for their personal safety was frightening and emotionally challenging. The bright spot – and Baldwin usually finds a "bright spot" – he is speaking in Harlem at Public School 180 and he fondly remembers how Harlem teachers and principal, Gertude Elise Ayer had helped him to realize his potential and to arguably save his life when he was a young student.

Baldwin is invited to speak to the teachers by Mrs. E. Sinnette, District Librarian, and co-instructor, with Mr. V. Pemberton, Community Coordinator of a semester-long staff development course: "The Negro: His Role in the Culture and Life of the U.S." Sinnette (1963; private correspondence) wants Baldwin to set the focus and tone of the course and writes in a letter to him:

As the person setting the tone of the entire course, may we ask that you devote major emphasis to the Negro child and his self-image. We believe that this more than anything else is the heart of our efforts in the course.

Baldwin's lecture is requested at a time when schools attended by African American students in Harlem are often staffed by teachers who have "washed out elsewhere in the system" Podair (2002, p. 154) and have been relegated to schools in Harlem.

Sinnette (1963) additionally informs Baldwin that the course will

> want to impress upon teachers who are often from a different cultural group what the Negro child, growing up in a ghetto, not seeing himself reflected in the history or in any part of the life of this country, whose flag he salutes each morning, must feel and subsequently reflect in his every thought, word and deed.
>
> *(p. 1)*

About 200 teachers are enrolled in the special in-service course that meets every week, on Wednesday, 3:30–5:10 beginning September 25, 1963 to January 22, 1964. Baldwin will speak, as he often does, extemporaneously, and without notes (his remarks are recorded on tape). The lecture that characterizes America, as it is, not mythologized, will be later changed to "A Talk to Teachers" and published in the *Saturday Review* December 21, 1963.

I doubt, if Billie Holiday's version of Harold Murry's song *Autumn in New York*, with the opening line "Autumn in New York, why does it seem so inviting?" is in Baldwin's thoughts as the 3:30 hour approaches. Love of country and duty to a cause and a people – a proud hopeful people – is why he is there to speak. New York City and the rest of America is not "inviting" to African Americans and their school-aged children

The New York City Board of Education administers and keeps in place some of the worse segregated schools in the nation. Schools African American and Latinx students attended in New York City have inferior facilities, less experienced teachers and severe overcrowding. Some schools are so overcrowded that they operate on split shifts, with the school day lasting only four hours for students (Kahn, 2016; Podair, 2002).

The Civil Rights movement, including memory of friends who have died fighting to have the humanity of African Americans respected and their minds challenged, along with wanting to help African American children anyway he can, is why Baldwin is there to speak. This talk to educators about African American children is one of several he has delivered this year.

The year 1963 has been up and down, for Jimmy Baldwin. The ups and downs running in no logical order. *Life Magazine* published a multipage photo essay, by Jane Howard of his visit to the South (the same one that I discover in my barbershop). Baldwin is anxious over how his criticism of Malcolm X – a person he considers a friend – in a recorded interview with another friend Kenneth Clark will be perceived by Malcolm and others. In the Clark interview, Baldwin argues that by preaching black supremacy, Malcolm is destroying a truth

68 Baldwin and Education

and inventing a myth. Also, Baldwin is still wrestling with the disappointment that he was not allowed to speak before Martin Luther King, Jr. gave the "I Have a Dream" speech at the March on Washington a few months earlier. He is forbidden to speak for the same reason Bayard Rustin, the March's main organizer, is forbidden. He is an openly gay black man (D'Emilio, 2003). Additionally, Baldwin is annoyed and disappointed about the outcome of a meeting he had set up with several other African American intellectuals and artists with Robert Kennedy, the Attorney General of the United States, over Kennedy's lack of understanding of racial injustice and the agency of African Americans.

Furthermore, the spring and summer months have been dreadful: much more than anyone should have to bear, especially, those living in a country that espouses "liberty and justice for all." The events crisscross though Baldwin's mind: April 12, Dr. Martin Luther King, Jr. is arrested and sent to jail in Birmingham; on June 12 the assassination of Mississippi activist, NAACP lawyer and friend Medgar Evers takes place when he pulls into his driveway and the 16th Street Baptist Church bombing, the assassination of four African American young girls – Addie Mae Collins, Denise McNair, Carole Robertson and Cynthia Wesley has occurred a little more than month ago, on Sunday, September 15.

It is after the brutal murder of the four young African American girls that Baldwin goes on a lecture tour through the South to raise money for the Congress for Racial Equality. He wants to do more, as much as he can do.

"That we are living through a very dangerous time," the opening line of Baldwin's speech has deep personal meaning to all listening, but in different ways. To many in the audience, it is Russia and the missile crises that comes to mind with those words. African American or European American, rich or poor, teacher or speaker, the Cuban Missile Crisis, the 13 days of political and military standoff between the United States and the Soviet Union is only a year old and the Cold War rivalry between the U.S. and USSR is hot and keeps Americans uneased. Duck-and-cover exercises for students, in case the USSR attacks America are a part of the official school curriculum (Onion, 2018).

Baldwin, however, is not speaking about Khrushchev or the Cold War, he is addressing how the inferior education African American children are receiving is causing a national crisis and he is encouraging teachers of African American students to go all out – "go for broke" – and teach them. Disrupt the factories of failure, the line between the classroom and prisons that schools where African American children attend have come to be. Baldwin (1963) states to the teachers:

> The society in which we live is desperately menaced, not by Khrushchev, but from within. To any citizen of this country who figures himself as responsible – and particularly those of you who deal with the minds and hearts of young people – must be prepared to "go for broke."

(p. 2)

Baldwin's charge – "go for broke" – to the teachers is not empty motivational rhetoric; he is not meeting with the teachers only to fulfill an obligation to speak. He is not merely keeping his promise to Mrs. Sinnette and Mr. V. Pemberton. Teachers were very important to his achievement as an artist and his fulfillment as a human: a *man*. Orilla Miller (who went by Bill), his teacher when he is young, is important because she never lies to him and never exercises the prerogative and cruelties Baldwin associates with whiteness (Als, 2019). Bill helped young Jimmy to understand the economics of racism, the role capitalism plays in keeping African Americans down and introduces him to aspects of culture (e.g., plays, films) that are available to him (Leeming, 1994).

Two other teachers, Countee Cullen and Herman W. ("Bill") Porter who were highly influential at another critical moment in his life, when he leaves the safety and comfort of his elementary school and moves to middle school, and faces the pressure the move put upon an effeminate, undersized African American young man with enormous eyes. Cullen, an icon of the Harlem Renaissance, known for his poetry accepts Baldwin into the Frederick Douglass School's literary club; he establishes a mentor–mentee relationship and spends hours working with him on both his fiction and poetry. In Cullen, Baldwin finds not only someone who helps him with his writing, but someone whose life experiences have similarities to his own.

Cullen however is displeased with Baldwin's forlorn, disheveled appearance and he is annoyed that life struggles are beating Jimmy down at such a young age. More so, Cullen has a big problem with the constant bitterness and anger of his stepfather toward Baldwin and others who help or try to help Jimmy.

Cullen is a much different African American man, than Jimmy's stepfather, as he resists and refuses to give into institutional racism. Cullen fights hard to raise himself up and the students he teaches. He treats Jimmy with respect and outwardly recognizes his potential. Young Jimmy, who has not yet worked through his sexual positionality, sees in Cullen, unlike his stepfather, a man who is not afraid to touch and not afraid to enter other people's lives and have other people enter his life. Further, Baldwin admires Cullen's flair. He is elegant, the tone and rhymes of his poetry are different than his African American contemporaries and he speaks French. Leeming (1994) states, "By his very presence Cullen pointed a way around the mentality of despair and proved that many roads out of the ghetto were possible" (p. 22). It is in Cullen's French class where the seed of going to France, which as Baldwin argues saves him, is planted in Baldwin's mind.

Bill Porter helps and influences Baldwin differently than Bill and Cullen. Porter is handsome, aloof and a Harvard graduate, who like Cullen instills in Jimmy the importance of self-reliance and discipline. Porter, the faculty advisor to *The Douglass Pilot*, the school magazine, makes Jimmy his editor-in-chief, which gives him a place to publish his writings. Leeming (1994) reports because of the citywide attention one of young Jimmy's essays receives, the insults and ribbing from his classmates changes to respect and provides opportunities for his friends

70 Baldwin and Education

and classmates (and greater city communities) to recognize and appreciate Baldwin's thoughtful and telling insights. With the new-found respect and praise Jimmy discovers his profession. Also, in Porter, Jimmy sees someone who, unlike his stepfather, is not in fear of the white-dominated world. Porter meets racism head on. Leeming (1994) describes Porter as being fond of telling a story about the time he takes Baldwin to the Forty-second Street public library to do some research. The research outing, besides validating what he learned from Bill about the importance of study and exploration into other resources (e.g., museums, art galleries) in order to learn and grow, teaches Baldwin how to use the library as a tool. Additionally, Baldwin learns that culture and learning, even when in a downtown library, museum, theater, is legally open to him. He has citizenship rights to visit and learn. Porter, Leeming (1994) posits, helps Baldwin to develop the "confidence to combat his father's skepticism about education and to overcome the stares of European Americans and the racial slurs of European American policemen, who sometimes say: 'Why don't you niggers stay uptown where you belong?'" (p. 23).

Baldwin, thus, is hoping and with words and passion, telling the 200 teachers and principals seated before him to do for the African American students they teach what Bill Miller, Countee Cullen, Bill Porter and Gertrude Ayer did for him. "Go for broke." Baldwin believes in the power of teachers to inspire their students, raise their consciousness and make a difference in their lives. He knows from personal experience what a caring dedicated teacher can do for a struggling student. About his teacher, Bill Miller, Baldwin will later say:

> I had been taken by the hand by a young white schoolteacher, a beautiful woman, very important to me. I was between ten and eleven. She had directed my first play … She gave me books to read and talked to me about the books and about the world: about Spain … Ethiopia, and Italy, and the German Third Reich; and took me to see plays and films, plays and films to which no one else would dream of taking a ten-year-old boy.

This chapter, "Baldwin and Education: Purpose, Freedom, Defying Mythmaking, Truth and Innocence" is guided by Baldwin's argument that schools should be revolutionary places and engines of self-awareness and realization, social justice and resistance. Knowledge and understanding of the five topics: purpose of education, "freedom is never given," myth-making, digging for and telling truth, and racial innocence discussed in this chapter are critical for the education of African American students.

Purpose of Education

With his state of the scene statement, that the current times are dangerous, and a revolutionary stance is needed on the part of teachers because of racism, oppression and poverty in America, Baldwin asks his audience if he may tell them his thoughts on the purpose of education. Baldwin, I imagine knows the "purpose of education" is the question, most teachers in the in-service session have considered, studied, even written about as a teacher-candidate. For Baldwin, however "the purpose of education" for African American children is much more than a 12-page composition to satisfy a course requirement; and if written well, that is to the instructor's satisfaction, to receive a course grade of "A." Understanding what education means, it's purpose – ideologically, politically, economically, socially and emotionally in a racist society; as well as how it is interpreted and acted upon can lead to life successes or failures. In a Du Boisean sense, education in an oppressed society can give one who is oppressed a ladder to climb over some of the walls of oppression that intersect along race, class, gender and other lines; but education can probably not enable them to completely escape.

Baldwin previously, four months before in May of 1963, had emphasized the purpose of education in a speech at Castlemont High School in Oakland, California to African American students. At the time, Baldwin tells the high school students, "the purpose of education and the reason it is necessary to become an educated person is a loaded question with very dangerous answers" (p. 2). Baldwin explains, on one level the purpose of education is to help one to "learn how to live with oneself"; on another level the purpose of education, Baldwin proffered, is to be able to discover more about the world including yourself and other people "both living and dead, past and to come" (p. 1). Baldwin argues that discovery should include the measure of your dignity; that is how one estimates one's self. At another level the purpose of education, taking into consideration that education occurs in a social context and has social ends, Baldwin argues is to determine what the purpose of education is for. However, speaking to New York teachers – about African American students – Baldwin argues the purpose of education

> is to create in a person the ability to look at the world for himself, to make his own decisions, to say to himself this is black or this is white, to decide for himself whether there is a God in heaven or not. To ask questions of the universe, and then learn to live with those questions, is the way he achieves his own identity.
>
> *(p. 2)*

Empower and Inspire: Learning that Education is more than About a Job

Education for African American people is always much more than attending school to get a good job, sharp car and beautiful apartment. Immediately (i.e., next day) upon Emancipation, African Americans demand and start to build schools so they can learn to read and write and openly continue their journey

72 Baldwin and Education

toward becoming educated. Young, old and very old physically and ideologically freed African Americans crowd in "schools" (e.g., sheds, under trees, abandoned buildings and new constructions) sitting and standing, occupying any-and-all space. African Americans argue being able to read and write is critical to establishing and defining one's humanity. Toni Morrison (1987) poignantly captured the moment in African American life when she stated, "Freeing yourself was one thing, claiming ownership of that freed self was another" (p. 87).

Education, Baldwin contends, should empower and inspire revolution. In speaking of "empower[ment]," Baldwin wants African Americans individually and collectively to take action to gain mental and physical freedom; to acquire agency to control the circumstances of their lives: and individually and/or collectively perform deeds that will improve the human condition for all African American people. "Freedom" Baldwin (1965) argues, "is not a word: it is a moral state of being, which must be reflected in a nation's institutions" (p. 3). Baldwin asserts that education must prepare African American children to understand how the web of racism engulfs and seeks to control the attitude and behavior of those who love and care for them and he points out that racism will come upon them too, when they enter school.

Baldwin (1963b) explains

> a black child, looking at the world around him, though he cannot know quite what to make of it, is aware that there is a reason why his mother works so hard, why his father is always on edge … He is aware that there is some terrible weight on his parents' shoulders, which menaces him. Therefore receiving an education to improve the human condition is critical to black students.
>
> *(p. 5)*

As Baldwin "talks to teachers," he along with being humble is deeply serious; he is not here to entertain. His purpose is to point out that the New York school system is destroying the minds and heart of African American children and to tell teachers that they have the power to eliminate this destruction in their classroom; as well as the opportunity to educate African American students on the real purpose of their education.

"Inspiring revolution" in education: resisting racism, calling out white supremacy, abandoning deficit ways of thinking about African American children and celebrating African American humanity, Baldwin tells the teachers is what they need to do. Inspiring revolution, Baldwin argues includes having a heightened consciousness, having agency and understanding Frederick Douglass' statement, "If there is no struggle, there is no progress" (p. 437).

Today "inspiring revolution" in education for African American students does not stop with using culturally relevant pedagogy and encouraging critical questioning but rigorously exercising ideas (e.g., liberty, freedom), ideals (e.g., "All

Baldwin and Education **73**

people are created equal") and practices (e.g., equality, equity). In addition, "inspiring revolution" includes instilling in African American students "hope." It also includes informing African American students of opportunities (professional, vocational) available to them and helping them to believe in themselves and to engage with life.

"Empowerment and inspiring revolution" for African Americans Baldwin (1963) concludes is not disloyal, nor mutinous because

> [I]f America is going to become a nation, she must find a way–and this child must help her to find a way–to use the tremendous potential and tremendous energy which this child represents. If this country does not find a way to use that energy, it will be destroyed by that energy.
>
> *(p. 5)*

John Dewey's argument that the primary purpose of education is not so much to *prepare* students to live a useful life, but to teach them how to live pragmatically and *immediately* in their current environment is popular among teacher candidates developing their education philosophy. So too, is George Counts' argument that the purpose of school is less about preparing individuals to live independently and more about preparing individuals to live as members of a society (Stemier, 2019). David Tyack (1988) looking back over the history of education argues that the purpose of education connects to the social and economic needs of society and the purpose of education, according to Labaree (1997) is a credentialing function (Stemier, 2019). However, Alvin Toffler (1970), a futurist when quizzed on the purpose of education in the 21st century states: "The illiterate of the 21st century will not be those who cannot read and write, but those who cannot learn, unlearn and relearn" (p. 414).

Baldwin would argue, whereas he respects the previous statements on the purpose of education; he does observe the absence of attention to African American people in a society normed on European American culture, values and ideology and omitting or playing down African American. Therefore, for him the purpose of education for African American students should be to teach them that racism is socially constructed, that the absence of, or marginalization of African Americans in the history and literature books they receive in schools is a social construction that maintains African Americans in a position of inferiority and European Americans in a position of superiority. Baldwin would resonate with Toffler's observation, because he believes much about America needs to be "unlearned," (e.g., myths of white supremacy); accurate history "learned" and full meaning of democracy "relearned."

Today, teachers of African American students who contended they "love children" and "want to help children learn" upon reading Baldwin should correct and/or change their curriculum and instruction. Racist myths, from Columbus discovering America to white males settling the West should be examined and changed; and the racism in the instructional labeling of African American students from "slow-witted" (1800s to 1900s) to "at-risk" students (2000 to present day) exposed and corrected.

Baldwin wants teachers of African American students to know African American history and to teach to change racist legacies of that history. Emancipation (1863) liberated African Americans from the land in the rural South, into the hands of European American city bosses who control the paved streets, and continue to own or control the food deserts and understock stores with poor-quality food in African American communities. European American city bosses or European American city and state legislators control the flow of money and economic empowerment (e.g., jobs) into African American communities as well as the overabundance of currency exchanges, liquor and one-dollar stores.

In addition, European American city bosses continue to relegate African Americans to segregated, overcrowded run-down housing that is furthered miserated by its location in communities of reduced hospital and health resources. Teachers of African American students, Baldwin would argue should use data from the pandemic to point out the disparities that have historically been part of African American communities. In 2020, Baldwin's argument: "American democracy is purposefully not adhering to the principles of equality for black people" continues to have validity. In communities where African Americans live there are absences of large grocery stores, even small grocery stores. According to Brooks (2014) "food deserts," areas where people live having a limited amount of affordable, healthy food are abundant in African American neighborhoods. Overall, marketing and selling in African American communities includes merchants overcharging for inferior goods (Elkins, 2016. In African American communities, there is a shortage of hospitals with 21st-century medical services (e.g., a shortage of trauma centers) and African American mothers experience higher rates of death or injury during childbirth than European American mothers. The coronavirus is disproportionately murdering African Americans; Violet Law (2020) reports "Racial minorities are disproportionately affected by health crises such as this one as a larger proportion of African Americans and Latinx have died from Covid-19" (p. 1).

Newkirk II (2018) reports: "Segregation is baked into the way people and institutions discuss health care at its most basic levels." Racial differences in almost every health outcome—from infant mortality to life expectancy—are obvious and pronounced, especially between European Americans and African Americans. Jessica Owens-Young (2020) argues "where we live matters for how long we live" (p. 1) and reports: neighborhoods with large African American populations tend to have lower life expectancies than communities that are majority European American, Hispanic or Asian. Owens-Young (2020) asserts,

> Such racial differences reflect the places in which different races live, not the individual characteristics of people themselves. Research shows that black communities are less likely to have access to resources that promote health,

like grocery stores with fresh foods, places to exercise and quality health care facilities.

(p. 2)

Further, African Americans have to continue to endure de facto segregation and micro aggressions throughout society. Structures and institutions of society (e.g., congress, universities, state governments, media and films) are operated and controlled to support European American interest.

A report compiled by the Transnational Racial Justice Initiative (2001), *The Persistence of White Privilege and Institutional Racism in US Policy*, defines white privilege as: "[A] system that accrues to whites (or European Americans) greater wealth, resources, more access and higher quality access to justice, services, capital—virtually every form of benefits to be reaped from US society— than other racial groups" (p. 7). It is because of systemic white privilege that there is impoverishment and injustice for the vast majority of people of color. "White privilege is more than a set of attitudes or individual opinions. It is an overarching, comprehensive framework of policies, practices, institutions and cultural norms that undergird every aspect of US society" (Transnational Racial Justice Initative, 2001, p. 7).

The Report's next observation is one that Baldwin points out in his work:

Too often, discussion of racial discrimination focuses solely on the effects on those who are oppressed as if there are no oppressors or beneficiaries. In this analysis, racial minorities are cast as 'problems to be solved' instead of victims of an unjust system.

(p. 7)

The *Racial Justice Initiative* conclusion offers the following observation:

The Government's efforts to address hate violence are inadequate. In the US and elsewhere, ethnic and racial minorities, migrants, refugees and displaced people are increasingly victims of violence and repression by the state as well as private, sometimes quasigovernment groups (sometimes known in the US as militias). Operating from a political framework of white supremacy and racism, these state agencies and private organizations are contributing to the development of a global "hate" movement.

(p. 8)

As I read the *Racial Justice Imitative* written two decades ago, re-read Baldwin's essays and interviews written six and seven decades ago, or longer, and read from many news sources about racial justice today – 2020 – I see Baldwin's statement "Education is indoctrination if you're white – subjugation if you're black" remains true.

76 Baldwin and Education

Another social condition that is illuminated in Baldwin's works is that African American people are forced to work for poor wages. Baldwin (1967) writes, "Our parents were lashed to futureless jobs, in order to pay the outrageous rent. We knew that the landlord treated us this way only because we were colored, and he knew that we could not move out" (p. 1). Since their arrival in America, African Americans remain a source of cheap labor or reduced pay for labor in comparison to European Americans. In 2017, African American men are paid 69.7 cents of the European American male dollar (Gould, Jones, Mokhiber, 2018); and the regard of their humanity is small or none ("Go back to your country" racist remarks by President Trump to four nonwhite congresswomen, Reps. Ayanna Pressley, Mass., Rashida Tlaib, Mich., Alexandria Ocasio-Cortez, N.Y. and Ilhan Omar, Minn., three of whom were born in the U.S. dominates the news coverage as I write (7/16/2019), showing that we still are living in "a very dangerous time").

For Baldwin the purpose of education is for us: you and me: "We the people …" to learn it is our responsibility to change society, change the social conditions in which African Americans and other people of color live if we think of ourselves as professional educators. Baldwin (1963) tells the New York teachers:

> Now if I were a teacher in this school, or any Negro school, and I was dealing with Negro children, who were in my care only a few hours of every day and would then return to their homes and to the streets, children who have an apprehension of their future which with every hour grows grimmer and darker, I would try to teach them – I would try to make them know – that those streets, those houses, those dangers, those agonies by which they are surrounded, are criminal. I would try to make each child know that these things are the result of a criminal conspiracy to destroy him. I would teach him that if he intends to get to be a man, he must at once decide that he is stronger than this conspiracy and that he must never make his peace with it.
>
> *(p. 5)*

Baldwin's declaration on the purpose of education to the teachers, is a declaration that needs be made today, several times over and then some. Education to get a good job and become a gold star consumer shopper needs to be contested, again and again.

Baldwin never hesitates to bring clarity to his prose, if there was a need. Therefore, he would, I believe not want his use of phrases "criminal" and "criminal conspiracy" to be misunderstood by readers. In a July 1968 interview with *Esquire* magazine, approximately four months after the National Advisory Commission on Civil Disorders established by President Lyndon B. Johnson to investigate the causes of the iconic race riots in 1967, released its report, Baldwin's meaning of "criminal" is described. The horrible conditions in which African American people are forced to live; and the "criminal conspiracy" are the policies (e.g., redlining, unfair labor practices, police anti-black violence) put in place by European Americans to keep African Americans in particular spaces. Baldwin argues that American democracy is purposefully not adhering to the principles of equality for African Americans and notes: one-way busing, a labor union based on the division of African American and European American labor, de jure and de facto segregated schools decades after the Supreme Court passed *Brown v. Board of Education* in 1954, the building of high-rise projects and the application of redlining to keep African Americans isolated.

Learning to Read the World, Searching for Truth and Thinking about Everything

The purpose of education for Baldwin includes each African American student being able to read the world (e.g., their own and others' conditions and opportunities), make life choices and offer help based upon the reading of circumstances and conditions. Baldwin demands a heightened consciousness on the part of African Americans so that each person knows how to look at the world for themselves and possesses the ability to make decisions on their own. Baldwin supports a Deweyan's belief that to maintain a robust citizenry and a sound democracy, learning and the "search for truth" must continue throughout life. However, Baldwin wants the "search for truth" to include European Americans examining historical and literary texts, traditions, customs, institutions and themselves to discover and eliminate the lies they learned in school and in their community about African Americans. Baldwin is concerned that racial democracy for African Americans, despite civil rights efforts, the election of an African American president and mayors in numerous big cities is far from a reality.

Following upon what he had previously told New York teachers is the purpose of education, and what he would do if he was a teacher of African American students in Harlem, Baldwin tells students in Oakland what he would do if he was their teacher. Baldwin (1963) says: "If I were your teacher my responsibility is to teach you to think ... to think about everything ... to discover the reason you and others do what you do" (p. 2). Baldwin's remarks are not direct to put any student down or to attack the Oakland school system; his interest is helping people, in this case African American students, to understand how power operates and threatens and often denies justice to African Americans. Baldwin speaks to the students in Oakland, the way he speaks to his younger brothers and sister and the way he speaks to his nephew in the letter he writes him. Baldwin isn't arrogant or overbearing; his words communicate kindness and thoughtfulness; inviting students' attention, not demanding it; nevertheless, Baldwin is concerned and speaks with urgency.

Learning to Consider Others

Baldwin's portraits of African American life is always richly human, when he speaks, and he hopes teachers will begin to see African Americans as he sees them: beautiful and proudly human, flawed, complex; very much the same as they are. Baldwin's portraits of African American life is also a statement to European American teachers that they no longer should feign superiority or act as if America is providentially their country alone. Instead, Baldwin argues, European Americans' claim of innocence, privilege and fragility must stop and African Americans must be completely welcomed into the national community; such is the text and subtext of Baldwin's remarks to the teachers.

The purpose of education as Baldwin argues is to heighten one's consciousness not only about self, but others. Baldwin illustrates awareness and compassion for another in an open letter to Angela Davis who is jailed and charged, but later found not guilty of participating in an attempt to free prisoners on trial at the Marin Courthouse in San Rafael, California. Baldwin in the open letter to Davis speaks in a language of compassion and with words that say be steadfast against the systems of oppression that is attacking her. Baldwin (1970/1971) writes:

> We know that we, the Blacks, and not only we, the Blacks, have been, and are, the victims of a system whose only fuel is greed, whose only god is profit. We know that the fruits of this system have been ignorance, despair, and death ... And we know that, for the perpetuation of this system, we have all been mercilessly brutalized, and have been told nothing but lies, lies about ourselves and our kinsmen and our past, and about love, life, and death.
>
> *(p. 1)*

Consideration of others, their life circumstances and condition, Baldwin argues is crucial and important to developing African American and European American relations. Baldwin knows that if European Americans are going to accept the humanity of African Americans, they will need to start thinking about them, outside of the spaces where African Americans work for European Americans or are taught by European Americans. In other words, Baldwin wants European Americans not to think of African Americans mainly as someone who does service works (e.g., maid, doorperson) or performs for them or shoots and dribbles, but as someone, people who could be their neighbor, doctor, lawyer and investment banker. Baldwin (1968) speaks of this dehumanizing oversight on the part of European Americans when he states:

> No one has ever considered what happens to a woman or a man who spends his working life downtown and then has to go home uptown ... We are a nation within a nation, a captive nation within a nation ... You talk about us as though we were not there ... we had no feelings, we had no ears, no eyes.

Consideration of others, that is, the consideration Baldwin has for students comes through loud and clear when Baldwin speaks to them in Oakland, California. Baldwin tells students he understands why some are bitter. Why some believe school is not beneficial and a waste of time. Baldwin professes, that, as their teacher he would not be angry at them, but would want them to think about things from a personal perspective; to examine their way of living; their style (e.g., dress, hair) in comparison to standards set by society and not be taken down or made a fool by it. Baldwin wants African American students to understand, that he understands, that things, such as dress (e.g., pants off the waist), hairstyle (e.g., naturals, dreads), dating relationships (e.g., unmarried people living together), music (e.g., rhythm and blues) is your generation asserting its independence.

Differentiating yourself from European Americans and some African Americans is arguably generational, "changing times" and should be understood and accepted that way. It not about good or evil, winners and losers. Baldwin (1963) posits

> It is your responsibility as young American citizens, to understand, that the standards, by which you are confronted, and which many of you are visibly and obviously victimized, and other of you, not so obviously, but equally victimized, are not the only standards.
>
> *(p. 2)*

Baldwin wants students to know, he accepts them for who they are, how they dress, how they act and the way they talk. He is in "love" with their humanity and wants them to know that white middle-class standards and styles are simply one of many standards and styles. Baldwin (1962) writes it as follows to his nephew: "There is no reason, for you to try to become like white people and there is no basis whatever for their impertinent assumption that they must accept you" (p. 4).

Looking out at the students, searching the audience, connecting with as many eyes and minds as possible, Baldwin wants his next words to stay with them throughout their life. To comfort them when necessary, because the words come with being born African American, understanding one's history and culture abounds. Baldwin (1963) states: "I am what time, circumstance, history, have made of me, certainly, but I am also, much more than that. So are we all" (p. xii). Baldwin, a native son of America, wants each and every set of eyes looking at him and set of ears listening to him to understand what it means to be a "native son" of America. Baldwin understands that for many African American students, racial injustice and alienation complicate their feelings of inheritance and belonging. Baldwin (1955) states: "I was forced to recognize that I was a kind of a bastard of the West" (p. 5). Questions such as, "What would I be if my ancestors had not been enslaved and brought to America" are left hanging.

Nevertheless, Baldwin wants African American students to know and he wants school systems across the country – to see as their purpose – to inform through

80 Baldwin and Education

policy and practice that African Americans are not to be confined to the dark corners of European American minds; not to be thought of as a statistic, or within the context of slums, violence and poverty. They (African Americans) are not a problem to be solved, but they are fellow citizens striving to resolve problems. Baldwin (1955) wanted African American students to understand "Negroes are Americans and their destiny is the country's destiny" (p. 42). "Finally," Baldwin (1963) says to the students and teachers in the audience: "if I were your teacher, I would beg you and insist that you fight with me, and not let me get away with anything, no matter how I may sound, I am only mortal" (p. 2).

The purpose of education for African American students is born out of a legacy – a thirst for knowledge. This legacy goes back to African American students who on the first day of Emancipation want to attend school more than do anything else. Teachers of African American students also have a legacy, one that needs to recapture. A legacy of dedication and commitment to the education of African Americans that was started in 1863 by African American men and women and European American men and women who come from different cities and town across the nation for the sole purpose to help newly emancipated African Americans fulfill their education dream. Arthur W. Foshay (1991) and others contended "The one continuing purpose of education, since ancient times, has been to bring people to as full a realization as possible of what it is to be a human being" (p. 3).

"Freedom is never given"

> Freedom is not something that anybody can be given. Freedom is something people take, and people are as free as they want to be.
>
> *James Baldwin, 1961*

In 1786, as the U.S. is establishing its independence, Thomas Jefferson writes, "I think by far the most important bill in our whole code is that for the diffusion of knowledge among the people, no other sure foundation can be devised for the preservation of freedom, and happiness" (p. 2). Schools, Jefferson claims are to make men free. Decades later, A. Philip Randolph places in sharp and clear perspective how freedom is achieved by African Americans. Randolph argues: "Freedom is never given; it is won." Baldwin, as he speaks to the teachers at P.S. 184, understands Jefferson's comment, its significance and its implication to Randolph's statement of fact. Baldwin wants the audience to know that for African Americans to become educated, that is to gain the academic and political tools including disposition (knowledge, skill and attitude) necessary to challenge a racist society and win; they will have to change the way they were teaching them.

African American will have to be taught to challenge the conspiracy they are forced to live in, Baldwin exclaims. African American students, at the very earliest of age, Baldwin argues must be informed that they are stronger than the racist conspiracy and they must be told to never make their peace with it. They must destroy it. Baldwin (1963) adds, referencing African American students:

> I would teach [them] that the press he reads is not as free as it says it is–and that he can do something about that, too. I would try to make [them] know that just as American history is longer, larger, more various, more beautiful, and more terrible than anything anyone has ever said about it, so is the world larger, more daring, more beautiful, and more terrible, but principally larger– and that it belongs to him.
>
> *(p. 5)*

Baldwin's message reminds the audience of current social and physical crimes against African Americans in general and African American children specifically and his delivery carries the emotional and social weight of the horrible times in South Carolina in 1740 and in other Southern states when laws are passed that prohibit enslaved people from being educated. Baldwin wants every adult in the audience to understand that history is not past, it is present; – and he wants the people in the audience to know that it is not African Americans who are afraid of becoming educated, but that European Americans are afraid of educated African Americans.

Baldwin's request to teachers early in his lecture, to discuss the purpose of education provides an opportunity for him to point out that schools where African American children attend since the Emancipation Proclamation was signed are resourced-poor, segregated and for the most part ignored by the local, state and federal government. Such schools, Baldwin notes are grossly inadequate as places to adhere to Jefferson's claim to make people free and to give them hope. Today, second decade of the 21st century, Baldwin's words still hold true, there is still a big resource difference between the schools that African American and European American students attend. Rebecca Bellan (2019) reports

> Funding disparities for city students are a nationwide issue: Public school pupils enrolled in urban districts receive on average around $2,100 less per pupil than their suburban counterparts, and $4,000 less than students who attend rural remote schools, according to a recent study by EdBuild. And within cities, kids in predominantly nonwhite districts receive less than kids in predominantly white districts—about $1,321 less.
>
> *(p. 7)*

The title of Baldwin's speech "The Negro Child – His Self-Image" is more in tune with Baldwin's growing beliefs about the heightened consciousness of current generations of African American students, than the title "A Talk to Teachers" at the time it is delivered. Students' self-image is a major education topic and discussion point during the 1960s, somewhat like the achievement gap today, but more devastating.

82 Baldwin and Education

However, fresh in Baldwin's mind, as he surveys his audience of northern teachers are the student protests in Tallahassee, Florida and Greensboro, North Carolina he reports on for *Mademoiselle* in 1960. Baldwin (1960) writes "History is a Weapon: They Can't Turn Back" after spending several days on Florida Agricultural and Mechanical University (FAMU): Upon observing and speaking at African American college student protests in the South, Baldwin comes up with the subtitle for his article: "They Can't Turn Back."

Baldwin reports, he is seeing a "new and freer negro" and this is the African American student, Baldwin wants his teacher audience to know about. Baldwin (1960) writes:

> I walk outside, waiting for my taxi and watching the students. Only a decade and a half divide us, but what changes have occurred in those fifteen years! The world into which I was born must seem as remote to them as the Flood. I watch them. Their walk, talk, laughter are as familiar to me as my skin, and yet there is something new about them. They remind me of all the Negro boys and girls I have ever known and they remind me of myself: but, really, I was never like these students. It took many years of vomiting up all the filth I'd been taught about myself, and half-believed, before I was able to walk on the earth as though I had a right to be here.
>
> *(p. 3)*

It is the self-image and agency of *these* African American students that Baldwin knows his teacher audience needs to learn about, because they don't know about them nor the formulation of their self-image. Richard Gibson, Jr. writes about his story at FAMU: "My Home on the Hill". Gibson, Jr. in 2015 includes the following in his story about his self-worth and agency.

> I entered FAMU amid the turmoil in the 1960s. I, along with my fellow FAMUans were deeply affected … "Walls of resistance" had begun to come down in Tallahassee. Not unlike the rest of the Deep South, Tallahassee had been a bastion of segregation. My professors would tell newly-arrived scholars that we had missed the "real fun" of FAMU student life … Tallahassee Movement of voter registration and lunch counter desegregation … of the 50s and 60s. While previous classes were concerned with … civil rights protests, my class … the sophomore and junior classes were interested in changing the direction of the university.

At North Carolina A&T Joseph McNeil, Franklin McCain, Ezell Blair, Jr. and David Richmond, four young men who didn't know one another before they met the fall of 1959 as freshmen, took seats at a white-only lunch counter at an F. W. Woolworth's in Greensboro N.C., in 1960. They order coffee, are not served; nevertheless, they remain at the lunch counter until the store closes that evening. One of the students tells a reporter: "We believe, since we buy books and papers in the other part of the store, we should get served in this part."

Baldwin wants his message to teachers about racism and oppression in school and society to inform them about how and why African American students feel as they do about themselves; their self-image, and how they feel about their teachers and school. "Schizophrenic," Baldwin argues can be the result of being an African American student in the American educational system, where myths, omissions, distortions and inaccuracies are the curriculum and where the African American community and local school are at opposite ends. Schools, Baldwin is pointing out are not meeting Jefferson's claim: to make men free, but was doing the opposite. Baldwin uses the term "schizophrenic," not in the clinical sense as a diagnosis of mental illness, but to discuss the results of white supremacy on African American students: invisibility in the school curriculum, labels of deficient and deviance, and hopeless as a student. Racism, as the Clarks' doll test study concludes is causing African American students to develop a negative self-image.

Ironically, as I was writing this chapter an article "Schools Grapple with Student Depression as Data Show Problem Worsening" by Evie Blad (2019) is given to me by a student. The *Education Week* article reports that the rates of mental-health incidents among teens and young adults have gone up over the last decade and argues that "Teachers and principals must be more versed in the warning signs of serious issues like mood disorders, anxiety, and suicidal thoughts so that they can better serve students in crisis." With Baldwin's statement of "schizophrenic" in mind, I read on to discover the suggested causes for the uptick in mental-health incidents which included: lack of sleep, social isolation (due to cell phone use and other technology), relentless and boring worksheets and lack of water intake. Racism as a possible factor is not discussed. Why not, I wonder?

Baldwin discusses "willful ignorance" (a topic I will return to later) as hiding in the purpose of education and in the curriculum selected for African American students, and arguably willful ignorance hides in research studies of depression on students. In *No Name in the Street*, Baldwin (1972) warns "Ignorance, allied with power, is the most ferocious enemy justice can have" (p. 149). "Justice" for African American students is helping them to take their freedom by appropriately including them in school policy and practice decisions.

Truth: Moral Principle of Freedom

Baldwin tells his audience how truth as a moral principle is important to African American people winning freedom, their belief in self and critical in their teaching. However, argues Baldwin, European Americans want to covet truth in order to control African Americans. Baldwin declares not only were African people brought to America as cheap labor, indispensable to U.S. economic, social and political growth and prosperity, they were treated like animals. Nevertheless, European Americans, Baldwin posits, for generations through multiple sources

84 Baldwin and Education

including school textbooks insisted African and African American enslaved people were treated "good": They are happy and satisfied with their treatment and way of life. Today, the discourse on the treatment of African Americans remains flawed; the truth about treatment remains hidden behind shadows created by policies and procedures. Linda Darling-Hammond (2001) explains: "Despite the rhetoric of American equality, the school experiences of African-American and other 'minority' students in the United States continue to be substantially separate and unequal. Few Americans realize that the U.S. educational system is one of the most unequal in the industrialized world, and that students routinely receive dramatically different learning opportunities based on their social status." In addition, Darling-Hammond (2001) contends, African American students and other students of color are concentrated in the least well-funded schools, and receive fewer instructional human and material resources. Baldwin argues European Americans continue to lie about the treatment and mistreatment of African Americans in order to justify treating them as less than human or as secondary citizens.

It is because European Americans hid truth from African Americans for centuries, and continue to lie to themselves today that it is almost impossible for an African American child to discover much about his or her actual history. But when African Americans "dig up their past" (Schomburg, 1925, p. 1) as the students at F.A.M.U. and North Carolina A&T were doing and discover their history, they start knowing and believing they are proud, beautiful, intelligent people, and their anger with the power structure that oppressed them causes them to demonstrate against it. It is for these reasons, Baldwin argues, that African Americans are not told the truth and European Americas are dogged in keeping African Americans in *their place*, preventing African Americans from having a major role in the American democratic project.

Baldwin tells teachers because America has never confronted it, that truth is a moral principle of freedom for African Americans; and because America has never dealt with the nation's lies about African Americans, we are in trouble. In *Notes of A Native Son: Many Thousand Gone* (1955) Baldwin speaks the following truth to European Americans about their perspective on African Americans that has high currency value today:

> It is only in his music, which Americans are able to admire because a protective sentimentality limits their understanding of it, that the Negro in America has been able to tell his story. It is a story which otherwise has yet to be told and which no American is prepared to hear. As is the inevitable result of things unsaid, we find ourselves until today oppressed with a dangerous and reverberating silence; and the story is told, compulsively, in symbols and signs, in hieroglyphics; it is revealed in Negro speech and in that of the white majority and in their different frames of reference. The ways in which the Negro has affected the American psychology are betrayed in our

popular culture and in our morality; in our estrangement from him is the depth of our estrangement from ourselves. We cannot ask: what do we *really* feel about him—such a question merely opens the gates on chaos. What we really feel about him is involved with all that we feel about everything, about everyone, about ourselves.

(James Baldwin, Collected Essay 1998, p.19)

Baldwin argues to be African American in America means that, you are denied truth and constantly forced to see yourself through European American eyes and denied the freedom to acquire a quality culturally relevant education and obtain employment that meets your knowledge and skill set. Instead, "you are the receptacle arm, you are the vehicle of, all the pain, disaster and sorrow which white America thinks it can escape" (Baldwin, 1955 p. 3). If you are black, your place is to bear the burden, do the dirty work, walk behind so white people can live the good life. Baldwin argues this is false reality, a denial of truth and European Americans need to understand there are major social problems in America that they need to address. Baldwin states

White people will have to ask themselves, precisely why they found it necessary to invent a n****r, because they invented him for reasons, and out of necessities of their own. And every white citizen of this country will have to accept the fact that he is not innocent, and that those dogs and those hoses, those crimes are being committed in your name.

(Baldwin, 1963, p. 5)

Returning to *Notes of A Native Son* and fast forwarding it into your – teacher, teacher candidate, professor – contemplations during the summer of 2020 as you watched racial awakening demonstrations and pondered your morality along with your return to school, Baldwin argues (in *Notes*) African Americans' history and their progress, relationship to all other Americans is kept in the social arena (e,g., justice, welfare, inclusion, recognition). African Americans are social and not a personal or a human problem, claims Baldwin. To think of African Americans, Baldwin contends – and you hear such rumbling in CoE and in schools – is to think of statistics, slums, injustices and violence as well as to be faced with an endless cataloguing of losses, gains and skirmishes. It, Baldwin professed is to feel virtuous, outraged, helpless, as though the African American continuing status among other American people were somehow analogous to disease – cancer, perhaps, or tuberculosis – which must be checked, even though it cannot be cured. But Baldwin (1955) argues

Our dehumanization of the Negro then is indivisible from our dehumanization of ourselves: the loss of our own identity is the price we pay for our annulment of his. Time and our own force act as our allies, creating an

86 Baldwin and Education

impossible, a fruitless tension between the traditional master and slave. Impossible and fruitless because, literal and visible as this tension has become, it has nothing to do with reality.

(p. 25)

Truth, absent in the classroom, encourages a toxic environment that invites, if not demands protest. Teachers of African American students must ask how do we protect an essential resource of democracy – the truth from the toxin of historical and contemporary lies that surround it (Ignatius, 2016)?

Digging for and Telling Truth

> The truth is a two-edged sword—and if one is not willing to be pierced by that sword, even to the extreme of dying on it, then all of one's intellectual activity is a masturbatory delusion and a wicked and dangerous fraud.
>
> *James Baldwin, 1972, p. 31*

James Baldwin (1998/1955) as Schlosser (2013) observes in "Autobiographical Notes" tells readers "his job is to examine attitudes, to go beneath the surface, to tap the source" (p. 3). And in *Notes of a Native Son*, Baldwin (1955) argues every artist's duty is to "dig down to where realty is" and tell America the truth about herself. "The things that people really do and really mean and really feel," Baldwin argues, "are almost impossible for them to describe, but these are the very things which are most important about them. These things control them and that is where reality is" (p. 5). Baldwin argues truth has an important role to play in African Americans' fight for equality and Baldwin states it is essential to speak truth. Baldwin understands that the difficulty of speaking truth is that it requires people to dig deep into their personal and institutional history, their prejudices and biases in order to transform themselves and their communities (The Inquirer, 2019). Throughout Baldwin's work, including his talks to teachers and students, Baldwin is brutally honest. He is a truth teller.

The path Baldwin chooses is not easy; it comes at a cost of personal criticism, personal health and days and months away from writing. Nevertheless, he constantly and intentionally makes the decision to speak truth and pursue justice. In doing so, Baldwin's critique of American life is often done by examining his own life and discussing the differences that are used by those in power to exploit and divide black communities (Johns, 2018, August 8).

Baldwin is forthright in speaking truth about himself, the way he looked, his bugged eyes, that he is gay. Baldwin learns to accept and appreciate the face and body that stares back at him when he looks into a mirror. During an interview with The Village Voice (Goldstein, 1984) Baldwin speaks about how queerness is experienced and how it is prioritized with skin color: "The sexual question comes after the question of color; it's simply one more aspect of the danger in which all Black people live" (p. 2).

Baldwin and Education **87**

Baldwin believes that speaking truth is not an act of defiance but an act of love, protest and transformation. Baldwin sees throughout society and in the schools he visits, that, because America is not truthful with itself about the life and conditions of African Americans and their seminal role in the U.S. achieving its stature and status of prominence throughout the world; that it doesn't know what to do with African Americans and their children. Schools are holding pens and "factories of failures" for African American youth. In *No Name in the Street*, Baldwin (1972) writes:

> The truth is that the country does not know what to do with its black population now that the blacks are no longer a source of wealth, are not long to be bought and sold and bred, like cattle, and they especially do not know what to with young black men who pose as devastating a threat to the economy as they do to the morals of young white cheerleaders.
>
> *(p. 432)*

Truth, good or bad, Baldwin concludes is an absolute. Besides schools serving as a vehicle for freedom, Baldwin argues schools must be places and teachers must be people who teach students to discover truth: truth about self and truth about society. Teaching truth, however, is a difficult task.

Baldwin wants teachers to be truthful in their action; to open their eyes to hyper ghettoization from testing and the deficit stereotyping of African American students. Baldwin wants teachers to examine their curriculum for bias and omissions and to have discussions with students about social injustices and efforts to make them feel inferior that they are dealing with in and out of school. While most teachers may assume that schools are safe places for children, Baldwin speaks truth and argues that schools are microcosms of society where racial, gender, sexual and class oppression are reproduced.

Surprisingly, I never discovered, in my research, that Baldwin sat down and held a discussion with a group of teacher educators or colleges of education deans. Nevertheless, from his talk to teachers and students, it is not difficult to imagine, that, had he done so, his critique of the education of African American students, his concern about the importance of speaking truth, and his protest against negative images of African American people would have been poignant. In a *New York Times* article (January 14, 1962), Baldwin speaks truth, the way he would want deans of colleges of education and professors of education to do: "As much truth as one can bear" (p.2), he says.

Baldwin remembers how Bill is truthful to him and presents him with opportunities so he can discover truth and learn about people and life in other places. Baldwin recalls how two African American male teachers, Countee Cullen and Bill Porter accept and encourage him academically and were truthful with him about things he should do to better himself. "Truth," speaking truth and pursuing truth, Baldwin knows, is important to African American survival. Also, truth is equally important to European Americans Baldwin (1963) argues:

What is upsetting the country is a sense of its own identity. If, for example, one managed to change the curriculum in all the schools so that Negroes learned more about themselves and their real contributions to this culture, you would be liberating not only Negroes, you'd be liberating white people who know nothing about their own history. And the reason is that if you are compelled to lie about one aspect of anybody's history, you must lie about it all. If you have to lie about my real role here, if you have to pretend that I hoed all that cotton just because I loved you, then you have done something to yourself. You are mad.

(p. 3)

Baldwin (1963) encourages teachers to teach students that they have the "the right and the necessity to examine everything, to search for truth" (p. 4). It is those parts of history that are covered in myths that erupt and cause crisis. Some European American teacher candidates in my classes experience a crisis upon reading Howard Zinn's (1980) *A People History of the United States*, a history of the American people from the point of view of the people and wonder why, criticism of the book notwithstanding, they were not exposed to *this* American history in school. Similarly, Anya Kamenetz (2018) reports on National Public Radio (NPR), an interview with James W. Loewen (referenced above) to publicize Loewen's new edition of *Lies My Teacher Told Me*, gave her the opportunity to reminisce about what she learned from reading the book in junior high school.

The book also taught a lot of history. It introduced me to concepts that still help me make sense of the world, like the "racial nadir" – the downturn in American race relations, starting after Reconstruction, that saw the rise of lynching and the Ku Klux Klan. In doing so, *Lies My Teacher Told Me* overturned one assumption embedded in the history classes I'd been sitting through all my life: that the United States is constantly ascending from greatness to greatness.

Kamenetz (2018) reports, when Loewen is queried about the new edition, he states:

I started out the new edition with the famous two photographs of the inaugural crowds of this guy named President Obama, his first inauguration, and this guy named President Trump, his first and maybe only inauguration. And you just look at those two photos and they're completely different. There's all kinds of grass and gaps that you see in the Trump photo…. What that does, I hope, is signal to every reader of the book: Yes, there are such things as facts here. You can see with your own eyes.

(p. 1)

Baldwin (1965/1998) argues the sooner students are exposed to their truthful history the more time and attention they can have to come to grips that history

> is not merely something to be read. And it does not refer merely, or even principally, to the past. On the contrary, the great force of history comes from the fact that we carry it within us, are unconsciously controlled by it in many ways, and history is literally present in all that we do. It could scarcely be otherwise, since it is to history that we owe our frames of reference, our identities, and our aspirations.
>
> *(p. 722)*

In addition, it is about truth – lies that were told to him – when Baldwin used the N-word midway into his talk. He speaks directly about the epithet that angers African Americans and attacks their self-image. Baldwin (1963) argues "In order for me to live, I decided very early that some mistakes had been made somewhere. I am not a 'nigger' even though you called me one" (p. 3). Looking directly into the eyes of his audience Baldwin (1963) proclaims: "But if I was a 'nigger' in your eyes, there was something about you – there was something you needed" (p. 3). Baldwin (1963) continues recounting lies that white people say about black people, such as they are lazy; they eat watermelon; and then concluded "if I am not what I've been told I am, then it means that you're not what you thought you were either! And that is the crisis" (p. 3).

A good third of my summer, 2019, is taken up serving as the intellectual leader for staff development meetings focused on racism because an elementary school European American student called an African American teacher the N-word. And, true to Baldwin's observation and like Baldwin, the teacher, Mr. C said: "No, that's not me," and recommended that the school (faculty and staff of mostly European American teachers) do something about the racism at the school. One third of the faculty/staff, approximately 24, decided to commit time during the summer to deal with some of the many manifestation of white supremacy at the school. Baldwin's identification that "some mistakes had been made," therefore initiating a "crisis" is as accurate today as in 1963 when Baldwin spoke. Racial progress, since Baldwin, although duly noted, continues to be, at best "inching along" as such incidents are frequent.

Myth-making

In his Los Angles speech, April 1963, Baldwin discusses the sinister side of myth-making, and how myth-making challenges African American agency to win freedom and to accept and appreciate self. Baldwin begins the discussion of myth-making, addressing attempts to eliminate the American Indians and how it is characterized. Baldwin posits,

90 Baldwin and Education

> I bet you … that not many American children, being taught American history, have any real sense of what that collision was like, or what we really did, how we really achieved the extermination of the Indian, or what that means.
>
> *(p. 3)*

Next, Baldwin discusses myth-making and African Americans' role in American social and economic growth. Baldwin argues that in order to "conquer" the country cheap labor was necessary. "And the man who is now known as the American Negro who is one of the oldest American citizens and the only one who never wanted to come here, did the dirty work" (Baldwin, 1963, p. 2). The American Negro, Baldwin argues, picked cotton and without his presence,

> without his strong back, the American economy, the American nation would have had major trouble creating capital. If one did not have the captive toting the barge and lifting the bale as they put it, it would be a very different country, and it would certainly be much poorer.
>
> *(Baldwin, 1963, p. 2)*

Myth-making to create identity undercut truth important to freedom represses others' self-image and causes citizens to be less active. Myths are grand narratives about African Americans, false and virulent, that sanction and codify white supremacy and fortify lies baked into biases and stereotypes. Myths along with lies about America is what prompted James Loewen (2018) to write *Lies my Teacher Told Me*. When asked about the biggest lie in his book, Loewen describes, how myths and lies come to be, along with serving as controlling factors.

> Usually when I'm asked, "What's the biggest lie?" I put my hand out in front of me slanting upward and to the right. And what I mean by that is the overall theme of American history is we started out great and we've been getting better ever since kind of automatically. And the trouble with that is two things. First of all, it's not always true.
>
> And the second part is what it does to the high school student. It says you don't need to protest; you don't need to write your congressman; you don't need to do any of the things that citizens do, because everything's getting better all the time.

Baldwin speaks bluntly not only about the self-image of African American students but about the image and identity of America, and how it comes to be. Baldwin argues that myths and lies are used to construct the image of America as white at a cost to the self-image of all other Americans. Baldwin (1962) writes in "Letter From A Region In My Mind":

> I want to suggest most seriously that before we can do very much in the way of clear thinking or clear doing as relates to the minorities in this country, we

must first crack the American image and find out and deal with what it hides. We cannot discuss the state of our minorities until we first have some sense of what we are, who we are, what our goals are, and what we take life to be. The question is not what we can do now for the hypothetical Mexican, the hypothetical Negro. The question is what we really want out of life, for ourselves, what we think is real.

(p. 6)

Baldwin challenges America's myth-making starting with the Pilgrims:

It's astounding to me, for example, that so many people really appear to believe that the country was founded by a band of heroes who wanted to be free. That happens not to be true. What happened was that some people left Europe because they couldn't stay there any longer and had to go someplace else to make it. That's all.

(Baldwin, 1963 p. 4)

In a later speech, Baldwin added:

Anybody who was making it in England, did not get on the Mayflower ... [and went on to say] This is important. It is important that one begin to recognize this, because part of the dilemma of this country is it has managed to believe the myth it has created about its own past.

(Baldwin, 1963, p. 4)

Ironically, in 2013, Robert Tracy McKenzie, chairperson of the history department at Wheaton College and the scholar who writes *Five Myths About the Pilgrims* reports: That the Pilgrims came to America in search of religious freedom is a myth. McKenzie argues the Pilgrims came to America to acquire "better and easier" living.

Baldwin points a finger at the myth of race in America because he wants teachers and students to be aware of the United States' creation myth – "its own unique, dramatic story intended to explain where we came from and who we are today" argues Jacqueline Jones (2013) in *A Dreadful Deceit: The Myth of Race from the Colonial Era to Obama's America*. Baldwin wants teachers to understand that race is a tool for maintaining American hierarchy and white privilege. Race that is "I am white" is used to tell African Americans that they are not as good as European Americans. Baldwin wants teachers and students to know that race has "no basis in biology or any longstanding, consistent usage in human culture. It is a product of collective imagination, not historical fact, and it exists outside the realm of rational thought" (Jones, 2013, p. 5).

The importance of education combating myths and discovering truth recently became more than a statement to discuss in teacher education or philosophy

92 Baldwin and Education

classes at the University of Wisconsin. When the then Wisconsin Governor, Scott Walker attempted to change the century-old mission of the University system by proposing to remove words in the state code that command the university to "search for truth" and "improve the human condition" and replace them with "meet the state's workforce needs." Whereas, the move highlighted the desire by some to keep truth in the dark and not be concerned about the human conditions of the less fortunate, it also called attention to none-stop attempts to make the purpose of education serve the oppressors at the expense of the oppressed.

Demystify Whiteness

Baldwin works to demystify whiteness, to help European American teachers to know that there isn't anything natural and normal about the physical, social and moral separation of European Americans from African Americans. Baldwin argues that redlining and ghettoization of African Americans, which forces African American students to live uptown in Harlem and European Americans to live downtown, is a social construction. Baldwin wants European American teachers to understand that racism is more than an individual belief, where the ignorance of an individual can be corrected by education, but that racism must be addressed as an institutional and systemic problem. He wants European American teachers to understand how racism (and whiteness) pervades America's cultural institutions, such as movies. In *The Devil Finds Work* (1967), Baldwin challenges the underlying assumptions in racialized feel-good films: *Guess Who's Coming to Dinner* and *In the Heat of the Night*, as well as racism in horror films such as *The Exorcist*, and black–white buddy films such as *The Defiant Ones*. Whereas these are yesteryear films, Hollywood like America is slow to change. Baldwin's analysis of films in *The Devil Finds Work* is useful to teachers today who communicate with or want to communicate with their students about life outside the four walls of schools. As I watch the *Game of Thrones* and *Homeland* award-winning television series, I often asked myself, what would Baldwin say about the token inclusion of African Americans and the roles of the few African American characters? What do such television series do to the self-image of African Americans? Since I couldn't ask Baldwin, I read comments on websites that African Americans visit. A comment by John Boyega, British black actor and star in *Star Wars* films captures much of what I read. Boyega told *GQ* magazine:

> There are no black people in Game of Thrones. You don't see one black person in Lord of The Rings. I ain't paying money to always see one type of person on-screen.

Baldwin argues Hollywood's fabrication of African Americans is not innocent but designed and inspired by racist ideology. Baldwin argues that "entertainment is not innocent" and entertainment (e.g., movies, television, magazines) shapes the country's consciousness (Obenson, 2015) and shapes groups' and individuals' thoughts of self: their self-image. The genocide of American Indians as entertainment is not innocent, nor are all the white heroes in film. About heroes in films, Baldwin (2017) states "Heroes, as far as I could see, were white — and not merely because of the movies, but because of the land in which I lived, of which movies were simply a reflection" (p. 2). Elahe Izadi (2017) in an interview with Raoul Peck, director of Baldwin's *I Am Not Your Negro*, discusses Baldwin's critique of *Guess Who's Coming to Dinner* (1967), a film about a liberal European American woman, and an African American doctor becoming engaged and the African American doctor meeting his partner's parents. Whereas Peck contends that Baldwin is pleased to see his friend Sidney Poitier as star of the film, there are nevertheless problems. Baldwin is proud to see Poitier's character as an educated, respectable, fully realized African American man, whose presence provides an example of what African American people can be when they are not oppressed. That said, Peck (Izadi, 2017) argues

> The message is, if you are an African American, in order to fit into the picture, you need to be very articulate, very handsome, have a PhD, be a doctor ... otherwise, you don't have any chance to get the girl in the movie. That was putting the bar very high for most black people.
>
> *(p. 1).*

"Respectability politics" (Higginbotham, 1993b) or the belief that conformity to socially acceptable or mainstream standards of appearance and behavior will protect members of marginalized groups from prejudice or systemic injustice, a term not defined as such during Baldwin's day, but very much at play.

Baldwin (1963, Los Angles) contends that for generations European Americans have lied about themselves: "they have put on the color of their skin a totally false value" (p. 6). Baldwin argues that for thousands of years European Americans have claimed they are better than everyone else, because they are white. However, Baldwin concludes the spiritual, political and actual results of this lie are morally and spiritually bankrupt and skin color has no importance to human life. Baldwin (1963) adds:

> I know that people have perished because of the color of their skin, but it is not because of the color of their skin, really. It is the value placed on it. It is because of what it means in the eyes of someone else or their own eyes
>
> *(p. 6)*

Baldwin (1963) speaking personally, as he often does, says:

> I want, from the very bottom of my heart for African Americans in this country to arrive, at, a real sense of who they are. I understand, that life being what it is,

94 Baldwin and Education

and power being what it is, that it is entirely possible that the world will have to lie to itself for the next two thousand years on the basis of color with the roles reversed.

(p. 6)

In the concluding paragraph of "History is a Weapon" an article written three years earlier, but that emphasizes the positive self-image and agency African American youth are adopting, Baldwin (1960) posits:

Americans keep wondering what has 'got into' students. What has 'got into' them is their history in this country. They are not the first Negroes to face mobs: they are merely the first Negroes to frighten the mob more than the mob frightens them.

(p. 1)

Baldwin adds

But these young people are determined to make it happen and make it happen now. They cannot be diverted. It seems to me that they are the only people in this country now who really believe in freedom. Insofar as they can make it real for themselves, they will make it real for all of us. The question with which they present the nation is whether or not we really want to be free.

(p. 2)

It has been almost 70 years, since Baldwin highlights young people, as the people to make freedom happen. Baldwin's observation is correct, in that young African American people of the 1960s fought and died for freedom and a respected self-image. In 2017, Zahara Hill writing in HuffPost identified 28 organizations that empower African American communities, many empowered by youth. Such organizations include Black Lives Matter, Black Girls Code, Million Hoodies, Black Youth Project, The Innocence Project and others. The existence of these organizations demonstrates that African American young people continue to have a heightened consciousness, are energized and active; they push back on respectability politics and they know they are somebody.

Teaching and Racial Innocence

"Racial innocence" often sits before me in my Introduction to Education class. Students who are newly admitted to the teacher education program and are taking their first education class. The vast majority or mostly all are European American women, who through the way they were raised (family, religion, 99% all-white schools); their sense of belonging to a particular social setting (small predominately white Wisconsin towns), or through their membership in particular institutions (church) display a natural confidence. Their sense of self is strong, their belief in their capacity to be an outstanding teacher is strong and their sense of morality is linked to the identity they derived from these associations. Such individuals are "innocent" as to how their moral identity has been constructed and the foundations on which it rests, social media and news media notwithstanding (Baddeley & James, 1991). They regard their view of the world as "normal" and their language – white standard English (WSE) – as common usage. As these students continue their journey to become teachers of all America children, they will need to face many moments of reckoning, where they confront and process much of what they were told about *Others* and their rights and privileges, spoken and unspoken by people who loved and cared for them, to learn it is completely false. The process of unlearning and learning severs bonds and re-establishes them with a genuine love only made possible by truth.

In 1962, James Baldwin calls out racial innocence as the "crime" of being willfully untouched by the racial injustices of American life. Racial innocence is ascertained through power; the power to control the flow of knowledge, which helps frame the telling of history and establishing America's innocence includes legitimatizing present-day claims of white superiority and black inferiority. Racially innocent is how European American people think, speak and act; and it is their attitude and behavior that gesture they have no role or responsibility in the racial conflict that is largely of their making. Baldwin (1963) argues it is "not permissible that the authors of devastation should also be innocent. It is the innocence which constitutes the crime" (p. 14). Racial innocence is deliberately being blind and in Baldwin's (1963) words "reassuring white Americans that they do not see what they see. And what they see is an appallingly oppressive and bloody history, known all the world over" (p. 72). Racial innocence as Kristine Taylor (2015) argues is in the very fabric of U.S. political rhetoric, policy formations and political institutions; and innocence is Americans' belief in their own blamelessness for the material realities of contemporary racism. Taylor (2015) also contends racial innocence is responsible for the "massive and willful ignoring of the actual history" of race in the United States (p. 16).

Toni Morrison (quoted in Edmundson, 1992) argues America is

> not history-less, but historical; not damaged, but innocent; not a blind accident of evolution, but a progressive fulfillment of destiny. In other words, as McClure (2016) argues the recurring trope of innocence is crucial for defining American self, as its very identity is wrapped in the bloodied layers of crimes against humanity related to settler colonialism and slavery.
>
> *(p. 55)*

Baldwin's scholarship, argues McCall (2018) provides a sustained critique of the (white) intellectual's pretensions to objectivity. Baldwin sees these pretensions as a function of European American innocence, a form of epistemic blindness that he claims is characteristic of white identity that manifests a retreat from reality that blinds European Americans to the tragic dimension of existence. African Americans generally lack the privilege of this blind innocence. Baldwin however argues African Americans are not fooled by claims of racial innocence. It is European Americans who are fooled or who fool themselves (Mura 2016). "Innocence" is a theme that Baldwin addresses in his work and the theme of racial innocence is not only a state of mind in teaching (and of teachers) but also a way of conducting business (e.g., policy and procedure) in schools.

Racial innocence is at play in teacher education programs when teacher candidates believe that they are prepared and/or can become prepared to teach students who are culturally different because they "love" children and agree to "sit in" on an ethnic studies course. The passage of *Plessy v. Ferguson* 1896: – "separate but equal" – a statute according to Justice Henry Brown "which implies merely a legal distinction between the white and colored races ... has no tendency to destroy the legal equality of the two races or reestablish a state of involuntary servitude" was a statement of racial innocence and it served for years, and it's legacy continues, as an attitude and behavior of European Americans. Racial innocence is in play in the *Swann v. Charlotte-Mecklenberg Board of Education*, in 1971, where the Court approves busing, magnet schools, compensatory education and other tools as remedies to overcome the role of residential segregation in perpetuating racially segregated schools. Racial innocence is at play within school policy, for example, *A Nation at Risk*, with its announced attention to equity and excellence, but where discussions of equity are muted, and in school programs and teaching where "color-blindness" – "I see all my students the same way" – prevails as African American students are suspended, called-out and placed in special education much, much more than European American students.

Findings from the Civil Rights Data Collection (2018), according to Moriah Balingit conclude: African American students faced greater rates of suspension, expulsion and arrest than their European American classmates and African American students – males and students with disabilities – are overrepresented in disciplinary action. Also, Balingit posits according to the Government Accountability Office (GAO) "These disparities were widespread and persisted regardless of the type of disciplinary action, level of school poverty, or type of public school attended" (p. 2).

Racial innocence prevails, when at the next meeting of educators, blame is totally or mostly placed on African American students and their families. Little if any attention is given to those responsible for the education of these students: the teachers, the teacher educators, the colleges of education where courses are taken to earn teaching and administrative licenses. Furthermore, the State Department of Education and local board of education claim willful ignorance about the racism inherent in their policies and practices.

Racial innocence, drawing on Baldwin's scholarship is also at play in other professions and occupations where those responsible (managers, teachers, principals, teacher educators) make unconscious or conscious claims of "innocence" and/or they are as "unaware of their political environment as the fish is of water." In "The Power of Innocence: From Politeness to Politics" an article by Simon Baddeley and Kim James (1991) the authors include the fish in water metaphor to examine "'innocent' managers who are "willfully ignorant" of their political environment. Baddeley and James's (1991) purpose for investigating innocence is they believed "an individual's ethnicity, class, nationality, gender, sexuality or religion has significance for the way they live-in and experience the world, and that these factors have become increasingly relevant to their job as managers (or teachers, principals, professors, etc.)." It follows Baddeley and James's (1991) argue that "political innocence" (racial innocence in the case of teachers and other educators) compounded a manager's (or teacher's) difficulties causing them problems understanding the implications of significant events going on around them.

In addition, Baddeley and James's (1991) conclude innocence can be powerful. Powerful, in the sense that innocent people control other people's lives and other people's understanding of the world; that innocent people (e.g., teachers) define through words and deeds of the dominant culture and normality; and that they control organizational resources. Further, Baddeley and James's (1991) discuss identity in the context of "powerful innocence"; these are lead managers, department chairs, principals who because of their position see themselves as "objective observers with minimal influence but who are unconsciously powerful definers of reality". The "powerful innocents" assume that *their* life is how life *is* and has to be for everyone (p. 114). Furthermore, Baddeley and James (1991) argue people's personal positions are arrived at and sustained by being with a group of people whose understanding of the world is similar to their own. Thus, their position is both sustained by other group members and contributes to the group. The last thing Baddeley and James (1991) contend, the fish discovers its water. Innocence derives its power through being comfortably and unreflectively surrounded by others of like mind. From this stance individuals cannot see themselves colluding with the larger flow of institutional direction nor its consequence.

"Racial innocence" hung heavy in the air in the room during Baldwin's "The Negro Child –His Self-image" lecture on that October day in New York City. "Americans' unknowingness" (Taylor, 2015), teachers' "willful blindness" (Balfour, 2001) and the assumption in American society that European American knowledge is superior and European Americans know best: "racial innocence" is what Baldwin (1963) knows he is up against – what he challenges when he speaks of information explicitly left out of the history text and ignored in other education text. Baldwin's truth challenges the racial innocence and superiority that comes with purposefully remaining "willfully blind" as well as teaching dehumanizing pedagogies in ways that lead African Americans to believe they are less than European Americans. Baldwin challenges the "powerful innocents," who assume that *their* life is how life *is* and has to be for everyone. Baldwin's argument declares that racial innocence is bogus and that European Americans' action toward African Americans is deliberate and intentional. Baldwin (1963) states "What I am trying to suggest to you is that it was not an accident, it was not an act of God, it was not done by well-meaning people muddling into something which they didn't understand (p. 4)." "Innocence" from a Baldwinian perspective, Balfour (2001) argues "is resistance to facing the horrors of the American past and present and their implications for the future ... a kind of deliberate blindness or deafness, a refusal to acknowledge uncomfortable truths" (p. 32). Innocence is when teachers and teacher candidates do not "go for broke" with assignments that help them to discover the importance of their life history when teaching students of different cultural backgrounds. Innocence is not participating fully in classroom discussions on race in small and large groups.

Jennifer L. Pierce (2012) argues in *Racing for Innocence: Whiteness, Gender, and the Backlash Against Affirmative Action* that European Americans narrate their story about themselves in ways that disavow any accountability for racism. European Americans not only deny responsibility, they are silent about their socialization into a racist society that is mythized in exceptionalism, whitewashed history, including the genocide of American Indians and the building of America on the backs of enslaved people. Racial innocence is supported by modes of stigmatization where deficit perspectives are rooted. Jonathan Rosa and Nelson Flores (2017) in "Unsettling Race and Language: Toward a Raciolinguistic Perspective" discuss how institutionalized hierarchies of racial and linguistic legitimacy are central to processes of modern subject formation. That is, racialized subjects are stigmatized for linguistic practices that are not middle-class and white. Thereby affording racial innocence to self-identified monolingual European American teachers in a study who viewed their bilingual Puerto Rican principal, who holds a doctorate in education, as intellectually and linguistically inferior, and ignored their "willfully blindness" to their own shortcomings (Rosa, 2016). Innocence, as one listen to friends, peers, strangers and family members is manifested in a myriad of ways, to escape one's role in a situation. However, as Taylor (2015) argues, commenting through a Baldwinian lens, "innocence does not mean materially *guiltless* or *faultless*, but rather *free from* or *untouched by*" (p. 329).

The same year, 1963, that Baldwin is explaining in "A Talk to Teachers" the devastating effects of racial discrimination on American society, particularly its effect on African American students, and arguing for change in teachers' deficit thinking toward their students, leading European American educators were arguing that African American students were "culturally deprived." Ira J. Gordon and Frank Riessman (1963) who in a *Research in Review* article: "The Culturally Deprived Child: A New View" delivered the opening address for the Conference on the "Education of Disadvantaged Children" held by the U.S. Office of Education in Washington, D.C., argue that although African American students are "culturally deprived" – inferior norms, values, skills and knowledge – they want to call attention to the positive features in the culture and the psychology of the lower income group; in particular their cognitive style. One major dimension of this style, Gordon and Riessman opine is "slowness" (p. 1). The opening of Gordon and Riessman's (1963) article/address includes a statement that reads like a note of compassion and support of racial innocence.

> There is now great interest on the part of practitioners and academic people in the problems of lower socioeconomic groups. We are nearing a major breakthrough in dealing with these questions. There is, I believe, considerable agreement regarding many of the recommendations for treating these problems (although there are some very different emphases). What is missing is a theoretical rationale to give meaning and direction to the action suggestions.

Gordon and Riessman (1963) believe they are exercising good intentions as they "call attention to the positive features in the culture and the psychology of lower income groups; – read *African American students* – in particular their cognitive style. One major dimension of this style is slowness" (p. 1). But, their critique, which "blames the victim" and their suggestions, nevertheless disparages African American humanity, holds up high European American humanity and racializes teaching African American children; while acting in innocence.

Baldwin (1979) in "If Black English Isn't a Language, Then Tell Me, What Is?" argues against such cultural deprivation theorizing, when he posits "the bulk of white people in America never had any interest in educating black people, except as it could serve white interest" (p. 2). Additionally, Baldwin (1979) argues:

> It is not the black child's language that is despised. It is his experience. A child cannot be taught by anyone who despises him and a child cannot afford to be fooled. A child cannot be taught by anyone whose demand, essentially, is that the child repudiates his experience, and all that gives him sustenance, and enters a limbo in which he is no longer black, and in which he knows he can never become white. Black people have lost too many children that way.
>
> *(p. 2)*

Racial innocence in schools allows European American students to act out and not be penalized while, African American students are sent to the principal's office. Racial innocence allows for the cause of the poverty in the home life of an African American student to be fully and squarely placed upon the student's parents' laziness and not hundreds of years of racial oppression in the U.S. According to Baldwin, not-seeing, the "innocence" is what "constitutes the crime." Racial innocence privileges the European American student running through the school hallway with polite words of: "slow-down and walk to your class" while systemic racism oppresses the African American student running through the school hallway with harsh shouts of: "Stop! Get over here!"

After Shock of Truth: Pam and Ann

Teachers leaving Baldwin's speech move quickly through the "canyons of steel" to their cars or the subway to go home. Teachers at Baldwin's lecture have much to ponder or forget. For most, their teaching philosophy, pedagogical methods and curriculum have just been severely criticized. Historical truths and beliefs have been called out as exaggerations or bald-faced lies. America is identified as a myth-maker and willful ignorance is charged and challenged. The education of African American children is defined as much more than preparing them to get a job and be good, polite, stay-in-your-community citizens.

You know some teachers have already dismissed Baldwin's remarks as civil rights theater. They are the ones who displayed "why doesn't he [Baldwin] hurry up and finish" in their eyes and were constantly squirming soon after the talk began. Their presence at the in-service is theater and the spirited applause they give the speaker is more that he is finished, than what he said.

Some other teachers are annoyed, almost insulted and have already dismissed Baldwin's remarks. They say to themselves: "I know how to teach *these* kids, I have been doing it for 15 years."

Besides, accepting Baldwin's statement, "that the structures in society are not made for African American students, but for someone else's benefit" ignores recent curriculum changes, and recent research that African American students are "culturally deprived" and it ignores the community participation underway in schools and gains achieved by the Civil Rights movement.

A few teachers silently welcome Baldwin's remarks and hope these staff development sessions will provide more of the same along with practical ideas. Curriculum ideas and instructional practices teachers can do daily in their classrooms. Yet, another group of teachers, African Americans, about 14, demonstrates a range of positive emotions in support of Baldwin. They believe they are too few in number and too spread-out across the school district to have an impact on the racism in school policies and practices.

You hear from behind, the familiar voice of Ann, who has taught across the hall from you for the last seven years. Rushing to catch up and now looking into your eyes, Ann says, "Pam, what do you think about the "Talk?" "What do you think about what he said to us, about us, our teaching and the hypocrisy of our country?"

Moving on, not answering, but giving her a quick glance. You say to yourself: "This man, James Arthur Baldwin, speaks about African American students, but in a different way than they are spoken about in the teacher's lounge, grad classes, the media; and a different way than I learned to think about African American, when I was growing up.

There is no deficit rhetoric about African American students and their families in his comments. He acknowledges their struggle and the poverty they live in; and argues that African American students' life circumstance should not determine their future and teachers have the power to help them achieve their dreams. His observations about society as well as the attitudes and treatment of African Americans are consistent with what I deep down know to be true, but ignore.

He comes across as honest. He doesn't claim that teachers are acting out implicit biases, he doesn't trash the New York Public School System or American society. Instead, respectful in tone and comments, he makes an urgent personal appeal to members of a profession, that are responsible for students' personal and professional success, to change their ideology on the education of African American children; to re-examine their knowledge of U.S. history and examine the way they consciously and unconsciously acknowledge African Americans' humanity.

The purpose of education, you hear Baldwin say, is about preparing African American students so they can engage successfully with the rest of the world as they keep in mind who they are, where they want to go and their plans to get there. Finally, you acknowledge to yourself that the comment that grabs you the most and the one you cannot let go is: "Because if I am not what I've been told I am, then you are not what you thought you were either!"

Again, you hear Ann: "Pam, Pam, what do you think about what we heard?" You look at her, tilt your head and ask her with somewhat heightened emotion: "What do you think! What do you think!" And quickly move on. You leave Ann gasping.

The Effect of James Baldwin's Words

Baldwin's words lean hard on teachers of African American students. They call into question teachers' innocence and challenge their rhetoric that "I want to teach because: 'I love children' and 'I want to help children.' Baldwin asks teachers to open their eyes – for their own good – to how racism constructs and keeps African Americans in a social status that renders them second-class citizens. Baldwin (1953) argues "People who shut their eyes to reality simply invite their destruction, and anyone who insists on remaining in a state of innocence long after that innocence is dead turns himself into a monster" (p. 2). However, Baldwin knows antiracist thinking and work is hard, most people don't want to engage, they don't want to consider their identity as a major area of investigation in their teaching.

European American teachers continue to see America as white and prefer to have all students assimilated into whiteness. And, while there may have been a required ethnic studies class for teacher candidates, or a "Talk to Teachers" lecture for classroom teachers, many European American teachers will teach for years without consciously believing that knowledge of African American history and culture is critical to successfully teach African American students. European American teachers have yet to fully believe that when the curriculum in schools is changed so that African American students learn about their history and culture

102   Baldwin and Education

and learn about their contributions to America, not only will it be beneficial for African Americans it will be beneficial for European Americans (Baldwin, 1963). Wanting to love and help African American students demands that European American teachers examine their "dysconscious racism" (King, 1991) and because of this continuing resistance the Talk in 1963 may be more appropriate today than it was then.

Speaking at New York City's Community Church in 1962, the year prior to talking to New York teachers, James Baldwin (1963c) delivers "The Artist's Struggle for Integrity" speech. The speech continues to be admired because of the way it deals with creative life at a time of a racial emergency. Baldwin, who has recent publications on the connection between art and society: "The Creative Process" (1962) and "As Much Truth as One Can Bear" (1962) tells his audience that "it is only the artist, as distinguished from the priest, the psychoanalyst, [and] the pope, who has really given us any real sense of what it is like to be alive." Baldwin posits "[t]he poets, (by which I mean all artists) are the only people who know the truth about us. Soldiers don't. Statesmen don't. Union leaders don't. Priest don't. Only Poets." ("The Artist's Struggle for Integrity".

As a teacher, I am obliged to pause, and respectfully consider, Baldwin's statement; not to disagree, but in search for the *teacher*, in this soliloquy. I am searching not for the teacher's *place* but the teacher's *role*, how the teachers contributes to someone – students – "being alive." Baldwin speaks graciously and glowingly about teachers; especially four teachers (including Gertrude Ayer, the school principal) who help shape his life, who put him on the path to become alive, and live. These teachers, to me, were artists in the way they work with James/Jimmy – their material. And it is important, not to lose memory of that.

Bibliography

Als, H. (2019). James Baldwin, restored. *the Paris Review*. February. https://www.theparisreview.org/blog/2019/02/15/james-baldwin-restored/. 4/11/2019.

Baddeley, S. and James. K. (1991). The power of innocence: From politeness to politics. *Management Education and Development*, 22, 106–118.

Baldwin, J. (1953/1985). A stranger in the village. In *The Price of the Ticket*. New York, NY: St. Martin's Press. pp. 79–90.

Baldwin, J. (1955). *Notes of a Native Son: Many Thousand Gone*. New York, NY: Beacon Press.

Baldwin, J. (1960). History is a weapon: They can't turn back. https://www.historyisaweapon.com/defcon1/baldwincantturnback.html. 7/17/2019.

Baldwin, J. (1962a). A Letter to My Nephew. *The Progressive*. (progressive.org). 12/4/2020.

Baldwin, J. (1962b). Letter from a region in my mind. *The New Yorker*, November 17. 12/4/2020.

Baldwin, J. (1963a). The fire next time. In *James Baldwin: Collected Essays*, ed. Toni Morrison. New York, NY: Library of America. (1998 [1963]).

Baldwin, J. (1963b). A talk to teachers. *The Saturday Review*. December 21.

Baldwin, J. (1963c). The artist's struggle for integrity. Community Church, New York City. James Baldwin – The Artist's Struggle for Integrity (An Excerpt), YouTube. 12/5/2020.

Baldwin, J. (1967). Negroes are anti-Semitic because they're anti-white. *The New York Times*. https://archive.nytimes.com/www.nytimes.com/books/98/03/29/specials/baldwin-antisem.html?mcubz=3. 8/9/2020.

Baldwin, J. (1965/1998). The white man's guilt. *Baldwin: Collected Essays*. *Ebony*. Editor, Toni Morrison. New York, NY: The Library of America.

Baldwin, J. (1966). A report from occupied territory. *The Nation*.

Baldwin, J. (1968). James Baldwin: How to cool it. Interview. *Esquire*. 70, 1. July. p. 49, 116. https://www.esquire.com/news-politics/a23960/james-baldwin-cool-it/. 6/28/2019.

Baldwin, J. (1970). An open letter to my sister, Angela Y. Davis. *The New York Review of Books*. https://www.nybooks.com/articles/1971/01/07/an-open-letter-to-my-sister-miss-angela-davis/. 6/28/2019.

Baldwin, J. (1972). *No Name in the Street*. New York, NY: Dial Press.

Baldwin, J. (1979). If Black English isn't a language, then tell me, what is? *The New York Times*. July 29. (odu.edu). 12/5/2020.

Baldwin, J. (1998). Autobiographical Notes. *The New York Times Book Review*. http://movies2.nytimes.com/books/first/b/baldwin-essays.html. 6/30/ 2019.

Balfour, L. (2001). *Evidence of Things Not Said: James Baldwin and the Promise of American Democracy*. Ithaca, NY: Cornell University Press.

Baldwin, J. (2017). *I Am Not Your Negro*. Film. Director Raoul Peck.

Balingit, M. (2018). Racial disparities in school discipline are growing, federal data show. *The Washington Post*. April 29. 12/4/2020.

Bellan, R. (2019). $23 million education funding report reveals less money for city kids. CityLab. https://www.citylab.com/equity/2019/03/education-nonwhite-urban-school-districts-funding-tax/585691/. 7/3/2019.

Bernstein, R. (2011, March 27). *Racial Innocence: Performing American Childhood from Slavery to Civil Rights*. New York, NY: New York University Press.

Bertran, M. and Mullainathan, S. (2004). Discrimination in the job market in the United States. J-PAL. https://www.povertyactionlab.org/evaluation/discrimination-job-market-united-states. 7/18/2019.

Blad, E. (2019). Schools grapple with student depression as data show problem worsening. *Education Week*. December. (edweek.org). 12/4/2020.

Brooks, K. (2014). Research shows food deserts more abundant in minority neighbor-hoods. *Johns Hopkins Magazine*. https://hub.jhu.edu/magazine/2014/spring/racial-food-deserts/. 7/17/2019.

Butler, P. (2018). The policing of black Americans is racial harassment funded by the state. *The Guardian*. https://www.theguardian.com/us-news/2018/jun/06/america-police-called-on-black-people-everyday-racism. 7/17/2019.

Coates, Ta-Nehisi (2014). The case of reparations. *The Atlantic*. https://www.theatlantic.com/magazine/archive/2014/06/the-case-for-reparations/361631/. 7/18/2019.

Counts, G. S. (1978). *Dare the Schools Build a New Social Order?*Carbondale, IL: Southern Illinois University Press.

Darling-Hammond, L. (2001). Inequality in teaching and schooling: How opportunity is rationed to students of color in America. *National Academy of Sciences*. https://www.ncbi.nlm.nih.gov/books/NBK223640. 8/10/20.

104 Baldwin and Education

de Marrais, K. B. and LeCompte, M. D. (1995). *The Way Schools Work: A Sociological Analysis of Education* (2nd ed.). White Plains, NY: Longman Publishers.

D'Emilio, J. (2003). *Lost Prophet: The life and times of Bayard Rustin.* Chicago, IL: University of Chicago Press.

Dewey, J. (1938). *Experience and Education.* New York, NY: Simon and Schuster.

Dewey, J. (1934). Individual psychology and education. *The Philosopher*, 12.

Douglas, F. (1857). 'West India Emancipation' speech delivered at Canandaifua, New York, August 4. *The Life and Writings of Frederick Douglass*, ed. Philip S. Foner, v. 2, 1950.

Elkins A. (2016). James Baldwin on police. Get-Tough. https://alexbelkins.com/2016/08/05/james-baldwin-on-police/. 7/17/2019.

Elisaoph, N. (1999). 'Everyday racism' in a culture of political avoidance: Civil society, speech, and taboo. *Social Problems*, 46, 4, 479–502.

Foshay, A. W. (1991). The curriculum matrix: Transcendence and mathematics." *Journal of Curriculum and Supervision*, 6, 4, 277–293.

Gibson, Jr.R. (2013,). My home on the hill: FAMU's Richard Gibson, Jr. April 8. Florida A & M University #MyHBCUMyStory. https://hbcustory.wordpress.com/2013/04/08/my-home-on-the-hill-famus-richard-gibson-jr-myhbcumystory. 3/15/2019.

Glass, A. (2019). Black students mount lunch counter sit-in, Feb. 1, 1960. February 2. https://www.politico.com/story/2019/02/01/greensboro-sit-in-1960-1135789. 3/16/2019.

Goldstein, R. (1984). An Interview with James Baldwin. "Go the Way Your Blood Beats." *The Village Voice.* 12/4/2020.

Gordon, I. J. and Riessman, F. (1963). The culturally deprived child: A new view. *Research in Review.* ASCD. (ascd.org). 12/5/2020.

Gould, E., Jones, J. and Mokhiber, Z. (2018). *Black workers have no progress in Closing earnings gaps with white men since 2000.* Economic Policy Institute. https://www.epi.org/blog/black-workers-have-made-no-progress-in-closing-earnings-gaps-with-white-men-since-2000/. 7/16/2019.

Hannah-Jones, N. (2018). Taking freedom: Yes, black America fears the police. Here's why. *Pacific Standard.* https://psmag.com/social-justice/why-black-america-fears-the-police. 7/17/2019.

Higginbotham, E. B. (1993a). *Righteous Discontent: The Women's Movement in the Black Baptist Church, 1880–1920.* Cambridge, Mass.: Harvard University Press.

Higginbotham, E. B. (1993b). Quoted in Randall Kennedy (2020) Lifting as we climb: A progress defense of respectability politics. *Harper's Magazine.* 12/10/2020.

Hill, Z. (2017). 28 organizations that empower black communities. HuffPost. https://www.huffpost.com/entry/28-organizations-that-are-empowering-black-communities_n_58a730fde4b045. 6/30/2019.

Hugo, Victor. (1862) *Les Misérables.* Trans. Charles E. Wilbour. New York, NY: Random House Modern Library. 1992.

Hugo, V. (1998). Quoted in *Victor Hugo's Conversations with the Spirit World: A Literary Genius's Hidden Life.* John Chambers. Rochester, VT: Destiny Books.

Ignatius, D. (2016). In today's world, the truth is losing. *The Washington Post.* https://www.washingtonpost.com/opinions/global-opinions/in-todays-world-the-truth-is-losing/2016/11/29/3f685cd2-b680-11e6-b8df-600bd9d38a02_story.html. 8/10/20.

Izadi, E. (2017). The best takedown of Hollywood comes from James Baldwin in 'I Am Not Your Negro'. *The Washington Post.* https://www.washingtonpost.com/news/arts-and-enterta. 6/30/2019.

Jefferson, T. (1786). To George Wythe. Paris, August 13, 1786. *American History*. http://www.let.rug.nl/usa/presidents/thomas-jefferson/letters-of-thomas-jefferson/jefl47.php. 11/3/2019.

Johns, D. J. (2018,). James Baldwin for the modern liberation movement. *Los Angeles Blade*. August 9. https://www.losangelesblade.com/2018/08/09/james-baldwin-for-the-modern-liberation-movement/. 3/18/2019.

Jones, J. (2013). *A Dreadful Deceit: The Myth of Race from the Colonial Era to Obama's America*. New York, NY: Basic books.

Kamenetz, A. (2018). "Lies my teacher told me," And how American history can be used as a weapon. *NPR, Education*. https://www.npr.org/2018/08/09/634991713/lies-my-teacher-told-me-and-how-american-history-can-be-used-as-a-weapon. 6/30/2019.

Khan, Y. (2016). Demand for school integration leads to massive 1964 boycott — in New York City. School Book. https://www.wnyc.org/story/school-boycott-1964/. 6/27/2019.

King, J. (1991). Dysconscious racism: Ideology, identity, and the miseduation of teachers. *The Journal of Negro Education*, 60, 2, Spring, 133–146.

King, M. L.Jr. (1947). The purpose of education. Morehouse College Student Paper, The Maroon Tiger. https://www.drmartinlutherkingjr.com/thepurposeofeducation.htm. 2/19/2019.

Labaree, D. F. (1997). *How to Succeed in School Without Really Learning*. New Haven, CT: Yale University Press.

Law, V. (2020). Coronavirus is disproportionately killing African Americans. Al Jazeera. April 10.

Leeming, D. (1994). *James Baldwin: A Biography*. New York, NY: Knopf.

Lind, D. (2015). The FBI is trying to get better data on police killings. Here's what we know now. VOX. https://www.vox.com/2014/8/21/6051043/how-many-people-killed-police-statistics-homicide-official-black. 7/17/2019.

Lippmann, W. (1941). Education vs. western civilization. *The American Scholar*, 10, 2, Spring, 184–193.

Loewen, J. (2018). *Lies My Teacher Told Me*. New York, NY: New Press.

Maguire, L. (2018). James Baldwin and racial justice. Philosophy Talk. February 12. https://www.philosophytalk.org/blog/james-baldwin-and-racial-justice. 3/19/2019.

McCall, C. (2018). Prophets in spite of themselves – Foucault and Baldwin on truth and innocence. *The New Polis*. http://thenewpolis.com/2018/05/12/prophets-in-spite-of-themselves-foucault-and-baldwin-on-truth-and-innocence-corey-mccall/. 2/24/2019.

McClure, R. D. (2016). Possessing history and American innocence: James Baldwin, William F. Buckley, Jr., and the 1965 Cambridge debate. *James Baldwin Review*, 2, http://dx.doi.org/10.7227/JBR.2.4.

McKenzie, R. T. (2013). Five myths about the Pilgrims. *The Washington Post*. https://www.washingtonpost.com/opinions/five-myths-abou. 3/11/2019.

Morrison, T. (1987) *Beloved*. New York, NY: Random House.

Morrison, T. Quoted in Mark Edmundson (1992.). Literature in living color. *The Washington Post*. July 7. https://www.washingtonpost.com/archive/entertainment. 7/4/2019.

Mura, D. (2016). White writing teachers (or David Foster Wallace vs. James Baldwin). *Journal of Creative Writing Studies*. https://scholarworks.rit.edu/cgi/viewcontent.cgi?referer=https://www.google.com/&httpsredir=1&article=1010&context=jcws. 2/3/2019.

Newkirk, V. R. (2018). America's health segregation problem. https://www.theatlantic.com/politics/archive/2016,/05/americas-health-segregation-problem/483219/. 7/17/2019.

Nowobilski, A. J.Running from Money: The puzzle of bars and liquor stores locating in black neighborhoods. Honor Thesis., Durham North Carolina: Duke University. https://sites.duke.edu/djepapers/files/2016/10/Nowobilski.pdf. 7/17/2019.

Obenson, T. A. (2015). Hey New York! 'The devil finds work: James Baldwin on film' Series kicks off tomorrow, Sept 11. Indie Wire. September 10. https://www.indiewire.com/2015/09/hey-new-york-the-devil-finds-work-james-baldwin-on-film-series-kicks-off-tomorrow-sept-11-148789/. 3/17/2019.

Onion, R. (2018). The teacher would suddenly yell "drop!" *Slate*. March 13. https://slate.com/human-interest/2018/03/are-duck-and-cover-school-drills-from-the-nuclear-era-a-useful-parallel-to-active-shooter-drills.html. 2/15/2019.

Owens-Young, J. (2020). Zip code effect: Your neighborhood determines your lifespan by as much as 30 years. Blue Zones. https://www.bluezones.com/2020/02/zip-code-effect-your-neighborhood-determines-your-lifespan/. 8/9/2020.

Pierce, J. L. (2012). *Racing for Innocence: Whiteness, Gender, and the Backlash Against Affirmative Action*. Stanford, CA: Stanford University Press.

Podair, J. (2002). *The Strike that Changed New York: Blacks, Whites and Ocean Hill –Brownsville*. Princeton, N: Princeton University Press.

Public Broadcasting System (PBS). (2016). Should the US pay reparation to black Americans?http://www.pbs.org/wgbh/point-taken/should-us-pay-reparations-black-americans/. 7/18/2019.

Rosa, J. (2016). Racializing language, regimenting Latinas/os: Chronotope, social tense, and American raciolinguistic futures. *Language & Communication*, 46, 106–117.

Rosa, J. and Flores, N. (2017). Unsettling race and language: Toward a raciolinguistic perspective. *Language in Society*, 46, 5, 1–27.

Schlosser, J. A. (2013). Socrates in a different key: James Baldwin and race in America. *Political Research Quarterly*, 66, 3, 487–499. https://repository.brynmawr.edu/cgi/viewcontent.cgi?article=1023&context=polisci_pubs.

Schomburg, A. (1925). *The Negro Digs Up His Past*. Schomburg Collection. 12/10/2020.

Shambaugh, J, Nunn, R. Anderson, S. (2019). How racial and regional inequality affect economic opportunity. Up Front. February. https://www.brookings.edu/blog/up-front/2019/02/15/how-racial-and-regional-inequality-affect-economic-opportunity/. 7/18/2019.

Stemier, S. (2019). Purpose of school. http://www.purposeofschool.com/contact/. https://www.teacherswithapps.com/the-goal-of-education-in-the-21st-century/.

Taylor, K. Y. (2015). *From #BlackLivesMatter to Black Liberation*. Chicago, IL: Haymarket.

The Inquirer (2019). Living black history: 4 African American leaders to learn from this month. *The Inquirer, Daily News*. February 1. https://www.philly.com/opinion/commentary/black-history-month-philadelphia-ida-b-wells-james-baldwin-20190201.html. 3/18/2019.

The New Polis (2018). Prophets in spite of themselves – Foucault and Baldwin on truth and innocence. (Corey McCall). May 12. http://thenewpolis.com/2018/05/12/prophets-in-spite-of-themselves-foucault-and-baldwin-on-truth-and-innocence-corey-mccall/. 3/18/2019.

Toffler, A. (1970). *Future Shock*. New York, NY: Bantam.

Toffler, A. (2014). Quoted in Shawn Stone. The goal of education in the 21st Century. July 2. https://www.teacherswithapps.com/the-goal-of-education-in-the-21st-century/. 7/4/2019.

Transnational Racial Justice Initiative. (2001). The persistence of white privilege and institutional racism in US policy. (raceforward.org).

Tyack, D. B. (1988). Ways of seeing: An essay on the history of compulsory schooling. In R. M. Jaeger (Ed.), *Complementary Methods for Research in Education* (pp. 24–59). Washington, DC: American Educational Research Association.

William, J. M. (2017). *James Baldwin: The FBI Files*. New York, NY: Arcade.

Zinn, H. (1980). *A People's History of the United States*. New York, NY: Harper Collins.

4

"GO FOR BROKE"

Additional Background on "Go for Broke"

Though Baldwin most likely borrowed the phrase "Go for Broke" from a 1951 film, its origin is rooted in U.S. military history when soldiers fought against overwhelming odds to defeat a stubborn enemy. "Go for Broke" is the motto of one of the most decorated units in U.S. military history, the Army's 442nd Regimental Combat Team (RCT). The 442 was a segregated World War II unit made up entirely of Americans of Japanese ancestry. At the start of WWII, Americans of Japanese ancestry, were distrusted by the federal government and barred from military service and placed in internment camps. However, the disbarment was removed in February 1943 and the 442nd RCT was activated and made up of Nisei volunteers. After the Nisei volunteers finished training for combat the following year, they were sent into battle. Their fighting earned nine Distinguished Service Crosses, more than tripling the 110th infantry battalion that earned three. As they fearlessly meet and defeat the German soldiers they face, they adopt "Go for Broke" as their motto; a motto they continue to live up to during their two years of service. The 442nd RCT and the 100th IB, before it joins the 442nd, earned an impressive score of awards, consisting of: 7 Presidential Unit Citations, 2 Meritorious Service Plaques, 36 Army Commendation Medals and 87 Division Commendations. Individual Nisei soldiers were awarded 18,000 decorations, including the following: 21 Medals of Honor, 29 Distinguished Service Crosses, 560 Silver Stars, 4,000 Bronze Stars, 22 Legion of Merit medals, 15 Soldier's Medals and nearly 9,500 Purple Hearts. The unit suffers many casualties, with 650 men lost, 3,700 wounded in action and 67 declared missing in action. To honor their sacrifices, April 5 every year is celebrated as National "Go for Broke" Day.

For the past 30 years, the "Go for Broke" National Education Center has been calling attention to the Nisei soldiers' valor and loyalty in the face of racial discrimination. The Center's mission is "To educate and inspire character and equality through the virtue and valor of our World War II American veterans of Japanese ancestry" (U.S. Department of Defense, 2019, p. 1).

This chapter discusses the metaphor "Go for Broke" that James Baldwin borrows and puts into practice. I imagine he borrows it, understanding its history, but more importantly, understanding the spirit and commitment to battle necessary for teaching African American students in a racist society. First, "Go for Broke" is discussed in the context of teaching African American students; next, it is illustrated by Baldwin in the Baldwin–Buckley debate; finally, Baldwin illustrates the concept of "going for broke" in "A Letter to My Nephew." These three examples of "Go for Broke" are indicative of the heightened consciousness, passion, and dedication James Baldwin puts into his craft.

"Go for Broke": Teaching

Though "A Talk to Teachers" is discussed in the previous chapter, this chapter focuses on the particular phrase Baldwin uses – "Go for Broke" – as he speaks to the teachers about how they should teach African American students. The full quote is: "So any citizen of this country who figures himself as responsible – and particularly those of you who deal with the minds and hearts of young people – must be prepared to 'Go for Broke'" (1963/1998, p. 678). The phrase "Go for Broke" is used by Baldwin to declare an all-out teaching effort against the forces of racism and oppression. Importantly, Baldwin wants teachers – who are tasked with the important job of *teaching the minds and influencing the hearts of young people* – to know their students are at risk because white supremacy does not want educated African Americans. Baldwin explains:

> [Y]ou must understand that in the attempt to correct so many generations of bad faith and cruelty, when it is operating not only in the classroom but in society, you will meet the most fantastic, the most brutal, and the most determined resistance. There is no point in pretending that this won't happen.
> *(1963/1998, p. 678)*

In "A Talk to Teachers," a few lines down from where "Go for Broke" and "determined resistance" are introduced, Baldwin addresses the paradox of education and the significance of teaching children to live with others.

The reward for "Go for Broke" teaching of African American students, Baldwin contends, is that as they become educated, they in turn will protest the oppressive conditions in which they live and hold the people responsible accountable. Baldwin (1963/1998) tells teachers they should remember that the educated child will examine society and the conditions in which they live, including the actions of the teachers, and demand accountability. "Why is my school closing?" "Why are there so few books about African Americans in the school library?" Why is our school the only one in the district with a zero-tolerance policy?" "Why was my great grandfather lynched?" "Why are there so few African American U.S. Senators?" "Why is my older brother always stopped by the police?" While these questions may make teachers uncomfortable, and some may, for some teachers, seem outside of the school's curriculum, students asking questions, their own questions and not the textbook's questions is an important step in "going for broke." Baldwin encouraged students to question and to question, and to question.

"Go for Broke" from a Baldwinian perspective means you teach in ways that educate students to make their own decisions, to make up their own questions and you teach students to handle the consequences of their decisions. Baldwin (1962a) contends that it is in the struggle with the aims of society and one's conscious awareness of society on which one's identity is defined and one's understanding of society is constructed. Throughout his writing, Baldwin is bluntly clear and definitive about the construction of his identity and his understanding of society. This is exemplified during a PBS interview with his good friend, the noted psychologist, Dr. Kenneth Clark. Baldwin (1963); in a response to Clark's question about the history of the founding of America, Baldwin addresses his identity that is forged out of his struggle with a racist society: "I am not a 'nigger,' I am a man!" stated Baldwin. The context for the question and response is Clark asking Baldwin: "What do you see? Are you essentially optimistic or pessimistic [about America and black and white relations]?"

BALDWIN: I'm both glad and sorry you asked me that question.... I can't be a pessimist because I'm alive. To be a pessimist means that you have agreed that human life is an academic matter, so I'm forced to be an optimist... But the future of the Negro in this country is precisely as bright or as dark as the future of the country ... What white people have to do, is try and find out in their own hearts why it was necessary to have a nigger in the first place, because I'm not a nigger, I'm a man, but if you think I'm a nigger, it means you need it.(Dr. Kenneth Clark interviews James Baldwin, 1963, Interview 3 of 3)

"Go for Broke," means you teach students to monitor the actions of the people who govern society. They cannot assume that those elected by the majority will do right by the minority or even the majority. They have to be on guard against authoritarianism and stand ready to protect their freedom. "Go for Broke," means "anyone who thinks of himself as responsible [must] examine society and try to change it and to fight it – at no matter what risk" (Baldwin, 1963/1998, p. 679).

"Go for Broke" is situational and contextual. It may include introducing a new math curriculum for students struggling with mathematics; it may be speaking up in a faculty meeting for staff development training on racism; and it may mean

"Go for Broke" 111

visiting the home of a student, who is not attending school because she feels alienated, in order to let her know that you and some other students believe she is smart and other students say she is fun to hang out with. That said, "Go for Broke" is not a singular swipe at racism, or a one or two and done bits of action. It is a sustaining daily struggle and more likely than not, is accompanied with challenges. Importantly, "Go for Broke" is based upon honesty and truth in teaching; designed "to make the world a more humane dwelling place" (Baldwin, 1962a, p. 1).

The need for teachers of African American students to "Go for Broke" is paramount, according to Baldwin (1963/1998) because any African American student who undergoes the American educational system runs the risk of becoming "schizophrenic." Baldwin's use of "schizophrenia," as I noted in Chapter 2, is not in the clinical sense of a mental disorder, but more akin to director of *Get Out* Jordan Peele's (2017) "sunken place." That is, as African Americans strive to increase their years of schooling, pursue positions in the profession or vocation of their choice, demand social justice, and appreciate their humanity and collected identity they are pushed back or held in place by systematic racism and find themselves, in Baldwin's (1963) term as "schizophrenic" and Peele's (2017) term as being in a "sunken place."

To "Go for Broke" according to Baldwin means acknowledging and doing something about racist acts when they occur. "All this (e.g., racism, whiteness) enters the child's consciousness much sooner than we as adults would like to think it does" (Baldwin, 1963/1998, p. 679). Therefore, teachers must put an immediate stop to racist actions. Tomorrow is a century too late, after lunch is avoidance and acting immediately, argues that yesterday, the day before and the day before that was the time to act.

To "Go for Broke" means establishing a classroom climate that rebukes antiblackness and promotes African American culture and teaches African American students they don't have to see themselves through the lens of whiteness, but through their own eyes. Baldwin contends that, whereas young African American students looking at the world around them, may not have the academic vocabulary (e.g., white privilege, interest conversion) to express what they see and what to make of it, they nevertheless learn from the reactions of their parents and other family members that something is not right or unfair, and this something is upsetting their loved ones. Baldwin (1963) put it this way in "A Talk to Teachers" because he wants teachers to understand the overall effect of systemic racism and why "going for broke" is so important.

> [A] black child, looking at the world around him, though he cannot know quite what to make of it, is aware that there is a reason why his mother works so hard, why his father is always on edge. He is aware that there is some reason why, if he sits down in the front of the bus, his father or mother slaps him and drags him to the back of the bus. He is aware that there is

112 "Go for Broke"

some terrible weight on his parents' shoulders which menaces him. And it isn't long – in fact it begins when he is in school – before he discovers the shape of his oppression.

(pp. 678–679)

Today, in the 21st century, legal segregation doesn't exist, therefore, the African American child will not be dragged to the back of the bus, but the African American child living below or slightly above the poverty line sees the financial weight on their families. They see their father or mother's concern as the family move often, sometimes causing children to double up with cousins, aunts and uncles; sleep on coaches, floors or in a van. They see and feel the absence of smiles and hearty laughter and comments of hope. Also, they see that their parents don't make enough to pay for food, and they too hesitate to ask for a second helping. According to the Pew Research Center's Patten and Krogstad (2015), the African American child poverty rate remains steady as other groups decline. Children make up 27% of the African American population, and 38% of African American children are in poverty.

The African American child living above the poverty line may not have the same experiences as the child in the above paragraph, but they, nevertheless experience systematic racism. They experience racism when their parents, who work as hard as their European American colleagues, are constantly overlooked as younger European Americans or European Americans who have not been with the company as long are promoted to senior positions, and their parents remain in place. They experience racism when they are asked to make do with clothes, shoes, no dental treatments (no braces) for another year or two. According to the Harvard Business Review's Michael Gee (2018) there are serious gaps in income, promotional opportunities, and advancement for minorities and women of all races.

The African American child at both income levels sees the effects of systematic racism as they observe their mother sit by the window and walk through their home anxiously, waiting for their older brother and sister to arrive home at night after being out with friends because she knows the history of police violence on black youth.

To "Go for Broke" as a teacher means opposing denials of racism as a continuing structural problem and questioning positions taken that deny the traumatic effect of violence on African American communities caused by structural racism. Racism, teachers who "Go for Broke" must point out, has continually denied African Americans access to opportunities and institutions from college campuses, to lunch counters, to the justice system. Whereas today African Americans are seen in these spaces, they still are not 100 per cent welcomed, often having to engage in "respectability politics" to fit into a given space and they have to continue to stand up for their rights. "I, Too Am Harvard," "I, Too Am Wisconsin,' is African American students on college campus showing that they belong; standing up for their rights.

"Go for Broke" **113**

To "Go for Broke" as a teacher means seeking to understand the everyday and academic false narratives about the failure of African Americans. Teachers must not buy into and regurgitate narratives of African American fathers as not being involved, missing, and having poor regard for their children. Mychal Denzel Smith (2017) writing in the *Washington Post*, offers a counter-narrative to the missing father thesis that I believe Baldwin would appreciate because he had a complex and bitter relationship with his own father. Baldwin's remained angry with his father throughout much of his life because his father wanted him to live his life based upon his beliefs, experiences and ideologies of racism in America. Baldwin's father was bitter toward European Americans because racism was destroying his life and he didn't want the same for his children (Leeming, 1994). Systemic racism took what could have been a normal father–son relationship and turned it upside down, making a father and son despise one another. At first, Baldwin took his father's bitterness toward him as one born out of his efforts to control him for his own pleasure; not understanding that his father didn't want his ambitious son to be crushed by a racist society as he pushed to have the freedom European American youth have. However, Baldwin (1984) would later write "The bitterness which had helped to kill my father could also kill me" (p. 222).

Mychal Denzel Smith (2017) says

> Growing up, the lesson was everywhere: Every major problem in black America can be solved if we addressed the problem of missing fathers … When a police officer was killed in Jersey City, in July 2014, a local television news reporter said on air that "the underlying cause" of the "anti-cop mentality that has so contaminated America's inner cities" was "young black men growing up without fathers.
>
> *(p. 7)*

A Reuters headline from 2007 for an article by Joyce Kelly proclaimed, "Father absence 'decimates' black community in U.S." (p. 1). Smith (2017) continues by critiquing Barack Obama. Smith argues that Obama has been one of the biggest advocates of the missing black father thesis. Obama, Smith contends, argues in a 2008 speech as a presidential candidate that too many black fathers are missing from too many lives and too many homes.

> They have abandoned their responsibilities, acting like boys instead of men. We know the statistics—that children who grow up without a father are five times more likely to live in poverty and commit crime; nine times more likely to drop out of schools and 20 times more likely to end up in prison.
>
> *(p. 1)*

Smith reported that Obama continues by stating, "They [black children] are more likely to have behavioral problems, or run away from home or become

114 "Go for Broke"

teenage parents themselves. And the foundations of our community are weaker because of it" (p. 1). Smith concludes his critique of Obama, quoting one of his iconic lines "I am a black man who grew up without a father and I know the cost that I paid for that." Smith (2017) offers the following counter-narrative to the black father thesis:

> Responsible fatherhood only goes so far in a world plagued by institutionalized oppression. For black children, the presence of fathers would not alter racist drug laws, prosecutorial protection of police officers who kill, mass school closures or the poisoning of their water. By focusing on the supposed absence of black fathers, we allow ourselves to pretend this oppression is not real, while also further scapegoating black men for America's poor societal conditions.
>
> *(p. 1)*

To "Go for Broke" is understanding that prior to the "missing father" thesis, the proclaimed cause of underachievement was a weakness in African American family structure due to matriarchal organization, or single-family African American households headed by mothers. To "Go for Broke" promotes conscious awareness; an enlightened understanding of the truth behind social injustices and inequality as well as pro and con debates among colleagues. In 1965, Patrick Moynihan, a Harvard sociologist and later three-term senator from New York, published "The Negro Family: The Case for National Action." The Moynihan Report, as it is commonly called, argues that the major obstacle to African Americans achieving economic, social and political equality is a large number of households led by women in African American communities. Moynihan contends that African American women are usurpers, African American men are emasculated, and African American urban life is a "tangle of pathology." Moynihan states, "A fundamental fact of Negro American family life is the often reversed roles of husband and wife" (p. 30). To "Go for Broke" is knowing the counterarguments against the Moynihan Report and taking action against its legacy that continues uninterrupted in schools today. For example, a counterargument to the Moynihan Report focuses efforts and critiques on systemic racism and sexism. The pivot to blaming African American women and mothers is a harmful and dehumanizing distraction that calcifies the underlying root and source of America's enduring sickness: institutionalized oppression.

Going for broke also means having a clear understanding of the role of the ally. Moynihan was trying to be an ally in helping President Johnson prepare his, "Freedom is not enough": Equal citizenship for Americans" address to the nation. However, Moynihan shows that an ally is not always a productive ally. "Blame the victim," ironically, became the shorthand for the Moynihan Report. Additionally, *The Atlantic* reports in 2015: "The Moynihan Report is a historical artifact best understood in the context of its time. Yet, it remains relevant today amidst current discussion of why racial inequality persists despite the passage of civil-rights legislation." Daniel Geary (2015), author of the article, adds, "Even those who do not see the report's analysis as pertinent to the present can learn how it shaped contemporary discourse. Fifty years later, the Moynihan Report is still a contested symbol among American thinkers and policymakers" (p. 1).

The Moynihan Report received severe pushback that has currency today in the African American community and serves an important part of the counter-narrative to the report. Bayard Rustin (1967), a prominent civil rights organizer and lieutenant of Dr. Martin Luther King, Jr., argues that Moynihan mainly focuses on the negative aspects of Negro life and neglects "the degree to which the 'abnormality' of some of the ghetto mores ... represents a desperate, but intelligent attempt on the part of a jobless Negro to adapt to a social pathology" (p. 422). Dorothy Height, civil rights icon and president of the National Council of Negro Women, argues,

> You need recognition of the fact that women have saved the family in crises of three hundred years, and there would be no family at all without what they have done. There are strengths in the family which should have been brought out by Moynihan.
>
> *(Osucha, 2015)*

Ralph Ellison, author of *Invisible Man*, argues that Moynihan "looked at a fatherless family and interpreted it not in the context of Negro cultural patterns, but in a white cultural pattern" (quoted in Epstein, 2007, p. 1). Ellison contends that the Moynihan Report treated people "as abstractions and ignored the complexity of actual experience" (quoted in Epstein, 2007, p. 1). Adding, in "Ghosts of Liberalism: Morrison's *Beloved* and the Moynihan Report," James Berger (1996) places Toni Morrison's (1989) often read and much admired *Beloved*, a book about slavery and racism in America in conversation with the Moynihan Report. Ellison continues: In doing so, Berger (1996) reminds readers that *Beloved* resists neoconservative and Reaganite denials of the persistence and normalization of racism in present-day society and shows how anti-blackness and sexism leads to trauma and violence in black communities. Ellison concludes noting *Beloved*, Berger (1996) argues, emphasizes African American culture and feminist agency to push back on Moynihan's negative characterization of black women. Finally, Berger (1996) according to Ellison contends that violence within the black community cannot be understood without considering that law, science, power and official knowledge have all been constructed under white supremacy and are legitimized through that lens first. The lives of others are secondary considerations.

To "Go for Broke" is teaching African American students that the "undesirable neighborhood" they may live in and the dangers they may face in their neighborhoods, as well as the suppression of their political and social rights such as voting, is not because African Americans are lazy or that they are inherently inferior to European Americans. It is because of societal resistance to African

116 "Go for Broke"

American advancement manifested in false arguments, such as African Americans being culturally and academically deprived and African American fathers and mothers failing to take advantage of opportunities. As Kevin Schultz (2015) argues, theses concerning the "lack of civilization" in African American culture or the notion that European Americans are the "advanced race" have a history that dates to the country's beginning. The creation of American slavery and American democracy are intertwined, beginning in the same time and same place, Jamestown in 1619.

"Go for Broke" Speaking/Speeches

James Baldwin's modeling of "Go for Broke" is showcased exceptionally well in 1965 when he debates conservative commentator William Buckley. In the subject "Has the American Dream Been Achieved at the Expense of the American Negro?" on the National Educational Television (NET) network. I encourage you to view the video before or after you read the text below. If you are new to Baldwin, read the text below first. If you have engaged with Baldwin before, it's your call.

> Location: The Cambridge Union
> Date: February 18, 1965
> Debate Topic: The American dream is at the expense of the American Negro
> Proposed by: David Heycock, Pembroke College
> Opposed by: Jeremy Burford, Emmanuel College
> James Baldwin speaks third
> William F. Buckley, Jr. speaks fourth

> Norman St. John-Stevas, M.P. introduces an edited version of a special debate in the week of the 150th anniversary of the foundation of the Cambridge Union.

Background

The debate is at the height of the Civil Rights movement. It is two decades after WWII, a war where African American soldiers fight heroically in Europe and employ the Double V campaign to promote the fight for democracy overseas and in the U.S. It is on the eve (March 21–25) of the Selma to Montgomery March. A bit more than two months earlier (August 6, 1965), the Voting Rights Act was passed marking an end to legal disenfranchisement; and a six-day rebellion against racism and unemployment in the Watts neighborhood of Los Angeles from August 11–16 has taken place. Also, it is a time of the Birmingham Children's Crusade when thousands of students left classrooms in Birmingham, Alabama, May 2–5 to march for civil rights.

In addition, it is a time when conservatives and others who are opposed to and/or want to slow down equal rights for African Americans are changing the language and tactics of European American resistance against African American progress: *Brown v. Board of Education* and the Civil Rights movement.

The anti-blackness behavior is demonstrated via tactics like "Southern strategy," the employment of racially coded rhetoric (e.g., avocations for states' rights) by politicians to appeal to white southerners (Franklin & Higginbotham, 2011) and "white flight" in Northern cities as European Americans move out of urban neighborhoods to the suburbs when African Americans move in (Franklin & Higginbotham, 2011).

Denial of economic opportunities, rise of neoliberalism, growth of racial innocence language and willful ignorance behavior are some of the many forms of white resistance that challenge termination of institutional racism. In many ways, it is also a time, very much like today, where conversations about race have yet to lead to the progress needed for America to become a true democracy. Remove the word "negro" from Baldwin's texts or speeches and replace it with African American and you are just about in the present moment.

About the Cambridge Union

The debate is held at the Cambridge Union Society at Cambridge University in England. The debate is iconized and is sometime referred to as the "Pin Drop" debate; noting that before each speaker spoke the room was so quiet that one could hear a pin if it dropped. The Cambridge Union is a debating and free speech society. American speakers before and after Baldwin–Buckley have included: Bernie Sanders, Jesse Jackson, Clint Eastwood, Buzz Aldrin and Ronald Reagan. This particular debate occurred on the occasion of the 150th anniversary of the Society.

About William F. Buckley

William F. Buckley, Jr. is founder and editor of the *National Review* (1955) and a major architect of the conservative movement of the late 20th century. Buckley "preaches undiluted conservatism" and anyone who observes him on *Firing Line* (1966–1999), the television program he hosts, will see him debate with guests on the issues of the day. Buckley isn't a student of common schooling. He was educated by private tutors in Paris when he was young and attended two English boys' schools in London, followed by a preparatory school in New York State. In 1943, Buckley attends the University of Mexico and serves three years in the U.S. army during WWII. After the war, in 1945, Buckley attends Yale University where he studies political science, history and economics. In 1951, he is recruited into the Central Intelligence Agency (CIA) and stationed in Mexico. Writing for *The New York Times*, Douglas Martin writes the following upon Buckley's death in 2008:

> William Buckley, with his winningly capricious personality, his use of ten-dollar words and a darting tongue writers loved to compare to an anteater's,

118 "Go for Broke"

was the popular host of one of television's longest-running programs, "Firing Line," and founded and shepherded the influential conservative magazine "*National Review*".... Republicanism but conservatism as a system of ideas — respectable in liberal post-World War II America. He mobilized the young enthusiasts who helped nominate Barry Goldwater in 1964 and saw his dreams fulfilled when Reagan and the Bushes captured the Oval Office.

Buckley argues African Americans are mainly responsible for their inability to achieve the American dream. Buckley (1969), with a "self-deceptive innocence about racism," reports saying to an African American man: "Your people, sir, are not ready to rule themselves. Democracy, to be successful, must be practiced by politically mature people among whom there is a consensus on the meaning of life within their society" (Bower 2003, p. 57). Buckley's argument stands in stark opposition to a then recent address to the nation by President Kennedy. On June 11, 1963, Kennedy delivers a "Report to the American People on Civil Rights." In the Report, Kennedy (1963) states:

> It ought to be possible, in short, for every American to enjoy the privileges of being American without regard to his race or his color. In short, every American ought to have the right to be treated as he would wish to be treated, as one would wish his children to be treated. But this is not the case.

Buckley's (1964) argument is that: "[s]egregation is morally wrong if it expresses or implies any invidious view of a race, not so if it intends or implies no such thing." To Buckley, the ideal of democracy and the privileges of being an American is for educated elites. As he speaks during the debate, somebody in the audience shouts,

> Mr Buckley, one thing you can do is to let them [African Americans] vote in Mississippi. Buckley responds: "I agree. Except, I appear too ingratiating. I think actually what is wrong in Mississippi is not that not enough Negroes have the vote but too many white people are voting."
>
> *(p. 3)*

The editorials in Buckley's *National Review* and on his television program *Firing Line* hold that "the civilization of the South will be degraded if black people are allowed to exercise their right to vote" (Tait, 2018, p. 1). Another argument by Buckley to maintain a racist America is that generation after generation of European immigrants have come to the United States and pulled themselves up by their bootstraps, working hard to give their children a good education and pushing the next generation into jobs and careers that ensure success. Why are African Americans the exception? Might there be something within the African American community that prevents it from rising up too (Schultz, 2015)?

Buckley, as Schultz (2015) explains, uses "blame the victim" arguments along with willful ignorance to dismiss the large and extensive structural resistance to African American achievement. Buckley willfully ignores the deliberate under-funding and closing of schools in African American communities, the devaluing of homes and property, poor infrastructure and streets in African American sections of towns and opportunities for employment, health and dental benefits and promotions that have long been a primary way European immigrants have risen to middle-class status.

Today, we see Buckley's argument within conservative neoliberal rhetoric that claims "justification" for continued racial domination and disadvantage in the name of "efficiency" (Dawson and Bobo, 2009). Joshua Tait (2018) in a *Washington Post* article: "Conservatives' self-delusion on race" writes on a topic at the heart of conservatism, that we hear in school and society and one advocated by Buckley: colorblindness. Tait's opening two sentences exemplify a rush to colorblindness and a denial of anti-blackness:

> Americans are at an impasse in their understanding of racism today. The activist slogan "Black Lives Matter" is met by the rejoinder "All Lives Matter" or "Blue Lives Matter.
>
> *(p. 1)*

Tait points out how conservatives (e.g., Donald Trump's statement of "I am the least racist person") with wide-eyed innocence strongly contend that they are not the bigots they are made out to be when charged with racism. Along with colorblindness and racial innocence, Buckley believes his ideas and those of the *National Review* "are at the fulcrum of genuine racial enlightenment", "non-racist," yet not ensnared in "dogmatic racial egalitarianism." He believes that both "segregation laws and integrating laws are equally wrong." Thus, according to Tait (2018), the strategies the *National Review* uses to stall black social and political advancements are legal colorblindness, law and order, free market dogmas, neoliberalism and frankness about racial "realities" (p. 1).

About James Baldwin

Today (2020), as I prepare to watch the YouTube video of the debate, I usually say to myself, "OK Jimmy, show me what it means to 'Go for Broke.'" Observing Jimmy is like watching a really good teacher work as he quickly connects to his audience. His speech, gaze and hand movements speak to each member of the audience individually and personally. He is respectful of his location and its history as a learned society, but he is still Jimmy, always real. His lead questions about race, economics and society are focused. In a setting where he is the star of the evening and only one of a few black people, Baldwin stands tall, defying any thought that he is out of place, in over his head, or doesn't understand his role

120 "Go for Broke"

and responsibility. He knows and embodies "I am a man," a declaration carried by civil rights protest marchers. Arguably, he knows that he is the first African American to speak at the Cambridge Union – but so what? Speaking to students at Castlemount High School or college students who protested in the South would be a more demanding audience for they are soldiers in the battle against racism.

You Could Hear a Pin Drop

Baldwin is not only prepared, he is ready. He will remind his British audience during the lecture that white superiority started in Europe and he is acutely knowledgeable of the history, literature and striving of African Americans. He is familiar with Du Bois' (1920/1999) observations on racism and imperialism, Baldwin's topic for the evening. Du Bois argued that racial capitalism from enslavement of African people, and anti-black notions of humanity, were "dashing this new religion of whiteness on the shores of our time" (Du Bois, 1920/1999, p. 18). Du Bois (1920/1999) posits in the "The Souls of White Folk,"

> The discovery of personal whiteness among the world's peoples is a very modern thing – nineteenth and twentieth century … This assumption that of all the hues of God whiteness alone is inherently and obviously better than brownness or tan leads to curious acts … the strut of the Southerner, the arrogance of the Englishman amuck, the whoop of the hoodlum who vicariously leads your mob.
>
> *(pp. 17–18)*

Baldwin's thoughts on whiteness were not far from Du Bois. Baldwin (1962a) posits:

> American Negro has the great advantage of having never believed the collection of myths to which white Americans cling: that their ancestors were all freedom-loving heroes, they were born in the greatest country the world has ever seen, or that Americans are invincible in battle and wise in peace … Negroes know far more about white Americans than that; it can almost be said, in fact, that they know about white Americans what parents—or, anyway, mothers—know about their children, and that they very often regard white Americans that way. And perhaps this attitude, held in spite of what they know and have endured, helps to explain why Negroes, on the whole, and until lately, have allowed themselves to feel so little hatred. The tendency has really been, insofar as this was possible, to dismiss white people as the slightly mad victims of their own brainwashing.
>
> *(pp. 101–102)*

Jimmy is ready!

Debate Topic: "Has The American Dream Been Achieved At The Expense Of The American Negro?" (Chosen by the Cambridge Union Society)

Audience: A packed room of more than 700 excited people are present. They are sitting and standing wherever they can squeeze in. Norman St. John-Stevas M.P., host of debate, states the following:

> Hundreds of undergraduates and myself, waiting for what could prove one of the most exciting debates in the whole 150 years of the Union history … I don't think I've ever seen the Union so well attended. There are undergraduates everywhere; they're on the benches, they're on the floor, they're in the galleries. And there are a lot more outside, clamoring to get in.

Opening Round: Two Cambridge students, David Heycock, representing the affirmative and Jeremy Burford, representing the opposing are each given five minutes to open the debate. Each first, offers welcoming comments and then presents their perspective on the topic. Heycock states that there is "consistent and quite deliberate exploitation of $1/9^{th}$ of the population in the U.S. and if one man in nine is prohibited from realizing his full potential, how can a society advance? Next Heycock draws from Martin Luther King, Jr.'s "Letter from Selma, Alabama Jail." In the "Letter" King writes about the lack of success of the Civil Rights Act of 1964 because people thought with the passage of the legislation racist actions would stop. Such is not the case, wrote King, because hundreds of blacks are jailed. Why? King (1965) explained:

> Why are we in jail? Have you ever been required to answer 100 questions on government, some abstruse even to a political scientist specialist, merely to vote? Have you ever stood in line with over a hundred others and after waiting an entire day seen less than ten given the qualifying test?
>
> *(p. 2)*

Jeremy Burford, the student who introduces Buckley, begins by arguing that the purpose of the debate is not to justify the Jim Crow treatment of African Americans but to prove the American dream is not at the expense of African Americans but rather "in spite of" it. Buford, citing an article in *U.S. News and World Report* (1963, July), argues that the per capita income of African Americans is the same as that of the people of Great Britain (Vaught, 2014). Following the introductions by the two students, Baldwin and Buckley are each allotted 15 minutes to make their case.

Baldwin: With only a small single sheet of paper – that he places on the lectern before him – Baldwin begins his lecture referring to himself as "kind of a Jeremiah" – a "prophet of judgment and hope" – one who is fearless in denouncing

122 "Go for Broke"

the evil of both the people and those who govern the people. Baldwin points out how systemic racism is continuing to resonate with the force it has for more than one-half a century ago. He discusses how slavery, marginalization and exclusion of African Americans are proof that the American dream is achieved at the expense of the Negro. The Mississippi sharecropper and Alabama sheriff – and today white racist police officers – who possess, at their personal core belief, a reality that compels them to believe that, when they meet an African American man, woman or child, this person is insane to attack the system to which they owe their identity. Baldwin declares African Americans have a second-class citizenship identity in a country where the stars and stripes to which they pledge allegiance, along with everybody else, does not pledge allegiance to them, despite the history of their family members serving and dying in U.S. wars. Baldwin addresses how oppression negatively affects the psychological state of African Americans, not only making them feel less but trapped because they can't prevent the same disaster from happening to their children.

Baldwin is both artist and teacher – his rhetoric is eloquent, and importantly, Baldwin makes the audience "conscious of the things they are not seeing," the nuanced effect of white supremacy – both the role of an artist and teacher. Baldwin posits: It [white supremacy] destroys, for example, a young black man's father's authority over him. His father cannot tell him what to do, he is governed by white supremacy. However, sadly, the young black man soon learns that white supremacy only cares for him as a field-hand or servant to white well-being and privilege. Baldwin (1965) asserts:

> By the time you are thirty, you have been through a certain kind of mill. And the most serious effect of the mill you've been through is, again, not the catalog of disaster, the policemen, the taxi drivers, the waiters, the landlady, the landlord, the banks, the insurance companies, the millions of details, twenty four hours of every day, which spell out to you that you are a worthless human being. It is not that. It's by that time that you've begun to see it happening, in your daughter or your son, or your niece or your nephew. You are thirty by now and nothing you

---

Baldwin's analysis is so powerful and clarifying that when I first read it years ago, it gave me a deeper respect and appreciation of the fathers and mothers of the students in my class. I saw them not as: Williams's dad, or Louise's mother. Instead, they were much more, individuals – African American humanity – to be admired, greeted with a warm hello, that truly means, "I am glad to see you. I hope all is well." Baldwin's analysis gave me a different way think about my parents, who were alive at the time. My mother, more so than my father, would discuss such statements with me. Mostly, she would talk and I would listen. My father, however, would stay up and watch Kup with me, on those Saturdays that I came home early – sometimes I came

have done has helped you to escape the trap. But what is worse than that, is that nothing you have done, and as far as you can tell, nothing you can do, will save your son or your daughter from meeting the same disaster and not impossibly coming to the same end.

Back to the Cambridge Union Society

Next, Baldwin turns to "expense," a key word in the debate: "The American dream is at the expense of the American Negro." Baldwin argues, African American bodies are sacrificed at the *expense* of the American dream and African Americans instead of receiving credit for their work are scorned and whipped. Baldwin asserts that there are several ways to address what *expense* means for the debate. However, for him, the many generations of cheap labor of the African Americans built the harbors, ports and railroads of the country, especially in the South. Baldwin, speaking on the behalf of African American people and taking *expense* into account, states:

> I am stating very seriously, and this is not an overstatement: ★**I**★ picked the cotton, ★**I**★ carried it to the market, and ★**I**★ built the railroads under someone else's whip for nothing. For nothing. [★**I**★ in original transcript.]
>
> *(p. 1)*

"For nothing," demands an exclamation point; maybe two – it is a deep reflective thought. Because, as Baldwin argues, not only is "my cheap labor" but it is also "the violation of my women and the murder of my children" (p. 1). The American dream, Baldwin argues, is at the *expense* of the African American!

Back to the Cambridge Union Society

As Baldwin continues during his remaining time, he exposes the hypocrisies (lies and myths) of liberalism: willful ignorance and white innocence that today contend that European Americans are besieged and

early to hang out with him and sometimes, he would get out of bed and come join and that would lead to me learning about his growing up in Georgia, being a U.S. solider in a segregated United States and attending Meharry Dental School. Baldwin's analyses and my discussion with my parents as an adult African American male also richly contributed to the narrative I employed to help my European American teacher colleagues better understand their students' families. African American people talking to European American people about race, I learned from Jimmy and my parents, is a challenge and all help is accepted.

Reparation to African Americans in some form probably will occur in your lifetime. African American people did not receive or were not able to keep the forty acres and a mule promised to them after the Civil War. Therefore, today as America engages in racial awaking, Baldwin's statement and thesis is gaining attention: "★**I**★ built the railroads under someone else's whip for nothing. For nothing." The history of the phrase "forty acres and a mule" that evokes the Federal government's failure to redistribute land after the Civil War is according to Black Past (2007) as follows:

> As Northern armies moved through the South at the end of the war, blacks began cultivating land abandoned by whites. Rumors developed that land would be seized from Confederates, and given or sold to freedmen. These rumors rested on solid foundations: abolitionists had discussed land redistribution at the beginning of the war, and in 1863 President Abraham Lincoln ordered 20,000 acres of land confiscated in South Carolina sold to freedmen in twenty-acre plots. Secretary of the Treasury Salmon Chase expanded the offering to forty acres per family.
>
> In January 1865 General William T. Sherman met with twenty African American leaders who told him that land ownership was the best way for blacks to secure and enjoy their newfound freedom. On 16 January that year,

victimized by "traumatic" conversations of race, with some European Americans arguing they are discriminated against as much as people of color. Robin DiAngelo, a retired sociologist and the author of *White Fragility: Why It's So Hard for White People to Talk about Racism*, echoes a message that Baldwin communicates to European Americans in the 1960s about their inability to understand their passive complicity in America's "white supremacist culture." DiAngelo (2018) posits, "Today we have a cultural norm that insists we hide our racism from people of color and deny it among ourselves, but not that we actually challenge it. In fact, we are socially penalized for challenging racism" (p. 50).

During the debate, Baldwin states:

> I have to put it this way – one's sense, one's system of reality. It would seem to me, the proposition before the House, and I would put it this way, is the American Dream at the expense of the American Negro, or the American Dream is at the expense of the American Negro.
>
> *(p. 1)*

Baldwin adds,

> One's reaction to that question – has to depend … in effect, [on] where you find yourself in the world, what your sense of reality is, that is, it depends on assumptions which we hold so deeply as to be scarcely aware of them.
>
> *(p. 1)*

Baldwin then turns his attention to segregation and begins explaining what it is and where it comes from. Baldwin argues segregation is inequality born of an unjust system in which individuals are only actors (Warner, 2012, p. 1). Baldwin argues that white supremacy was born in Europe and that segregation between black and white people is considered such a natural system of reality by European Americans that they wonder

"Go for Broke" 125

why African Americans are attacking the system to which they owe their identity. Baldwin points out how the system of segregation affects African Americans and European Americans and how it destroys both groups. About European Americans, segregation and its resulting legacy (e.g., Jim Crow, de jure and de facto segregation) give them a false feeling of superiority and the belief that they have the right to overtake and subjugate (e.g., African people) and annihilate Indigenous people in America. Segregation gives European Americans, to quote again) "the strut of the Southerner, the arrogance of the Englishman amuck, and the whoop of the hoodlum" (p. 18).

Mindful of his 15-minute limit, like a teacher who understands the importance of connecting the conceptual and historical dots before the bell rings, Baldwin addresses how white supremacy affects white people. Baldwin argues,

> Sherman issued Special Field Order No. 15. The order reserved coastal land in Georgia and South Carolina for black settlement. Each family would receive forty acres. Later Sherman agreed to loan the settlers army mules.
>
> Less than a year after Sherman's order, President Andrew Johnson intervened, and ordered that the vast majority of confiscated land be returned to its former owners. This included most of the land that the freedmen had settled.

> they've [white people] been raised to believe … that no matter how terrible their lives may be … and no matter how far they fall, no matter what disaster overtakes them, they have one enormous bit of knowledge in consolation, which is like a heavenly revelation: at least, they are not Black.
>
> *(p. 2)*

Baldwin, however, testified that what has happened to European Americans is much worse than what has happened to African Americans because European Americans do not understand the evils within themselves. Baldwin stated:

> But he [white man] doesn't know what drives him to use the club, to menace with the gun and to use the cattle prod. Something awful must have happened to a human being to be able to put a cattle prod against a woman's breasts, for example. What happens to the woman is ghastly. What happens to the man who does it is in some ways much, much worse.

"Much, much worse," Baldwin contends, because the white man currently lives a "good life" in a civilized nation, embedded with prosperity, which claims to celebrate its love of freedom and humanity worldwide. Baldwin concludes:

> It is a terrible thing for an entire people to surrender to the notion that one-ninth of its population is beneath them. Until the moment comes when we,

the Americans, are able to accept the fact that my ancestors are both black and white, that on that continent we are trying to forge a new identity, that we need each other, that I am not a ward of America, I am not an object of missionary charity, I am one of the people who built the country—until this moment comes there is scarcely any hope for the American dream. If the people are denied participation in it, by their very presence they will wreck it. And if that happens it is a very grave moment for the West.

Baldwin's life work includes letting European Americans know that segregation is detrimental to them and those they love; and that those who govern have no problem putting their foot on the neck of poor European Americans, if they don't do as they are told. Baldwin (1972) states:

And what the white students had not expected to let themselves in for, when boarding the Freedom Train, was the realization that the black situation in America was but one aspect of the fraudulent nature of American life. They had not expected to be forced to judge their parents, their elders, and their antecedents, so harshly, and they had not realized how cheaply, after all, the rulers of the republic held their white lives to be. Coming to the defense of the rejected and the destitute, they were confronted with the extent of their own alienation, and the unimaginable dimensions of their own poverty. They were privileged and secure only so long as they did, in effect, what they were told but they had been raised to believe that they were free [my emphasis].

(p. 183)

Baldwin's comment: "how cheaply, after all, the rulers of the republic held their white lives to be" encouraged me to read a review of two books, *White Trash: The 400-Year Untold History of Class in America* by Nancy Isenberg and *Hillbilly Elegy: A Memoir of a Family and Culture in Crisis* by J. D. Vance, by Alec MacGillis (2016) in *The Atlantic*. The review was informative about poor European Americans; the next generation of people, that Baldwin was referencing. My takeaway from MacGillis' review is that Baldwin's analysis holds true today. MacGillis contends the government and corporations each did their part to weaken organized labor, which once boosted wages and strengthened the social fabric in rural areas and the rust belt where many Europe Americans live. And, although, the government has accelerated the decline of coal for environmental reasons; the government has done awfully little in the way of remedies for those affected. MacGillis concludes the review with a statement that parallels Baldwin and then some:

The most painful comparison is not with supposedly ascendant minorities— it's with the fortunes of one's own parents or, by now, grandparents. The

"Go for Broke"   127

demoralizing effect of decay enveloping the place you live cannot be underestimated. And the bitterness—the "primal scorn"—that Donald Trump has tapped into among white Americans in struggling areas is aimed not just at those of foreign extraction. It is directed toward fellow countrymen who have become foreigners of a different sort, looking down on the natives, if they bother to look at all.

Additionally, I wonder if Baldwin's comments about European Americans having to judge their parents and ancestors causes frictions and steadfast willful ignorance between European American teachers who "Go for Broke" and those who struggle with it.

Baldwin's thoughts on the effect of white supremacy on African Americans are further elaborated in the essay "Many Thousand Gone," where Baldwin (1955/1984) describes how the horrors and shamefulness of segregation play on the thoughts and feelings of the average African American. How segregation and white supremacy eats at one's sense of self, community and humanity.

> [T]here is, I should think, no Negro living in America who has not felt, briefly, or for long periods, with anguish sharp or dull, in varying degrees, and to varying effect, simple, naked, and unanswerable hatred; who has not wanted to smash any white face he may encounter in a day … to break the bodies of all white people and bring them low, as low as that dust into which he himself has been and is being trampled; no Negro, finally, who has not had to make his own precarious adjustment to the "nigger" who surrounds him and to the "nigger" in himself.
>
> (p. 39)

Segregation of African American and other people of color continues to be played out; America racial awaking, notwithstanding, Christian E. Weller (2019) reports shortly before COVID-19 took over, the U.S. labor market had seen a record 109 months of uninterrupted job growth, with the overall unemployment rate falling to its lowest level in 50 years. However, African American workers continued to face more hurdles to get a job, never mind a good one, than their European American counterparts. They continued to face systematically higher unemployment rates, fewer job opportunities, lower pay, poorer benefits and greater job instability. Weller (2019) adds these persistent differences reflect systematic barriers to quality jobs, such as deliberate discrimination against African American employees as well as occupational segregation—whereby African American workers often end up in lower-paid jobs than European Americans—and segmented labor markets in which African American workers are less likely than European American workers to get hired into stable, well-paying jobs.

Winners by a Landslide

Although both speakers exhibited rhetorical excellence, the attending audience voted 540–160 Baldwin the victor. In the minds of the audience, Baldwin has successfully argued that "The American Dream Has Been Achieved At The Expense Of The American Negro." Baldwin received a standing ovation from the Union, a phenomenon that the narrating host claims he "had not seen in the Union … in all the years [he had] known it." David Leeming, Baldwin's biographer, in *James Baldwin: A Biography* said the following about the debate: [T]his was one of his [Baldwin's] greatest speeches, and all of Buckley's wit and reasoning prowess had little effect against what the audience recognized as genuine power" (1994, p. 244).

Baldwin has only hours to enjoy the brilliant and powerful way he went for broke. Less than 72 hours later while in London having dinner with his sister Gloria, he is informed that his friend Malcolm X is assassinated (Leeming, 1994).

"Go for Broke": Writing – "A Letter to My Nephew"

Texting is the thing today, and I appreciate its value and admire the necessary skills. I particularly admire how fast thumbs move when texting. Thumbs are showing off their skillset; strutting their stuff. But to receive a letter, paragraphs and pages of words written to you, about you and your life – I am not talking about cleverly constructed junk mail – is very special! Rarely heard of today.

Super special, in a class of its own is Baldwin's letter to his nephew; carefully composed and beautifully written. However, I must admit, I did received such a "letter" from my father. Of course, not with the eloqence of Baldwin's missive. For, if you are an African American young man or woman, you receive this letter, more than once, especially when you are about to leave the house to hang out with friends … no stamps needed.

James Baldwin has a fondness for letters. Jimmy is a letter writer. He enjoys writing and receiving letters in turn. In his Estate, there are letters from many notable names of his time: Lorraine Hansberry, Nina Simone, Bobby Seale, William Styron and Jacqueline Kennedy Onassis (Leeming, 1994). One of my delights, when I was at the Schonberg Library researching Baldwin's archives was reading some of the many letters he received from different people. I was particularly interested in the collection of letters because I had written him a letter in the early 1980s, and received a reply. Many of the letters are from everyday people, many congratulating him on an article or book he had written or an interview he had done, but most are invitations for him to come and speak. There are requests after requests from everywhere.

Baldwin is a social being, according to David Leeming, and communicates with his mother, Emma, through a continual stream of letters. Emma's letters to her son, according to Leeming (1994), "were full of advice of the kind mothers tend to give sons whose lives are in danger" (p. 10). Some letters from mother to son are stern or reprimanding (Leeming, 1994). Emma, or "Birdie" as she is called by some, worries about Jimmy's smoking, drinking and partying, and tells him so in her letters to him – Emma wants her Jimmy to "keep the faith."

Baldwin's letter to his nephew, James, that I discuss below, while eloquent in capturing and making public an important, potentially lifesaving conversation between African Americans of older and younger generations, also brings attention to the role of "literacy" and "voice" in African Americans' lives. Baldwin's letter – the letter-essay as a personal–political form – to his nephew and, more recently, Ta Nehisi Coates' (2015) letter to his son, Samori (*Between the World and Me*) are fruits of an historical struggle sustained by the hope and suffering of African American people. For African Americans, a *letter* to one's nephews, nieces, uncles, aunts or mother invites reminiscing about an achievement that had its beginning during enslavement when enslaved African Americans risked having their fingers cut off if they attempted written communication with another family member or someone they loved who had been sold and taken away. Letters – be they scraps of paper with a few important words about the condition of a loved one or describing the hope a person has; suffering they or some loved one or friend has endured, or a warning carrying great meaning. While perhaps it is time not to overly fuss over the achievement of letter writing, it nevertheless was hard fought and won against white supremacy.

Though *the act* of writing letters to a loved one, during enslavement, was in itself, a show of activism; activism is also at work in the content of the letters, where there are acts of repudiation against the characterization of African Americans as: "worthless," "idle" and "ignorant." Three terms used to falsely define and describe African Americans. Letters – or *the* letters – written by African Americans, according to Pamela Newkirk (2009), editor of *Letters from Black America*, have a history that can be traced back to the 1730s when poet Alexander Pope published his correspondences as literary works. In Newkirk's "*Letters*" the hopes, dreams, fears and suffering of African Americans are expressed. Similarly, *Word by Word: Emancipation and the Art of Writing* by Christopher Hager describes the horrors and evil of enslavement: the forbidding of African Americans to read or write and how a few enslaved African Americans acquire literacy and voice despite fierce prohibition.

The act of writing letters in defiance of states' antiliteracy laws (Alabama, Georgia, Louisiana, North and South Carolina, Virginia) was a potent form of self-empowerment. Letters gave voice to oppressed African American men and women who were controlled by the whip during the day. The letters demonstrate agency performed in the secrecy of darkness with the aid of small candle-light or moonlight as African Americans tell the true story of their enslavement. The letters written by enslaved and recently emancipated African Americans establishes a relationship between literacy and freedom. The relationship between literacy and freedom – full democratic freedom – is how I see Baldwin "going for broke" in "A Letter to My Nephew." An open letter written by Baldwin is

130 "Go for Broke"

activism and a protest, hoping to bring together a people, enlighten the outside world, and share tactics of survival and resistance.

Addressed to his nephew and namesake (with whom African Americans readers were invited to identify), the letter is also indirectly meant for readers of the liberal magazine *The Progressive*, in which it first appears. As a shrewd parenthetical aside, Baldwin anticipates outcries over his analysis of racism:

> I hear the chorus of the innocents screaming, "No! This is not true! How *bitter* you are!"—but I am writing this letter to *you*, to try to tell you something about how to handle *them*, for most of them do not yet really know that you exist.
>
> *(1963, p. 6)*

"A Letter to My Nephew" demonstrates Baldwin's all-out effort – " going for broke" – to communicate to his nephew on the 100th anniversary of the Emancipation Proclamation of 1863; the day Abraham Lincoln declares all enslaved people held in rebelling states are to be free (Franklin & Higginbotham, 2011); that he, James, is not being treated equally and why that is. Baldwin explains to James the circumstances of his life: "You were born where you were born and faced the future that you faced because you were black and for no other reason" (1963, p. 7).

Baldwin wants James to understand that it is not because of the music he chose to listen to or the way he wears his pants that he isn't loved, and his humanity isn't full appreciated. It is because he is *black*! Baldwin wants James to know that his youth had been defined by his skin color, and to Baldwin, the horrific ordeals – lynching, police brutality, segregation, verbal reputations – made over black skin color is what infuriated him.

> I was thirteen and was crossing Fifth Avenue on my way to the Forty-second Street library, and the cop in the middle of the street muttered as I passed him, "Why don't you niggers stay uptown where you belong?" When I was ten, and didn't look, certainly, any older, two policemen amused themselves with me by frisking me, making comic (and terrifying) speculations concerning my ancestry and probable sexual prowess, and, for good measure, leaving me flat on my back in one of Harlem's empty lots.
>
> *(Baldwin, 1963, pp. 19–20).*

Skin color notwithstanding, Baldwin wants James to know "there is really no limit to where you can go" and what you can do. Baldwin tells James his destiny is up to him. He must work hard to achieve greatness and prove his countrymen wrong: "You were not expected to aspire to excellence: you were expected to make peace with mediocrity" (Baldwin, 1963, p. 7).

The themes of "high expectations" and "hard work" are central to discourses around academic excellence and African Americans making it out of the ghetto during Baldwin's time and are implicit and explicit in his words to James. Baldwin tells James, harking back to Phillis Wheatley, Fredrick Douglass, W. E. B. Du Bois, Anna Julia Cooper, Zora Neale Hurston, Augusta Savage, Bessie Smith and others who gave America black intellectual thought, music and culture: "Know from whence you came and take no one's word for anything, including mine—but trust your experience" (1963, p. 8).

Besides telling James about his circumstances, Baldwin explains to James that his countrymen will claim innocence for their past racist behaviors and attitudes. But Baldwin tells James, he does not want him to be fooled or taken in: "It is the innocence which constitutes the crime" (1963, p. 6).

Next, Baldwin says the "innocent" will scream in chorus: "No! This is not true!" (1963, p. 6). Today, "innocence" continues to be claimed, by the ancestors of those who first claimed it. Choruses sing out in schools and other American institutions: We have nothing to do with racism; we are not racist.

"Innocence," Baldwin tells James, is manifested in schools and other supposedly democratic places as willful ignorance: And willful ignorance operates in many guises – "I didn't know" being one of the more popular expressions. Young James likely does not have books of interest in the school library because the committee in charge of ordering books *didn't know* what to order; or argue publishers *don't have* books with African American characters who are scientists, doctors or lawyers. "Innocence" is attested, despite the small amount of effort necessary to become knowledgeable (computer access notwithstanding). "Innocence" is observed outside of school during discussions over "Black Lives Matter" versus "All Lives Matter." "Black Lives Matter" is considered controversial. Baldwin tells James that the claims of innocence have continued for centuries to wash him away, stating, "I am writing this letter to you, to try to tell you something about how to handle them, for most of them do not yet really know that you exist" (1963, p. 6).

"Going for broke" is fueled by passion and stick-to-it-ness (much in common with responsibility and wholeheartedness described in Chapter 2) that Baldwin emphasizes at the beginning of "A Letter to My Nephew": "I have begun this letter five times and torn it up five times" writes Baldwin (1963, p. 3). Whenever I read those lines, I feel Baldwin's anxiety; not anxiety due to annoyance, but a strong desire to get it right because of its importance. Baldwin knows his letter is not like the statement in a person's last will and testament or like the letter a solider leaves behind to loved ones before going off to battle. This letter is about James' present and future life. A plan of how to "live while black: African American in America." Also, when I read "A Letter to My Nephew," I am reminded of teachers, often teachers of the p/K-6, who pore over their lesson plans; changing and making modifications with each and every one of their students in mind … because they have discovered what it means to love children and want to help children.

To "Go for Broke" includes teachers having a critical consciousness, in this case, about the needs of African American children living in a racist society.

Baldwin acquires his critical consciousness at an early age. When he is a teenager, he is greeted by a renowned African American female pastor, who asks: "Whose little boy are you?" Baldwin sees the question, a question asked by both pastors and pimps in his community, as an attempt to attract naive people to their "racket" as he simultaneously becomes aware of his personal need and desire to belong. "I unquestionably want to be *somebody's* little boy," Baldwin (1963) asserts, so "when the pastor asks me, with that marvelous smile, 'Whose little boy are you?' my heart replies at once, 'Why yours'" (pp. 28–29). Here, Baldwin represents African American students' need and desire to belong and society's (e.g., uncle, teacher) responsibility to them. Hatton (2016) illuminates: "This boy is but one of many children that Baldwin describes in his writing who can only be saved (spiritually, politically, physically) by a communal sense of responsibility to one another" (p. 2). Hatton (2016) explains that African American children stand as reminders that society is beholding—that is, to hold dear—it's every member.

"A Letter to My Nephew" also demonstrates a heightened critical and political consciousness to pursue equity and social justice because Baldwin publishes the "Letter to My Nephew" in *The Progressive* (1962b). "Since 1909, *The Progressive's* aim is to amplify voices of dissent and those under-represented in the mainstream, with a goal of championing grassroots progressive politics". When Baldwin publishes "A Letter to My Nephew" it is a critical moment in African Americans' fight for their civil rights. Two months prior to Baldwin's article, James Meredith, an African American with nine years in the U.S. Air Force, has attempted to enroll at the all-white University of Mississippi. Meredith's attempt to enroll brings out Confederate battle flags and protests that turn into a riot on the Ole Miss campus. Two people are killed, hundreds wounded and many others are arrested. President Kennedy is forced to call out the National Guard and send some 31,000 Guardsmen and other federal forces to enforce order (Franklin & Higginbotham, 2011). Tensions between African Americans and European Americans is high and escalating.

Baldwin (1963) tells James that European Americans perpetuate lies and myths about African Americans to diminish their sense of self-worth and increase their own. His mother has worked around them all of her life, but they don't know she even existed. Baldwin (1963) explains to James that if someone continually hears that they have no power or value, they eventually start to believe it. Proselytizing, such as, white doctors and lawyers are better than black doctors and lawyers, white schoolteachers are better educated than black schoolteachers, Harriett Tubman's picture is more suited for a $2 dollar bill than a $20 dollar bill and so forth, tends to make people more likely to accept powerlessness and inferiority as an indisputable fact rather than an outrageous injustice, Baldwin (1963) tells James. Thus, Baldwin cautions his nephew against believing what white society says about him and to him, because they are only concerned about themselves. Baldwin (1963) argues: "Please try to remember [James] that what they believe, as well as what they do and cause you to endure, does not testify to your inferiority, but to their inhumanity and fear" (p. 8).

"Go for Broke" **133**

Preceding this, Baldwin (1963) declares:

> I accuse my country and my countrymen, and for which neither I nor time nor history will ever forgive them, that they have destroyed and are destroying hundreds of thousands of lives and do not know it and do not want to know it.
>
> *(p. 5)*

Speaking truth and being honest are foundational stones of "going for broke." In "A Letter to My Nephew," Baldwin publicly exclaims to the readership of the social justice-minded *The Progressive*, how and why James and other African Americans are living in horrible conditions and why they are having horrific experiences in America: Baldwin (1963) states:

> You were born into a society which spells out with brutal clarity and in as many ways as possible that you are a worthless human being. They want to place a collar on you, place boundaries on what you can and cannot do, where you can live, and whom you may marry.
>
> *(Baldwin, 1963, p. 7)*

The rhetoric of "worthlessness" is a racially-scarring, false discourse from enslavement, Jim Crow and racial segregation that Baldwin wants James and other African American children to put behind them. Instead, Baldwin wants James to know that New York would not be the great city it is without African Americans and that African Americans are indispensable to the U.S. economy. However, in order for European Americans to justify and soothe their guilty consciences about African American enslavement and their animal-like treatment, myths had to be invented and lies told – that African Americans deserve to be treated as less than human: "worthless."

Baldwin demands that James and other African American children see their humanity as beautiful and know that they will grow up to be proud, honorable men and women. He wants them to understand that although "born under conditions not far removed from those described in London hundreds of years ago by Charles Dickens," their ambitions should not be settled (Baldwin, 1963, p. 6). They should not make peace with mediocrity. "Worthless," "bah humbug!"

> If you know whence you came, there is really no limit to where you can go.
>
> *(Baldwin, 1963, p. 8)*

Baldwin's honesty with his nephew were words of truth some of *The Progressive* readership may not have wished to read, let alone think about. "Going for broke," demands that popular myths and lies be debunked in favor of truth. Next, in "A Letter to My Nephew," Baldwin takes up the difficult task, a task

134 "Go for Broke"

that is challenged today, of telling James what he must do to survive. Baldwin understands that James and other African American youths are angry about the past 400 years and how institutions, behaviors and attitudes of European American people today replicate the past. Nevertheless, Baldwin unhesitatingly and pragmatically argues: "The really terrible thing, old buddy, is that you must accept them [European Americans]. And I mean that very seriously. You must accept them and accept them with love. For these innocent people have no other hope" (1963, p. 8).

From my research, I didn't discover how James reacted to the statement from Uncle Jimmy. Baldwin is dearly admired today by many, and celebrated today by many progressive groups, including Black Lives Matter. Nevertheless, his "transformative love" of white people thesis is sometimes challenged. Janelle Hanchett's (2016) "A letter to James Baldwin because I have some questions about the love thing" is an example of a challenge, from which I openly and graciously borrow.

Hanchett (2016) argues that racism in 2016 remains very much as it did in 1962, when Baldwin wrote his nephew. "Today black people continue to 'tremble' and white people remain unconcerned; black people insist they matter but white people don't have to see, nor listen or be a bit curious about the life and condition of black people" (p. 1). Hanchett (2016) argues that despite black people following Baldwin's directions on how to survive and take charge of their lives, they are still perishing. "History books have been written, race conversations have taken place 'to free white people trapped in a history they don't understand,' but they don't listen" (p. 1). European Americans, or to use Baldwin's word, "my countrymen," don't listen, Hanchett contends, because throughout their lives they have heard that African Americans are inferior in every imaginable way. Hanchett (2016) states

> I know what it feels like to learn *from unidentified sources, from the air you breathe, from something, somehow, some way,* that your race is *just a little better* but you are for sure *not racist* because "racist" is a slur and not hiring someone because of the color of their skin is not something you would ever do. You have black friends.
>
> *(Hanchett emphasis, p. 2)*

Such reasoning, Hanchett writes, is what worries her about Baldwin's transformative love thesis. Additionally, Hanchett asserts, "I feel the silence in my bones of the [white] people around me and the ones doing mental gymnastics to justify police brutality and I wonder if they know in their gut, they're wrong." Hanchett maintains many white people find it difficult to act because to act is to be committed, and to be committed is to be in danger of losing their identity. Concluding, Hanchett (2016) states:

> I'm kinda tired of "love." I hear a lot about it but don't see much action. I'm tired of anything that doesn't make us USE OUR ACTUAL BODIES to

dismantle our place, a place that was never actually ours, a place that was stolen, ripped off, burned and murdered for.

You say love IS what makes our feet move.

You say this is how you make change, and you said do not be afraid. I know you weren't talking to me. I'm not black and I'm not your nephew.

But I am afraid.

Because I wonder when *all* white people will feel this pain as their pain and this perishing as their perishing and stand up and set the stars aflame themselves, shake the earth themselves, become an immovable pillar in the fight for the moment when, as you say, the "dungeon shook, and the chains fell off."

So I'll keep fighting, in love, I guess.

And hope to god you're right

(p. 2)

Hanchett's (2016) argument is compelling and it demands attention. It also is an invitation to "Go for Broke," as Baldwin argues, and to "keep fighting, in love," as Hanchett asserts. Baldwin tells James that he and his generation must be strong. First, they must draw upon the love of one another – the love of family and friends – and communicate with each other. Baldwin writes: "[Y]ou were [born] to be loved ... hard at once and forever to strengthen you against the loveless world" (1963, p. 6–7).

Next, Baldwin lets James know he understands, as Hanchett argues about the anti-blackness that exists today. He knows that he is suffering because of it. Baldwin states:

Remember that: I know how black it looks today, for you. It looked bad that day [you were born], too, yes, we were trembling. We have not stopped trembling yet, but if we had not loved each other, none of us would have survived. And now you must survive because we love you, and for the sake of your children and your children's children.

(1963, p. 7)

"Going for broke" also means understanding that in the second Letter in the volume *The Fire Next Time*, "Down at the Cross: Letter from a Region in My Mind," Baldwin (1963) is more forceful about the failure of American democracy for African Americans and argues that black life in urban ghettoes is "the measure of equality, citizenship and democracy denied" (Muyumba (2008, p. 1). "Going for broke," thus, demands that teachers understand the dilemma that African American students are in – thus, consequently they are in – as described by Baldwin in 1962 and more recently, 2015, by Ta-Nehisi Coates in *Between the World and Me* ... and parents before their children go out for the evening.

Baldwin continuing with his "love" thesis argues

136 "Go for Broke"

these men [European Americans] are your brothers—your lost, younger brothers. And if the word *integration* means anything, this is what it means: that we, with love, shall force our brothers to see themselves as they are, to cease fleeing from reality and begin to change it. For this is your home, my friend.

(1963, pp. 9–10)

Baldwin (1963) speaks candidly that racism is the child of white supremacy and power; similarly, he references European Americans who lack understanding of the role of their ancestors in building and maintaining racism as "the innocents." Yet, Baldwin knows, and wants James and the readership of *The Progressive* to know, that many European Americans know about white supremacy and know they are benefitting from white supremacy, but don't want to change. Written during the same decade as Baldwin's Letter, "The National Advisory Commission on Civil Disorders Report" organized by President Lyndon B. Johnson (July 28, 1967) to investigate the urban rebellions erupting in cities across the nation between 1964 and 1967, argues "white racism—not black anger—turned the key that unlocked urban American turmoil and that from every American new attitudes, new understanding, and, above all, a new will is necessary" (p. 1). The Report also argues that the US is moving into a two-class society: one black and one white. Baldwin (1963), as I note above, makes a similar observation comparing the horrible conditions of the areas where African Americans live (e.g. Harlem) to Dickens's central London, an area synonymous with poverty and crime.

"Going for broke," as Baldwin demonstrates in "A Letter to My Nephew," demands a political disposition that is hopeful. Baldwin asks James and other African Americans to love their countrymen who deny their humanity; to develop a transformative love for their oppressor (while still holding them accountable) that awakens them to their racist acts, educates them about equity, social justice and their willful ignorance. Baldwin knows this is a different belief than the ones Hanchett espouses. Nevertheless, Baldwin (1963) proceeds, telling James,

I know what the world has done to my brother and how narrowly he has survived … and this is the crime of which I accuse my country and my countrymen, and for which neither I nor time nor history will ever forgive them.

(p. 4)

But Baldwin (1963) contends "one must strive to become, tough and philosophical concerning destruction and death, for this is what most of mankind has been best at since we have heard of man" (p. 5).

"A Letter to My Nephew" is James Baldwin's plea to future generations of African Americans. The essay is an outstanding illustration of "Going for Broke."

It is insightful, stocked with "mother and father wit," consciousness and brutal honesty. Its proactive approach to dealing with institutional oppression and everyday racism is an excellent model for African American youth.

A final illustration of "going for broke" brings us back to the brave members of the 442nd RCT in World War II that started this chapter. On December 2011, more than 450 Japanese American soldiers of World War II were honored with the Congressional Gold Medal, the highest civilian award for service given by the United States, because they lived by their motto: "Go for Broke." Thus, "Go for Broke" is much, much more than a "motto" or "metaphor," but the action of committed people – soldiers, teachers, and others – who go all out despite the obstacle of racism for a just cause.

Pam and Ann: What do you think?

A soft tap grows louder on the classroom door, as Ann enters holding two coffees. She hands Pam a coffee and speaks before she sips from the other one. "Well! You never answered me, yesterday. You kept walking. I am very serious. What do you think about what James Baldwin said yesterday?"

"I answered you," Pam, slightly irritated, responds, "I asked you, 'What do you think?'"

"Ok, Ok," Ann sighs, "since I am the curiosity cat, I will go first … if you promise you will tell me. To begin, I liked the way he spoke to us; no sarcasm or irony, but with passion, urgency and respect. He speaks like we are smart people who have power to help African American children have a rewarding education. '*It is your responsibility to change society if you think of yourself as an educated person.*' I scribbled down that line".

"Him, with his picture on *Time* magazine and that beautiful story in *Life*. It was the picture and story that made me come yesterday. I have never been in the same room with anyone who was on the cover of *Time*."

"Ann, get on with it!" Pam urges. "It's almost time to pick up the kids. What did you learn?" "But," Pam continues, "Are you frightened by anything, he said? Because I am frightened. The hair on my neck rose when he said: '*Because, if I am not what I've been told I am, then it means that you are not what you thought you were either.*'"

"And, I became annoyed as he argued that our teaching makes the students 'schizophrenic'… What have African Americans contributed to civilization … and did they really help to build New York? That's news to me, I never read about that anywhere. But I do believe African parents work hard and most are not lazy … However, we do have a number hanging about when we come and leave school … men standing on the corner. Why aren't they working?"

"Pam, he wasn't saying we – you and me – were making African American children 'schizophrenic' but, the New York Public School System and the educational system in America is making African American students schizophrenic"

138 "Go for Broke"

replies Ann. "But, you're right … Pam, that's us. I never thought about the schooling of African American children in the way he describes it. And, from the way he describes the education of African American children, it doesn't sound good. It sounds awful."

"But no, Pam, I don't feel frightened by anything James Baldwin says, but heightened … wanting to know more. He speaks of his reality and the reality of the students we teach in ways I don't think about. Systemic racism, I haven't thought about that idea, since I was in my political science class in college. Yet, as I listen, he is characterizing what I learned. And, he argues society doesn't want people who think, especially African Americans: *'no society is really anxious to have that kind of person around, what societies really, ideally, want is a citizenry which will simply obey the rules of the society.'* The civil actions by African Americans in both the North and South is protesting that idea".

"Pam, he calls us – white people – who don't push back or resist racial injustice 'racists,' without using the word. Downtown, I see African Americans glared at, verbally rebuked or treated invisible. Black lives don't matter – I see it … but don't acknowledge it. This is the way it has always been!"

"Baldwin argues the way we act is not Christian. You, me, all of us that worship every Sunday, singing and praying like we are chosen people, are phony … That it is not an act of God that African Americans are treated the way they are treated and forced to live in the poor conditions they live. I looked down and kept my head down when he said, 'It was not an accident, it was not an act of God, it was not done by well-meaning people muddling into something which they didn't understand. It was a deliberate policy hammered into place in order to make money from black flesh.' Then, when he went off on 'identity' I wanted to walk out, but couldn't because I would have been too noticeable. Instead, I scribbled his words down. Pam, listen to this. What do you think about it?"

> What is upsetting the country is a sense of its own identity. If, for example, one managed to change the curriculum in all the schools so that Negroes learned more about themselves and their real contributions to this culture, you would be liberating not only Negroes, you'd be liberating white people who know nothing about their own history. And the reason is that if you are compelled to lie about one aspect of anybody's history, you must lie about it all. If you have to lie about my real role here, if you have to pretend that I hoed all that cotton just because I loved you, then you have done something to yourself. You are mad.

"Pam, I am not mad, you are not mad. Yet, what he is saying rings true. We know Columbus didn't discover America. He was lost and Indians were already here. Also, publications by African American authors tell Baldwin's story, but our history and literature books by most European Americans don't".

"My grandmother called last night from New Orleans, the one that sends me – us – those delicious pralines, that you like so much, to tell me, to be careful. She knows I teach in Harlem and she's afraid of a black–white riot. When I told her, that James Baldwin was our speaker, she almost dropped the phone. She told me that he had been traveling throughout the South, stirring up trouble. She said, she saw him on television, and he is big trouble. Talks like he has the all the answers."

"When I said, Grandie Alice, he's nice, smart and kinda cute, she hung up. I knew the 'cute' thing would get her. I love her, but, it's a different world in the South where she lives. When Baldwin said after Reconstruction there was a bargain between the North and South. That African American who were liberated from the cotton fields were, not really liberated, but simply delivered to city bosses, sidewalk pavement and urban tenements. I thought of her, the racism that I see, but chose not to see; what we in the North see, but chose not to see."

"But, speaking to her, sharpens my thinking about what Baldwin is saying; and he shook me up when he said: 'Because if I am not what I've been told I am, then it means that you're not what you thought you were either! And that is the crisis.' It grabbed me. I never thought I was racist. I am a good ... white ... person."

Bibliography

Anderson, M. D. (2017). Why the myth of meritocracy hurts kids of color. *The Atlantic*. https://www.theatlantic.com/education/archive/2017/07/internalizing-the-myth-of-meritocracy/535035/. 10/30/2019.

Baldwin, J. (1962a). The creative process. In *Creative America*. New York, NY: The Ridge Press. Retrieved from https://openspaceofdemocracy.files.wordpress.com/2017/01/baldwin-creative-process.pdf.

Baldwin, J. (1962b). A Letter to My Nephew. *The Progressive*. (progressive.org). 12/4/2020.

Baldwin, J. (1963). *The Fire Next Time*. New York, NY: The Dial Press.

Baldwin J. (1965). Baldwin vs. Buckley. Net Educational Television (NET). https://www.youtube.com/watch?v=oFeoS41xe7w. 7/1/2019.

Baldwin, J. (1972). *No Name in the Street*. New York, NY: The Dial Press.

Baldwin, J. (1984). *Notes of a Native Son*. Boston, MA: Beacon Press. (Original work published 1955).

Baldwin, J. (1998). A talk to teachers. In T. Morrison (Ed.), *James Baldwin Collected Essays* (pp. 678–686). Ann Arbor, MI: The Library of America. (Original work published 1963).

Bellot, G. (2017). Baldwin vs. Buckley: A debate we shouldn't need, as important as ever. Literary Hub. https://lithub.com/baldwin-vs-buckley-a-debate-we-shouldnt-need-as-important-as-ever/. 5/4/2019.

Berger, J. (1996). Ghosts of liberalism: Morrison's Beloved and the Moynihan Report. JSTO/PMLA. 111, 3, 408–420. May. 4/26/2019. https://www.jstor.org/stable/463165?seq=1#page_scan_tab_contents.

140 "Go for Broke"

Black Past (2007). Forty acres and a mule. https://www.blackpast.org/african-american-history/forty-acres-and-a-mule/. 8/11/20.

Brown, D. (2016). Cissy Marshall recalls day of Brown v. Board of Education decision. *The Washington Post*. August 20. https://www.washingtonpost.com/news/local/wp/2016/08/20/. 4/16/2019.

Buckley, W. (1964). Quoted in W. F. Buckley and Gore Vidal (1968). *Gore Vidal: The United States of Amnesia* and *Best of Enemies*. (educationandthearts.blogspot.com). 12/5/2020.

Buckley W. Quoted in C. A. Bower (2003). *Mindful Conservatism*. Lanham: N.J.: Roman & Little Field.

Coates, T. N. (2015). *Between the World and Me*. New York, NY: Random House.

Dawson, M. C. and Bobo, L. D. (2009). One year later and the myth of a post-racial society. *Du Bois Review: Social Science Research on Race*. 6, 2, 247–249. Institute for African and African American Research. https://dash.harvard.edu/bitstream/handle/1/10347165/One%20Year%20Later%20and%20the%20Myth%20of%20a%20PostRacial%20Society_DBR.pdf?sequence=1. 5/3/2019.

DiAngelo, R. (2018). *White Fragility: Why It's So Hard for White People to Talk About Racism*. Cambridge, Mass.: Beacon Press.

Du Bois, W.E.B. (1994). *The Souls of Black Folk*. New York, NY: Dover Publications. (Original work published 1903).

Du Bois, W.E.B. (1999). The souls of white folk. In W.E.B. Du Bois (Ed.), *Darkwater: Voices from Within the Veil* (pp. 17–29). New York, NY: Dover Publications. (Original work published 1920).

Eckart, K. (2017). Promoting self-esteem among African-American girls through racial, cultural connections. *University of Washington News*. December. 21https://www.washington.edu/news/2017/12/21/promoting-self-esteem-among-african-american-girls-through-racial-cultural-connections/. 7/27/2019.

Epstein, J. (2007). Ralph Ellison, a biography, by Arnold Rampersad. Artist as hero. *Washington Examiner*. https://www.weeklystandard.com/joseph-epstein/artist-as-hero. 4/27/2019.

Field, R. D. (2016). Humans are genetically predisposed to kill each other. *Psychology Today*. https://www.psychologytoday.com/us/blog/the-new-brain/201610/humans-are-genetically-predisposed-kill-each-other. 5/11/2019.

Frable, D. E. S. (1997). Gender, racial, ethnic, sexual, and class identities. *Annual Review of Psychology*, 48, 139–162. https://msu.edu/~bartonf/wra135/Gender.pdf. 7/27/2019.

Franklin, J. H. and Higginbotham, E. B. (2011). *From Slavery to Freedom: A History of African Americans, 9th edition*. New York, NY: McGraw-Hill.

Geary, D. (2015). The Moynihan report: An annotated edition. *The Atlantic*, September 14. https://www.theatlantic.com/politics/archive/2015/09/the-moynihan-report-an-annotated-edition/404632/. 5/8/2019.

Gee, M. (2018). Why aren't black employees getting more white collar jobs? *Harvard Business Review*. February, 28. https://hbr.org/2018/02/why-arent-black-employees-getting-more-white-collar-jobs. 7/27/2019.

Hanchett, J. (2016). A letter to James Baldwin because I have some questions about the love thing. *https://www.renegademothering.com/2016/07/11/letter-james-baldwin-questions-love-thing/*. Blog [renegademama]. 5/26/2019.

Harrison, M. S. and Thomas, K. M. (2009). The hidden prejudice in selection: A research investigation on skin color bias. *Journal of Applied Social Psychology*, 39, 1, 134–168. https://abcnews.go.com/images/Politics/Colorism_JASP_Article.pdf. 7/27/2019.

Hatton, N. De J. (2016). "As though I were one of their possessions, as, indeed, I am": James Baldwin as Literary Ancestor. International Conference: "A Language to Dwell in": James Baldwin, Paris and International Visions. American University of Paris, Paris, France. http://faculty.ucmerced.edu/nhatton/presentations/though-i-were-one-their-possessions-indeed-i-am-james-baldwin-literary. 5/28/2019.

Hawkins, D. F, McKean, J. B., White, N. A. and Marin, C. (2017). *Roots of African American Violence: Ethnocentrism, Cultural Diversity, and Racism*. Boulder, CO: Lynne Rienner Publishing.

Ingraham, L. (2018,). "Shut up and dribble." The Ingraham angle. Fox News. February 18.

Kelly, J. (2007). Father absence "decimates" black community in US. Reuters. 12/5/2020.

Kennedy, J. F. (1963). Report to the American People on Civil Rights. CBS News. 12/5/2020.

King, Jr.M. L. (1965). A Letter from a Selma, Alabama, jail. https://www.pdffiller.com/jsfiller-desk15/?projectId=294602232&expId=4946&expBranch=3#500a0a43cea6422398c9ace1d0f58794.

Leeming, D. (1994). *James Baldwin: A Biography*. New York, NY: Knopf.

MacGillis, A. (2016). The original underclass. *The Atlantic*. September. https://www.theatlantic.com/magazine/archive/2016/09/the-original-underclass/492731/. 8/11/20.

Marom, D. (2008). William F. Buckley Jr. is dead at 82. *The New York Times*. https://www.nytimes.com/2008/02/27/business/media/27cnd-buckley.html. 5/11/2019.

Moynihan, P. (1965). The negro family: The case for national action. Retrieved from https://web.stanford.edu/~mrosenfe/Moynihan's%20The%20Negro%20Family.pdf.

Muyumba, W. (2008). Notes on native understanding. *The New Black Magazine*. July 12–13. http://www.thenewblackmagazine.com/view.aspx?index=1477. 5/27/2019.

Newkirk, P. (2009). *Letters from Black America*. New York, NY: Farrar, Straus and Giroux.

Osucha, E. (2015). Race and the regulation of intimacy in the Moynihan Report, the Griswold decision, and Morrison's paradise. *American Literary History*, 27, 2, 256–284.

Patten, E. and Krogstad, J. M. (2015). Black child poverty rate holds steady, even as other groups see declines. *Fact tank*. Pew Research Center. July 14. https://www.pewresearch.org/fact-tank/2015/07/14/black-child-poverty-rate-holds-steady-even-as-other-groups-see. 7/27/2019.

Rainwater, L. and Yancey W. L. (1967). *The Moynihan Report and the Politics of Controversy*. Cambridge, Mass.: MIT Press.

Report of the National Advisory Commission on Civil Disorder. (1968). New York: Bantam Books.

Rustin, B. (1967). Why don't Negroes …. In Lee Rainwater and William L. Yancy, Editors. *The Moynihan Report and the Politics of Controversy*. Cambridge, Mass.: MIT Press. pp. 417–426.

Schultz, K. M. (2015). William F. Buckley and National Review's vile race stance: Everything you need to know about conservatives and civil rights. *Salon*. https://www.salon.com/2015/06/07/william_f_buckley_and_national_reviews_vile_race_stance_everything_you_need_to_know_about_conservatives_and_civil_rights/. 4/27/2019.

Smith, M. D. (2017). The dangerous myth of the "missing black father". *Washington Post/Chicago Tribune*. January 10. *https://www.chicagotribune.com/news/opinion/commentary/ct-missing-black-fathers-obama-20170110-story.ht*. 9/27/2019.

Snyder, T. (2017). *On Tyranny: Lessons from the Twentieth Century*. New York, NY: Crown Publishing Group.

Tait, J. (2018). Conservatives' self-delusion on race. *The Washington Post*. October 5. https://www.washingtonpost.com/outlook/2018/10/05/conservatives-self-delusion-race/?utm_term=.36faaba18e44. 5/3/2019.

U.S. Department of Defense. (2019). Go for Broke: Unit's motto now a national day. April 4. https://www.defense.gov/explore/story/Article/1805390/go-for-broke-army-units-motto-now-a-national-day/. 7/8/2019.

Vaught, S. (2014). James Baldwin vs. William F. Buckley, Jr. for the soul of America. Academia.edu. https://www.academia.edu/14434498/James_Baldwin_vs._William_F._Buckley_Jr._for_the_Soul_of_America.

Warner, J. (2012). Why James Baldwin beat William F. in a debate, 540–160. Inside Higher Ed. April 8. https://www.insidehighered.com/blogs/education-oronte-churm/why-james-baldwin-beat-william-f-buckley-de.

Weller, C. E. (2019,). African Americans face systematic obstacles to getting good jobs. Center for American Progress. December 5. https://www.americanprogress.org/issues/economy/reports/2019/12/05/478150/african-americans-face-systematic-obstacles-getting-good-jobs/. 8/11/2020.

Zamalin, A. (2014). Reconstructing the nation: African American political thought and America's struggle for racial justice. CUNY Academic Works. https://academicworks.cuny.edu/gc_etds/399.

5

STUDENTS BE YOU

Developing Identity, Defying Place, Taking Role

> Children have never been very good at listening to their elders but they have never failed to imitate them.
>
> *James Baldwin, 1960*

James Baldwin speaks honestly and directly to African American students about their identity, place and role in America, and systemic racism in schools and the U.S. In a "Letter to My Nephew" and at a speech at Castlemont High School in Oakland, California, Baldwin on May 8, 1963 delivers a straightforward – "brutal" by his account – address to African American youth. Baldwin tells the students at the urban and majority African American school, his remarks will be "brutal" because he wants to make his point absolutely clear. The speech, "Living and Growing in a White World" although only three typewritten pages long, with another three typewritten pages of Q&A speak directly to African American students about their identity, place and role in society.

"It Was Necessary"

> I left America because I doubted my ability to survive the fury of the color problem.

Before Baldwin speaks to the Castlemont students and writes the letter to his nephew, he has spent years in Europe gathering and crystalizing his thoughts and developing clarity about what he will later extemporaneously say during numerous, lecturers, speeches and interviews about identity and African Americans' place and role in a racialized United States. Baldwin's time in Europe is a time for self-discovery.

144 Students be You

Leaving America, Baldwin contends is necessary. He is feeling overwhelmed and fearing self-destruction. For 22 years he has lived in overpriced Harlem poverty; put up with a stepfather who he believes doesn't love him; served as the major care giver of seven younger brothers and sisters; served three years as a junior preacher, then broken with the church and Christianity; watched his stepfather succumb to tuberculosis and mental illness; avoided getting caught up in a major race riot in his neighborhood; and grieved over the suicide death of a good friend, Eugene Worth, an African American political activist who leaped off the George Washington Bridge into the Hudson River. Besides the day-to-day challenging conditions generated by systematic racism, Baldwin is overwhelmed because America is retreating from its constitutional obligations to African Americans. Racialized violence including lynchings are happening to African Americans daily and the action of the Federal Government is slow or not at all. Anti-lynching laws are stalled in Congress and racial segregation is so overt and blatant that German prisoners of war are permitted to urinate in the same latrine as white U.S. soldiers, however, African American soldiers are forced to urinate in segregated latrines.

Baldwin, to my way of thinking (and perhaps yours) is feeling like some of the teachers and professors I have met along the way, who leave the profession because structural racism and white privilege is too much for them to bear. It was not as if they had another job waiting, but they needed to get out. It was too much for them to teach African American students using a curriculum and implementing instruction that belittles or denies both African American students' humanity and their own humanity; neglects historical and contemporary truth and teaches students to imitate European Americans more than it teaches them to think and serve other African Americans (Woodson, 1933).

To teach feeling constantly overwhelmed by racism or with heightened anxiety because of institutional and individual racism I heard them say, was "too hard, unprofessional." "TeachingWhileBlack," leads to African American and Latinx educators being singled out to be on "race" committees, and if they are African American and female – two in one – even better because the number of committees they are assigned are increased. Baldwin's feelings of "living in overpriced Harlem poverty," I relate to African American professor colleagues, who spoke to me about a need to leave the profession or search for a new job because the institution – over-imagined ivory tower – did not want them conducting research (e.g., using theoretical lens, investigating sites) they wanted to conduct. TeachingWhileBlack leads to European American supervisors and administrators "pulling faculty of color over" when evaluations from classes enrolled with mostly European American students come in, or when African American professors wanted to attend an education conference or colloquy where African American or Latinx educators gather.

Baldwin chose Paris, as the place to go in Europe because his mentor Richard Wright, who has achieved literary fame with the publication of his novel *Native*

Son is living there with his family. In addition, Baldwin has learned that African American painters, jazz musicians, novelists and journalists; an African American community of about 500 people fed up with the racism in America have found a degree of relief in the French capital and generally on the other side of the Atlantic (Kramer, 2001). Josephine Baker, W. E. B. DuBois, Langston Hughes and others have discovered less fuss is made over the color of their skin and they are able to live and perform to the full extent of their ability; their humanity is embraced, and their skills and ability prized.

This is what Baldwin wants; not to be put into a box and have his professional and personal life defined by U.S. history, lies and myths about African Americans' professional and social development and their individual identities. Baldwin's life dream is to become a writer, and he states, "I began plotting novels at about the time I learned to read" (Baldwin, 1955, p. 1). However, Baldwin doesn't want to be "merely a Negro; or, even, merely a Negro writer" (Baldwin, 1985, p. 171); and he notes "I wanted to find out in what way the specialness of my experience could be made to connect me with other people instead of dividing me from them" (Baldwin, 1959, p. 137).

In what are often called "Paris Essays" (1950–1961): "Encounter on the Seine: Black Meets Brown" (1950), "Stranger in the Village," (1953), "A Question of Identity," (1954) and "The Discovery of What It Means to Be an American," (1959) Baldwin writes about his "displacement" and journey of self-discovery that informs his thinking about his identity, and, place and role in America. Baldwin, as Matthew Clair (2014) writes will admit to his insecurity, and he understands that his insecurity is rooted in an understanding of the place and role society imagines for him. Yet, as Baldwin (1961) will relate in *Nobody Knows My Name*, being alone in Paris is motivation to reconstruct his American experience and identity in ways that are disorienting as well as liberating, causing him to say:

> the color of my skin had stood between myself and me; in Europe, that barrier was down.... It turned out that the question of who I was, was not solved because I had removed myself from the social forces which menaced me – anyway, these forces had become interior, and I had dragged them across the ocean with me. The question of who I was had at last become a personal question, and the answer was to be found in me.
>
> *(p. 1)*

Baldwin is not bashful about discussing his identity; that he is a homosexual black man. He doesn't harper on it, nor does he hide it; he is who he is. When a reporter asks Baldwin about how he feels starting out as a black, poor and homosexual writer, concluding, "You must have thought, 'Gee, how disadvantaged can I get?'" Baldwin smiles, and says: "No, I think I hit the jackpot" (James Baldwin, interview, Florida Forum, Miami, WCRT, 1963. YouTube).

146 Students be You

Baldwin's discussion of identity considers social, personal and religious aspects of identity and the self-realization and self-fulfillment of the individual. The autobiographical "Paris Essays" discuss personal identity, mainly Baldwin's; group identity: Americans living in Paris and other parts of Europe, and possible solutions for achieving identity. "Identity," Baldwin understands is much of what life is about and if you are African American "identity" is a determinant of life or death, poverty or plenty, a good evening out or insulting stares, remarks or worse.

Throughout the "Paris Essays" Baldwin discusses the implications of racism on both the oppressed and oppressor and addresses how racialized history influences identity and African American place and role in society; and he illuminates how European Americans hold fast and tight to their privilege and refuse to accept reality including the countless injustices for which they are responsible. For Baldwin, racial history is something that can't be dismissed. Referring to Joyce's notion of history as a nightmare, in "Stranger in the Village" Baldwin (1955) states history is a "nightmare from which no one can awaken" (p. 2). Thus, racial history ever present and inescapable, influences the identity of both African Americans and European Americans.

Chapter 5: "Students be You: Developing Identity, Defying Place, Taking Role" is written with the expectation – and hope – that teachers of African American students will have the "brutal" courage, Baldwin has on the afternoon he speaks at Castlemont High school in Oakland and when he writes the letter to his nephew.

The "Paris Essays" have meaning and application for schools and classrooms where African American students are enrolled. There are numerous in-school experiences where African American students are "Strangers in the Village," where African American and European American students have an "Encounter on the Seine: Black Meets Brown". "A Question of Identity" is played out at PK-college. And, every school day during the academic year, African American students engage in a "Discovery of What It Means to be an American".

Chapter 5 continues with Baldwin's discussion of "identity," "place," and "role" found in the "Paris Essays" and next discusses African American students' identity, "place" and "role" as found in the Castlemont speech and "A Letter to My Nephew."

"Paris Essays": Self Discovery, Identity, Determining Place and Role

> The place in which I'll fit will not exist until I make it.
>
> *James Baldwin, 2009*

> The American Negro has arrived at his identity by virtue of the absoluteness of his estrangement from his past.
>
> *James Baldwin, 1955*

Developing one's identity, according to an article in *Psychology Today*, by Heshmat (2014) largely concerns the question: "'Who are you?' What does it mean to be who you are are?" (p. 1)? Heshmat (2014) argues identity formation is a matter of "finding oneself" and developing and making nurturing choices that are consistent with one's true self. Baldwin, following Heshmat's (2014) reasoning was opposed to identity identification that was myopic, limiting restrictive, or static. Baldwin's exile affirms his opposition to different categories of political, racial and cultural identity because they entrap the individual (Kramer, 2001). Baldwin was concerned with categories that prevent fluid, diverse, plural identities.

James Baldwin learns much about himself, his culture, other African American people, Europeans and Africans once he lands in Paris, on November 11, 1948 at the age of 24, unpublished, $40 in pocket, hungry, unable to speak a word of French and needing to immediately find his mentor, Richard Wright. Paris, in 1948, Susan Henneberg (2015 reminds us, is still recovering from four years of Nazi occupation during World War II. The City of Light that had been made dark is returning to its "sophistication and liberality" (Yardley, 2014). Many buildings need renovation and some working-class areas need to be rebuilt. Food and gasoline are still rationed and jobs for people from America are scarce. In order to stretch his money, Baldwin lives in a series of cheap hotels – rue du Dragon, rue de Verneuil – and is one time jailed because, after complaining to an American friend that his hotel rarely changes his sheets, his friend brings him sheets taken from another hotel. The maid at the hotel where Baldwin is staying, recognizes the sheets are not of that hotel and calls the police.

A criminal charge is lodged then dropped. Baldwin, however, is jailed for a week and during this time asks himself, if his flight from home is the cruelest trick he has ever played on himself, since it has led him to such a low point. Baldwin posits "I could never in my life have imagined – lower, far, than anything I had seen in that Harlem which I had so hated and so loved, the escape from which had soon become the greatest direction of my life" (quoted in Leeming, 1994, pp. 69–73). Divested, Baldwin realized as Henneberg (2015) observes: "Prejudice toward those people perceived to be at the bottom of society was everywhere" (p. 1). Upon returning to his hotel room after his court hearing Baldwin attempts suicide by tying the bed sheet around his neck, tying the sheet to a ceiling pipe and standing on a chair. However, when he kicks the chair away, the pipe breaks, drenching the room with water. Embarrassed and angry with himself, Baldwin leaves the hotel, more determined than ever to fulfill his dream to become a writer.

An Inauspicious Beginning?

During his early days in Paris, Baldwin lives a Bohemian lifestyle, like he lived in Greenwich Village in New York (Mabanckou, 2014) and engages in an all-out search for his literary and personal identity. Baldwin frequents Arab cafes,

148 Students be You

connects with European American students and artists, befriends African students and establishes friendships with African Americans living in Paris; and writes essays – "Paris Essays" – about these encounters (Entrée to Black Paris, 2010). It is during these early years that Baldwin begins to discover his own literary identity, his own place and role as a writer, African American and man. It is during his period of self-discovery that Baldwin writes an article: "Everybody Protest Novel," for *Zero*, a new magazine that will help to establish him as a writer, and very much his own person, expressing his own unfiltered ideas. In the article, Baldwin criticizes writers who use their stories for social protest: fiction where a social problem is dramatized by its effect on the protagonist.

Uncle Tom's Cabin, a book by Harriet Beecher Stowe published in 1851, initially sells more than 300,000 copies in under two years, and goes on to sell more than a million copies. A book that Baldwin admires and reads several times during his youth, the "crown jewel" of anti-slavery protest novels receives merciless criticism from Baldwin for its dishonesty and pulling on people's heart strings. *Uncle Tom's Cabin* writes Baldwin (1955) "is a very bad novel, having, in its self-righteous, virtuous sentimentality, much in common with Little Women" (p. 14). More significantly than his attack on Stowe for sacrificing the humanity of her African American characters, is Baldwin's attack on Richard Wright, his mentor, for doing the same thing. In "Alas Poor Richard," Baldwin levels a blistering critique of Richard Wright's *Native Son*. Baldwin argues the subtext of the novel maintains a continuous support of the monstrous legend it is written to destroy: African Americans as monsters, absence of humanity and complexity. Baldwin (1955) states: "Below the surface of this novel there lies, as it seems to me, a continuation, a complement of that monstrous legend it was written to destroy" (p. 22). Baldwin (1955) couples the protagonists of *Uncle Tom's Cabin* (Uncle Tom) and *Native Son* (Bigger Thomas) together. "Bigger is Uncle Tom's descendent, flesh of his flesh" (p. 22), Baldwin argues conveys, that the characters in *Native Son* are not real, "untethered from reality" and they are separate from the common and painful life of African Americans. About this lack of reality, including poor identity formation, Baldwin (1955) writes:

> It is remarkable that, though we follow him [Bigger Thomas] step by step from the tenement room to the death cell, we know as little about him when this journey is ended as it did when it began; and, what is more remarkable, we know almost as little about the social dynamic which we are to believe created him. Despite the details of slum life which we are given, I doubt anyone who has thought about it, disengaging himself from sentimentality, can accept this most essential premise of the novel for a moment.
>
> *(p. 27)*

Baldwin knows rough living, growing up in Harlem. Baldwin understands that despite poverty, cramped, freezing in the winter and hot in the summer, living conditions and a feeling of hopelessness because of racism and classism, an African American youth – 20-year-old Bigger Thomas – is not a flattened person, a one-dimensional stereotype without any humanity. Grotesquely evil, yes, in that he murders and burns the body of a young European American woman in the furnace of the mansion where he lives and then rapes and kills his girlfriend and drops her body down an air shaft. Humiliated, yes in that he works as a chauffeur for wealthy European Americans who have richly benefited from their whiteness. But a person void of feelings, absent of humanity, Baldwin argues lacks reality. Paramount, also, is that Baldwin does not want African American male youth identified as Bigger Thomas with their place being a prison cell and their role monstrousness. Baldwin (1955) argues:

> But our humanity is our burden, our life; we need not battle for it; we need only do what is infinitely more difficult – that is, accept it. The failure of the protest novel lies in its rejection of life, the human being, the denial of his beauty, dread, power, in its insistence that it is his categorization alone which is real and which cannot be transcended.
>
> *(p. 23)*

Because of the criticism of his novel, Wright angrily ends his friendship with his mentee. Baldwin, however, argues that he had not purposely come after Wright. Nevertheless, Baldwin has set himself apart from Wright and established his own literary identity. "Identity" established, editors of other magazines began to request articles from the man who has successfully attacked both the "crown jewel" and most recently celebrated protest novels. Baldwin's new writings would constitute the "Paris Essays."

No Invisible Man *Searching for True Self, a Stable Cultural Identity*

Searching for one's true self is evident in Baldwin's first "Paris Essay": "Encounter on the Seine: Black Meets Brown." Baldwin (1955) writes about his search for self, living in Paris: what it means to be both black and American. Baldwin reflects on African Americans: their anguish brought on by capture, enslavement, segregations and continuous systematic racism. Baldwin speaks of a people – his people – who suffer alienation, had their identity stolen from them but are continually fighting to survive and create their own identity. Baldwin (1955) states:

> The African before him [the Black American] has endured privation, injustice, medieval cruelty, but the African has not yet endured the utter alienation of himself from his people and his past. His mother did not sing "Sometimes I Feel Like a Motherless Child," and he has not, all his life long,

150   Students be You

ached for acceptance in a culture which pronounced straight hair and white skin the only acceptable beauty.

(p. 124)

Baldwin's statement, and the work of Stuart Hall (1996) that argues "identities are never unified [they] are increasingly fragmented and fractured; never singular but multiply constructed across different, often intersecting and antagonistic, discourses, practices and positions" (p. 4) reminds me of the time I was a child attending church. Whenever I would hear the song "Sometimes I Feel Like a Motherless Child" I would become sad, because the adults around me became sad. Some crying. At the time, I wondered why are they sad? Because, in some cases the mothers of the adults crying are standing next to them or seated only a few rows away. They are not motherless, I tell myself. Nevertheless, I don't rack my brain about it. I conclude it is a crazy-adult thing, and I just want church over, so I can go and play. It isn't until, years later when I read "Encounter on the Seine" that I have an "aha" moment, a flash back to me squirming in a pew and understand why there is sadness all around me. Africa, the mother country of black people and according to science: all people, is what the song is about. The mothers of some of the mothers who had had their mother taken from them during enslavement are overcome with grief, they are motherless. They don't know what happened to their mother, they have little knowledge about the life they lived.

Music (e.g., spirituals, work calls and chants) as I dig deeper is central to African American history and humanity. I discover Frederick Douglass (1845) and Du Bois's (1903) observations that black music is proof of black people's identity as human. Douglass argues "I have sometimes thought that the mere hearing of those songs would do more to impress some minds with the horrible character of slavery than the reading of whole volumes of philosophy on the subject" (p. 14) and Du Bois (1903) connects music to black people's humanity when he posits music is one of the few means of expressing "the articulate message of the slave to the world" (p. 156). Baldwin (1955) in "Many Thousand Gone" also argues

It is only in his music, which Americans are able to admire because a protective sentimentality limits their understanding of it, that the Negro in America has been able to tell his story. It is a story which otherwise has yet to be told and which no American is prepared to hear.

(p. 25)

"Motherless Child" as the Negro Spiritual is also known has a great deal to do with identity: "Who am I?" "Where on the Continent of Africa do, I as a black person – an African American – come from?" "Which country?" During enslavement, black families were torn apart; family members sold and required to move on or die. Many are forced to take on a racist white man name. Black identity and culture are fractured and demoralized, yet it survives. And although alien from African and Europen cultures, African Americans, Baldwin argues, are connected to both cultures in ways neither Africans nor Europeans can imagine. In "Encounter on the Seine: Black Meets Brown," *Notes of a Native Son*, Baldwin (1955) explains, "This alienation [of black Americans from Africans] causes the Negro to recognize, he is a hybrid. Not a physical hybrid merely: in every aspect of his living he betrays the memory of the auction block and the impact of the happy ending" (pp. 123–124). In other words, "hybridity" means that the black experience since 1619 cannot be separated from the complex black/white engagement that shapes every and all areas of American history (Kramer 2001),

> In white Americans, he [the African American] finds reflected – repeated, as it were, in a higher key – his tensions, his terrors, his tenderness. Dimly and for the first time, there begins to fall into perspective the nature of the roles they have played in the lives and history of each other. Now he is bone of their bone, flesh of their flesh; they have loved and hated and obsessed and feared each other and his blood is in their soul. Therefore he cannot deny them, nor can they ever be divorced.
>
> *(Baldwin, 1959, p. 123)*

Ironically, Baldwin learns in Paris, that both African Americans and European Americans are defined by their American identity; and, their black and white difference is an individual thing; an American thing. Whereas, African Americans and European Americans are friendly to one another when they meet, they do not huddle up, like long-lost friends. Baldwin contends when African Americans encounter European Americans, they engage in meaningless chit-chat within a context of willful ignorance and distrust. Similar encounters take place on school yards and in school hallways and cafeterias – African American students and European American students don't engage in meaningful discussion of race in America and school officials rarely or only occasionally set up candid ongoing discussions about racism; or actively encourage such discussions. Much like, how Black History Month is handled, it is limited and superficial. "Willful ignorance," "things are getting better," "racial progress is being made" is exercised by European American students and European American school officials. They do not wish to discuss the racism that continues to exist in the U.S. nor why there is less attention given to skin color in France and other European countries.

Baldwin notices, in Europe, European Americans are somewhat intimidated when they see an African American so far from home; and African Americans don't raise the race question with European Americans because they believe it will be a futile exercise and false hope to think European Americans will learn from the discussion and take this knowledge back to the U.S. with them. Thus, Baldwin argues, African Americans and European Americans do not discuss the history and politics of racism in America, or current racial problems in the U.S.

152 Students be You

except in guarded snatches. When African Americans and European Americans meet in Paris, they have small talk about the Eiffel Tower and debate: Is the Mona Lisa smiling?

In "Encounter on the Seine: Black Meets Brown," Baldwin explicates a complex issue in black identity formation. Baldwin points out that because Europeans have not studied American's racism, especially how systemic racism operates throughout the 50 states, there is a tendency for them to learn about racism in the U.S. from the media; films and news stories about life in America. Such learning, Baldwin contends gives a false narrow interpretation of African Americans: mostly always poor, absence of agency and resiliency, unmotivated, lacking education, rarely the hero or heroine. Such narrow and universally so perceptions galls Baldwin because it clouds the real identity of African Americans as Americans. Baldwin contends, it is only with African Americans' true story that their identity since 1619 in America can be constructed. Baldwin (1955) argues, only by accepting this reality can African Americans accept their uniqueness and the uniqueness of their experience, and thereby set free the spirit so long anonymous and caged.

The uniqueness of the African American experience lessens cordiality when they meet Africans from French colonies living in Paris. Africans harbor feelings of distrust, alienation and guilt toward African Americans because of enslavement and that they no longer are bound to Africa. Africans identify African Americans with U.S. imperialism that exploits and takes advantage of Africa and Africans argue that the U.S. is not fair to Africa as it is to European countries. Moreover, Africans frown on African Americans for buying into America; in that, Tony Morrison argues "In this country American means white. Everybody else has to hyphenate" (Morrison, 2015, p. 16).

On the other hand, Africans feel guilty because their ancestors escaped enslavement and are connected to their home county. Mabanckou (2014) posits an African man does not harbor the same fear of rootlessness as an American man of color, even though he has endured history's injustice, and, unlike an American man of color, has not "all his life long, ached for acceptance to a culture which pronounced straight hair and white skin the only acceptable beauty" (Baldwin, 1955, p. 124). Mabanckou (2014) adds that sometimes Africans display exaggerated self-confidence because they come from a continent defined by borders and a sovereign nation, which they are optimistic, will one day be emancipated and free from the bonds of dependence on colonial power. African Americans, on the other hand according to Mabanckou are in a battle to be acknowledged and have their identity embraced. That said, Baldwin believes that black Africans and African American, instead of seeing the diasporic experience only through the lens of alienation and miseries should look on it – moving forward – as a positive opportunity for cultural fusion, mediation and creativity (Kramer, 2001). In "African-Americans" in Paris, Baldwin (1959) posits, "We could be considered the connecting link between Africa and the West, the most real and certainly the most shocking of all the African Contributions to Western life" (p. 21).

Baldwin's discussion of "cultural opportunities" between Africans and African Americans and his observation that "living in another land can influence identity and the way one sees their home country and sees other people" leads me to think about the small but growing number of African students in U.S. schools and how they see African Americans, European Americans and other people of color. According to Monica Anderson (2017), a senior researcher for the Pew Research Center, in 2015 there were 2.1 million African immigrants living in the United States, up from the 881,000 in 2000 and a substantial increase from 1970 when the U.S. was home to only 80,000 foreign-born Africans. Some African immigrants are children, and some will soon have, if not already, children in U.S. classrooms. From reading Baldwin, it suggests that African students' identity formation would be served if a truthful history is taught about England, France, Italy and the United States and their failure to give African countries home rule after WWI; and if African Americans and African immigrants had school time to begin working through 400 years of alienation and distrust in order for both to embrace their black identity.

Living *in White Villages*

"Stranger in the Village" (1955) the final essay in *Notes of a Native Son* is about "race relations, cultural inheritance and psychic dislocation" (Gehlawat, 2019). Baldwin is a transatlantic transplant from America to Europe; black diasporic identity in European culture; or in more contemporary language: a black body and black identity in a white populated space under a white gaze. In the essay, Baldwin, at times: astonished, amused or outraged, describes his visit to a small remote village in Switzerland of about 600 people who have had only minimal to no personal contact with black people. Baldwin a "stranger," he thought at first, because his race, skin color and hair are different, realizes there is something deeper at play. He remains a "stranger," the second time he visits, within the year, as much as the first time he visited. Baldwin (1955) posits, "But I remain as much a stranger today as I was the first day I arrive, and the children shout Neger! Neger! As I walk along the street" (p. 165). Baldwin concludes that the people of the village, although not unkind, fail to see and accept that he is a human, just like them.

The essay, a case of the African American experience from the end of WWII (1945) to the present day also shows the struggle for black voice and self-representation; and the rediscovery of a black man's (Baldwin's) identity as an African American. Baldwin calls attention to the madness of racism and the guise of white innocence as it is employed to reduce the sight and presence of him, from a three-dimensional complicated, complex human being to a dehumanized "sight" (Gehlawat, 2019, p. 5). Baldwin argues that such a radical dislocation at a physical and psychic level epitomizes the historical alienation and the continuing present-day alienation of the African American. Baldwin describes how when European

154 Students be You

Americans maintain their innocence and alibis – observed in the Academy as 'I can't find an African American or Latinx candidate for the advertised searched position' – it causes them to become a monster. Baldwin (1955) argues, "People who shut their eyes to reality simply invite their own destruction, and anyone who insists on remaining in a state of innocence long after that innocence is dead turns himself into a monster (p. 178). Baldwin calls attention to how European Americans have separated their history, in the telling of the story of America from African American history, thereby creating a false American history, in that the history of whites in America and black in America are forever intertwined and cannot be told as separate stories. Further, Baldwin calls attention to the complex and complicated relationship between African Americans and European Americans in America: their proximity, mutual interdependency, and shared difference from white and black people elsewhere in the world; calling attention to singularity of the American crisis at the "color line."

The essay is one of my favorite Baldwin's pieces, first, because of the way it explores and addresses race and place in American identity, and discusses how Baldwin will not be denied establishing his identity; as a human being and not an object. However, in doing so Baldwin (1955) acknowledges, and points out that this quest is a never-ending struggle because "People are trapped in history and history is trapped in them". (p. 182). That said, Baldwin (1955) argues

> What one's imagination makes of other people is dictated, of course, by the laws of one's own personality and it is one of the ironies of the black–white relations that, by means of what the white man imagines the black man to be, the black man is enabled to know who the white man is.
>
> *(183)*

Another reason I like the essay is because of its identification with and relevance to the lived reality of so many African Americans (Jackie Robinson, James Meredith, Barack Obama) in America who enter heretofore white spaces or spaces where the "Other" has been kept out, and how it speaks directly to "identity;" and the development of one's identity. A singular African boy or girl who is a student in a multiracial classroom or a student in an all African American, all European American or all Latinex classroom will influence the identity of students in each of the classrooms and will have his or her identity influenced. Dealing with – accepting or resisting – a "stranger," influences how a person sees herself/himself, and teaches, "Who are you?"

"Stranger in the Village" also addresses how, Baldwin like many African Americans who come to be in a white dominated spaces handles alienation: ignores negative comments, the white gaze and establishes their own identity so they are not looked upon as an object or a freak. Ironically, as I read the last sentence in "Stranger in the Village": "It did not occur to me – possibly because I am an American – that there could be people anywhere who had never seen a Negro" (p. 197).

Students be You **155**

I connect the statement to the comments of African American students in honors and AP classes who comment on how they are initially looked upon by their European American classmates when they enter the classroom: as people they have never seen before. The African American student in an honors class with all European American students is very much a "Stranger in the Village," a person trying to adapt to a world defined by European Americans who are trying to protect their identity (e.g., history, culture) and continue the reign of white supremacy. Deborah Mathis (2002) in "Yet a Stranger: Why Black Americans Still Don't Feel at Home" echoes Baldwin's thesis, however Mathis isn't describing a black man in a remote village in Switzerland, but African Americans in their home country, in America: Mathis (2002) reports that African Americans continue to be segregated spiritually, emotionally and sometimes physically from the rest of the country. Mathis (2002) contends a good deal of racism has gone underground, become more insidious and a "steady diet of indignities, disillusions, rejections, and suspicions" continue to confront African Americans. Mathis (2002) argues hopes, and ambitions are poisoned making them feel like strangers in the U.S.

Additionally, for those of us – African American and Latinx tenure track hires – who joined a university faculty during the late 1960s, early 1970s, up through the 1990s and in some places later, we are strangers in the village. Reading Baldwin's essay is a reminder that you don't have to travel to a Swiss village to be treated as a stranger.

Is the Grass Green on the Other Side?

In "A Question of Identity," Baldwin writes about the "American student colony" in Paris. He discusses former WWII American soldiers who decided to stay in Paris after the war and study at French universities. Baldwin is curious about why some of the former soldiers are successful in this endeavor and why others are not. Baldwin observes that although the former soldiers had different experiences during the war, some have been in combat and some have had other roles, they nevertheless have a common bond, something deeper than being a student in Paris. Baldwin discovers that the common bond is that all are fascinated by and with the French: their food, culture, history, everything. About the unsuccessful students, Baldwin learns, they hold an idyllic view of Paris, they have minimal knowledge of French history; little understanding of the life and living of French people, and they struggle with the French language. Baldwin discovers when their idealized conception of Paris and France is deglamorized these students soon head back to America; eager for "home cooking and culture." The former soldiers who are successful, Baldwin concludes are studious about French history and culture. They often live with a French family and their close friends are French. However, despite their deep enculturation dive, Baldwin notices that these students also have problems, usually because of a generalized, fantasized view of America held by French people. The French see America as the shining

156 Students be You

city on a hill where idealism and individualism is the rule and African American and European American relationships are good, not horrific. Such false or mythologized fascination of America conflicts with the successful students' romanticized thoughts and ideas about the French. Ultimately, most of these students, Baldwin observe, also leave France for America; eager to rejoin with family and friends and engage in African American culture and life.

Baldwin surmises that from experiencing another country, the students in the American colony in France gain a clearer understanding of their own country. And, when Baldwin applies his analysis to himself, he realizes that he, like all the American students who live in Paris, learn a great deal about the struggle for identity, by observing and analyzing others. As Baldwin examines his own growth, he better understands the struggle one encounters and endures to find his/her true identity.

I Am an African American

In "The Discovery of What It Means to be An American," Baldwin addresses the difficulties as an African American to locate one's place and role in a racialized society and "identity": that is who one is as a black person in America. Systemic racism and power make it difficult to discover one's true self. Baldwin contends that he could not develop his identity or distinguish his role or place living in the U.S. Baldwin (1955) posits:

> I do not think that I could have made this reconciliation here [U.S.]. Once I was able to accept my role – as distinguished from "my place" – in the extraordinary drama, which is America, I was released from the illusion that I hate America.
>
> *(p. 19)*

In Europe, Baldwin contends he doesn't feel cut off or oppressed because of racism. Baldwin (1955) declares for the first time in his life I "can reach out to everyone, that he [is] accessible to everyone and open to everything" (p. 8). He declares, "[w]hat Europe still gives an American – or gave us – is the sanction, if one can accept it, to become oneself. No artist can survive without this acceptance" (Baldwin, 1961, p. 9). This extraordinary feeling inspires Baldwin to lose the racial trauma associated with being "merely a negro writer" and discover that skin color is not an impediment. Baldwin begins to accept his "own weight and his own value" (p. 20). It is during his time in Europe that Baldwin looks deeply into himself and concludes it is time to cast off habits that are holding him back: he acquires a heightened consciousness of his ability as a writer, accepts his physical appearance, and homosexuality and demonstrates the ability to stand up to others. Writing about this time, first describing his feelings of being down and out; he discusses going to the remote Swiss village, taking along with him two records by Bessie Smith and his typewriter.

It is in the Swiss village as he looks deeply into himself that Baldwin writes, "I began to try to re-create the life that I had first known as a child and from which

I had spent so many years in flight" (p. 138). Baldwin contends it is through listening to Bessie Smith, her tone and cadence, that he is able to journey back to his early childhood and "remember the things I had heard and seen and felt. I had buried them very deep" (p. 138). Such "finding of oneself," Heshmat, (2014) argues is central to identity formation and developing and making nurturing choices that are consistent with one's true self.

It is also during this European experience, a period of nine years – living life and writing the "Paris Essays," completing *Go Tell it on the Mountain* and writing his first play, "The Amen Corner" that deals with a man's search for self-identit – that Baldwin comes to accept that Europe is a part of his identity and inheritance and to acknowledge that slowly but surely he is accepting the status of being a black American without shame or remorse. Europe, however, Baldwin contends is not without problems for black people. Although not constrained, Baldwin nevertheless knows, and doesn't wish to forget, that Europe is the land where the slave trade is developed, and the concept of race is constructed.

Going Home, Going South

> Maybe home isn't a place but an irrevocable condition.
>
> *James Baldwin, 1956*

In July 1957, James Baldwin, the writer, with clearer knowledge of himself as a man: African American homosexual; and with a better understanding and preparation for his role and place as a black artist – *an artist* – boards an ocean liner bound for New York. Living in Europe helps Baldwin to understand that although he is the *Other* in America, he is as American as any Texas GI. He has lived in Europe one year, less than a decade, and has concluded that the freedom he was seeking had always been within him; always, it has been in his hands and he is responsible for its development. "Once I found myself on the other side of the ocean," Baldwin tells the *New York Times*,

> I could see where I came from very clearly, and I could see that I carried myself, which is my home, with me. You can never escape that. I am the grandson of a slave, and I am a writer. I must deal with both.
>
> *(Daniel, 1987, p. 1)*

Bone (1965) observed that his time in Europe gives Baldwin many things, including:

> It gave him a world perspective from which to approach the question of his own identity. It gave him a tender love affair which would dominate the pages of his later fiction. But above all, Europe gave him back himself.
>
> *(p. 2)*

158 Students be You

Another thing Europe gives Baldwin is an understanding that being an artist, his literary work does not place him in a marginal social position, because in Paris, art and literature are an integral part of culture rather than an inappropriate activity for a "regular guy." As Kramer (2001) concludes, understanding that writing is honorable work helps Baldwin embrace his lifelong artistic dream and he begins to feel that he has finally escaped from a dark tunnel and can see the open sky. Baldwin also comes to understand, as Leeming (1994) observes, that "the black artist was a prophet of freedom, not only freedom for his own race but freedom for all those suffocating under the repressive blanket of emotional safety and innocence" (p. 136).

The European odyssey has been rough and one Baldwin will continue to reference throughout his life. Jail, more than one attempt at suicide and many days with no or little money gave serious character to Baldwin's odyssey. Homer would smile and Harriet Tubman would applaud.

Aboard the ship, Baldwin relaxes somewhat, and acknowledges to himself, he is an established author. *Go Tell it on the Mountain*, his first novel is published and is highly acclaimed; *Notes of a Native Son*, which contained the "Paris Essays" is published in 1955; his second novel, *Giovanni's Room*, although controversial, nevertheless, positions him as a fast-rising literary star and his appearance on the cover of *Time* magazine is less than a decade away. The Parisian experience has helped Baldwin to understand his racial "role" in the U.S. (Kramer, 2001) and about being an American writer. "The American writer in Europe," Baldwin (1959) would later say, "is released … from the habit of flexing his muscles and proving that he is just a 'regular guy' … [now,] he realizes how crippling this habit has been" (p. 6).

Over the past year, Baldwin has become increasingly concerned about the racial violence against civil rights protesters demonstrating peacefully and the menacing actions taken toward young African American children enrolling in heretofore all European American schools. Baldwin explains, "I could simply no longer sit around Paris discussing the Algerian and the African American problem. Everybody was paying their dues, and it was time I went home and paid mine." (See Pavlic, 2018 because confusion exists around when Baldwin makes the statement.)

When Baldwin's boat docks at New York harbor, the Civil Rights Act of 1957 is being debated in Congress. The Act designed to protect the rights of African Americans and other minoritized people will become the first federal civil rights legislation passed by the U.S. Congress in 82 years, since Reconstruction and the Civil Rights Act of 1875. The Civil Rights Act of 1957 is signed into law by President Eisenhower on September 9, but not before Southern senators led by Senator Richard Russell of Georgia protested.

Russell, in a speech on the United States senate floor argues with fixed bayonets the Federal Government is overriding southern tradition.

Students be You **159**

[The] bill is cunningly designed, vested in the Attorney General's unprecedented power to bring to bear the whole might of the Federal Government, including the armed forces if necessary, to force a comingling of white and Negro children in the state-supported public schools of the South ... to force the white people of the South at the point of a Federal bayonet to conform to almost any conceivable edict directed at the destruction of any local custom, law or practice separating the races and enforce a comingling of the races through the social order of the South.

(Russell 1957, July 2, 1957)

The Civil Rights Act of 1957 aimed to ensure that all African Americans can exercise their right to vote, established the Civil Rights Division in the Department of Justice and a Civil Rights Commission within the executive branch with the authority to investigate discriminatory conditions and recommend corrective measures, and kickstarted the 1964 Civil Rights and the 1965 Voting Rights Act.

Within months after his arrival, *Harper's Magazine* and *Partisan Review* commissions Baldwin to write on the civil rights movement, and thereby he takes his first trip south. A northern African American's first trip south, during Baldwin's day is usually filled with apprehension and excitement. Baldwin, Leeming (1994 argues, talks repeatedly about traveling south, his fears and his vulnerability as an African American man and a potential victim. In "A Fly in Buttermilk" Baldwin (1958) writes:

The South had always frightened me. How deeply it had frightened me – though I had never seen it – and how soon, was one of the things my dreams revealed to me while I was there. And this made me think of the privacy and mystery of childhood all over again in a new way. I wondered where children got their strength – the strength, in this case, to walk through mobs to get to school.

(p. 163)

Baldwin has made two trips south before he speaks to the students at Castlemont High School. These trips will help shape the message he will deliver to the students as well as help him in his continuous journey of self-discovery and help him to discern his place and role: bearing witness and being an artist.

Baldwin flies from New York to Charlotte, North Carolina. Charlotte is his first destination because he is emotionally shaken by a photograph of Dorothy Counts, a 15-year-old African American female being menaced by an angry shouting white mob as she enters a high school attended heretofore only by European American students in Charlotte and he wants a first-hand account about desegregation in the South.

Upon arrival in Charlotte, Baldwin discovers that Dorothy Counts' father, Reverend Counts has withdrawn his daughter from the school with all European

160 Students be You

American students and placed her in the "separate but equal school." Baldwin, does, however, interviews Gus Roberts, an African American male who integrates another high school with only European American students. According to Leeming (2014), Baldwin discovers during his interview of Gus Roberts, that he has been taunted, threatened, received numerous anonymous racist phone calls and forced to eat alone in the school cafeteria. About Gus Robert, Leeming (2014) notes, Baldwin observes that "pride and silence were his weapons" (p. 140). Yet, Baldwin wondered about the emotional and psychological effect the experience is having on Gus.

Baldwin interviews Harry Golden, the editor of *The Carolina Israelite*, Julian Sheers, an editor of *The Charlotte News* and the principal of Gus Robert's school, whom he describes as formal but supportive of Gus Robert. The principal, while supportive of Gus Roberts, does not believe in racial integration of schools; nevertheless, Baldwin grows to like him, because although he is a racist, Baldwin recognizes within him "complex and redeemable humanity" (p. 140). Baldwin also discovers during his visit to Charlotte that the so-called liberal white southerner, is an emotional, but not really a liberal person when white flesh has to touch black flesh. Attending an antiracist speech in Charlotte, Baldwin is taken about how nervous white people are about shaking his hand: "touching his flesh as equal to theirs" (Leeming 2014, p. 141). This is especially so with white women. Leeming (2014) argues, Baldwin feels he is a sexual object, the living version of a myth.

Leaving Charlotte, Baldwin flies to Atlanta where he meets Martin Luther King, for the first time. Upon King's advice, his next stop is Birmingham, Alabama and then Montgomery, Alabama to see the results of the bus boycott. In Montgomery, Baldwin observes the attitude of European Americans defeated by the bus boycott. Baldwin posits

> beneath their cold hospitality [they] are mystified and deeply hurt. Hurt, because, they have been betrayed by black people, not merely because black people have declined to remain in their 'place,' but because they [black people] have refused to be controlled by the town's image of them.
>
> *(Leeming, 1994)*

While in Montgomery, Baldwin meets Coretta King after church at a dinner.

Baldwin continues his interviews, traveling to Nashville, Tennessee and Little Rock, Arkansas; and along the way his interviews and observations develop into published articles of his journey. Baldwin concludes when his first trip south comes to a close that he has "bared witness" to unusual commitment and dedication to social justice on the part of African Americans in general, but especially African American youth. Their efforts, Baldwin contends are unique in American history. King's nonviolent approach to obtain civil rights for African Americans is a wonder to behold and a privilege to be

Students be You   161

a part of. Yet, Baldwin wonders if the nonviolent approach will do it, if it will be enough to eliminate systemic racism. European Americans, he now knows, better than ever want to maintain white power and privilege.

About Baldwin's travels, Amiri Baraka (1987) would say:

> This man traveled the earth like its history and its biographer. He reported, criticized, made beautiful, analyzed, cajoled, lyricized, attacked, sang, made us think, made us better, made us consciously human.... He made us feel ... that we could defend ourselves or define ourselves, that we were in the world not merely as animate slaves, but as terrifyingly sensitive measurers of what is good or evil, beautiful or ugly. This is the power of his spirit. This is the bond which created our love for him.

"No Moral Distance Between San Francisco and Birmingham"

"[T]o transition from spectator to witness is a long and difficult process. It requires a return to the past, and understanding of this country in its totality" (Gyarkye, 2017). It is this James Baldwin, with an understanding of America and with almost a decade of self-discovery and identity formation in Europe; over five years as a national literary scholar, leading public intellectual; and extensive travel throughout the South and the rest of the country on behalf of the Civil Rights movement "bearing witness" for social justice, who visits the Oakland Bay Area and while in Oakland speaks at Castlemont High School.

It is the spring of 1963 and KQED Film Unit invited James Baldwin to investigate racism in San Francisco (Cherian, 2014). During his visit to the Bay Area, he is accompanied by a mobile film unit that comes along to record his interviews. Baldwin visits Hunter's Point and Potrero Hill, two areas devastated by unemployment to talk with community leaders and unemployed youth. Baldwin sees all around him structures and messages of dispossession and despair that are engulfing the areas where African Americans live and he sees the forces of gentrification and urban renewal lying in wait. *Take this Hammer* is the resulting film from Baldwin's interviews and leads to one of Baldwin's (1963) more memorable comments at the time: "There is no moral distance ... between the facts of life in San Francisco and the facts of life in Birmingham. Someone's got to tell it like it is. And that's where it's at."

Castlemont High School

> Not everything that is faced can be changed, but nothing can be changed until it is faced.
>
> *Baldwin, 1953*

162 Students be You

> One must find, therefore, one's own moral center and move through the world hoping that this center will guide one aright.
>
> *Baldwin, 1963*

On May 8, 1963, the students and faculty could not have found a more profound and knowledgeable person to speak on "Living and Growing in a White World" than James Baldwin. The author of the best seller, *The Fire Next Time* entered the Knights' auditorium of the predominantly African American Castlemont High School to deliver considerably one of his two greatest speeches aimed at African American students' education. Baldwin discusses identity, the impact of history, causes of students' actions, students' norms, life in and out of school and the role of African American students. These two speeches, minus a few dated words (e.g., Negro) notwithstanding, are as theoretically and pragmatically relevant today as the day they are delivered because they address American society as it is and not the myth. In both speeches, " A Talk to Teachers" and "Living and Growing in a White World," Baldwin offers his perspective on education and how African American students should be taught and he discusses how students can become more involved in school and society where they are marginalized or exiled. Baldwin's speeches, like his novels and essays, address ideology and power, explore identity and engage in self-examination. They, as Louis Pratt (1978) argues, "shed the light of reality upon the darkness of our illusions" (p. 5). Baldwin proclaims black lives matter before there is a hashtag.

The Message

In the two speeches, "Living and Growing in a White World" (discussed below) and "A Talk to Teachers," Baldwin discusses the paradox of education for African American students, argues that the classroom in not separate from the world outside of the school, and encourages students to learn their history and to question everything. Both speeches are delivered with a sense and tone of urgency directed at teachers and students. Baldwin wants teachers to change viewing African American students as deficit, to push aside the way a racist system has taught them [teachers] to see African American people; but instead see African American students as equal in every way to their humanity and highly capable of academic learning, However, to do so, Baldwin knows, teachers will know, such thinking will challenge their self-interest; but not to do so, Baldwin wants them to know will bring "fire."

In "Living and Growing in a White World," Baldwin speaks caringly and bluntly to the African American students, telling them to be more assertive. They should raise questions, refuse to judge themselves by and adhere to others' cultural standards, examine the realities in which they live, learn about self and self-love. Baldwin argues that African American students don't want to live in U.S. society as it is structured but should want to change it, to include their needs and interests and make it fair to all who live in the U.S. Baldwin, a strong advocate for students knowing their history knows the curriculum taught in schools where African American students attend does not inform them that the heritage and culture of the country – Africa – where their great grandparents were stolen from has been purposively devastated to fuel European American economics and social desires. African American students know little of W. E. B. Du Bois and his observations in *The World and Africa*, about how African culture was destroyed. Du Bois (1947 states:

> With all this went the fall and disruption of the family, the deliberate attack upon the ancient African clan by missionaries. The invading investors who wanted cheap labor at the gold mines, the copper and tin mines, the oil forests and cocoa fields, followed the missionaries. The authority of the family was broken up; the authority and tradition of the clan disappeared; the power of the chief was transmuted into the rule of the white district commissioner. The old religion was held up to ridicule, the old culture and ethical standards were degraded or disappeared, and gradually all over Africa spread the inferiority complex, the fear of color, the worship of white skin, the imitation of white ways of doing and thinking, whether good, bad or indifferent. By the end of the nineteenth century the degradation of Africa was as complete as organized human means could make it. Chieftains, representing a thousand years of striving human culture, were decked out in second-hand London top-hats, while Europe snickered.
>
> *(p. 78)*

The 1960s, however, is a new era, a time when African Americans are engaged in an all-out demand for equality and respect. This generation has long put into the rearview mirror notions of only some African Americans making it (Du Bois's "talented tenth") or vocational "uplift" that confronted their great grandparents and their mothers and fathers (Washington, 1895). Gone or striving to put behind them, Du Bois's (1903) observation, that African Americans are always "measuring one's soul by the tape of a world that looks on in amused contempt and pity," (p. 11) "Black is Beautiful" is the social and political outcry and although its emphasis on black identity for some is to upend negative associations that some Americans, including African Americans, felt toward all things black; for others, the social and political outcry is the recognition of African American culture and heritage and a pronouncement of African American "striving" (Du Bois, 1903), celebrating their cultural identity (Jones, 1973) and demanding their humanity be fully prized.

African American "striving," develops out of the demands of returning WWII African American soldiers and African Americans in resistance to second-class citizenship; the defiance of Emmett Till's mother, Mamie Till, who has an open

164 Students be You

casket funeral for her murdered 14-year-old son whose body is brutalized, his eyes gouged out, in order for the world to see the evil and horror of white supremacy; the passage of *Brown v. Board of Education* (1954) knocking down the bogus "separate but equal" doctrine; the Montgomery bus boycott (December 5, 1955–December 20, 1956) and the growing Civil Rights movement. In addition, African American striving develops because Africans countries are rising up and U.S. global leadership demands that America shows nations of the world, especially Asian and African countries that it treats everyone equally, including African Americans. Jones's (1973) addressing the significance of the emerging African countries, argues independent African nations gave African Americans a sense of pride and dignity that they had never felt before; as the U.S. is forced to receive African diplomatic and economic missions and treat them with the same courtesy shown Europeans.

Past African Americans' "strivings" signal to African American youth of the 1950s and 1960s, they have a heritage and culture with which to identify and equality is their constitutional right, therefore, they should make every effort to obtain their civil rights. It is a time when African Americans exercise their voice, press for their constitutional rights and address their American identity, exemplified in Malcolm X's (1964) "Ballot or Bullet" speech that spoke to militant black nationalism.

> No, I'm one of the 22 million black victims of the Democrats. One of the 22 million black victims of the Republicans and one of the 22 million black victims of Americanism. *[applause]* And when I speak, I don't speak as a Democrat or a Republican, nor an American. I speak as a victim of America's so-called democracy. You and I have never seen democracy – all we've seen is hypocrisy. *[applause]*

The students who come to listen to Baldwin on that spring day, like many African American students, come with thoughts about their personal identity and their racial identity; American and African heritage. They want to hear Baldwin's thoughts on the Civil Rights movement: challenges, progress, what they can do to help, and to ask questions. They have concerns.

Baldwin knows he is addressing an audience of proud, dedicated African American youth who are tired and angry about being disrespected by European Americans. For example, in *Take this Hammer*, a film Baldwin makes during this same time he is on the West Coast, Famios Bell (aka Jackie Bell) says to Orville Luster, the film producer: "I'll tell you about San Francisco. The white man, he's not taking advantage of you out in public, like they're doing down in Birmingham, but he's killing you with that pencil and paper, brother!"

Baldwin has seen with his own eyes the critical role young people are playing in the Civil Rights movement. He sees young people at civil rights meetings, observes youth as they march, and hears about their imprisonment and, for some, death. Baldwin is aware of the strength and courage of nine African American students in Arkansas – Little Rock Nine – who desegregate Central High School; and he knows about the "Greensboro Four," students at North Carolina AT&T State University who protest segregation at a Woolworth's department store in 1960.

Baldwin too is fired up. He said when in Europe, he could not bear to sit in Paris, "polishing my fingernails," trying to explain Little Rock to the French, while children ran daily a vicious gauntlet in order to get to school.

To begin, Baldwin wants African American students to understand that although their "countrymen" work diligently to turn African American people into abstractions, a profound African American presence is in every sphere of American culture and produces a hybrid national identity, and now a multicultural society. In *Notes of a Native Son*, Baldwin (1959) writes:

> One of the things that distinguishes Americans from other people is that no other people has ever been so deeply involved in the lives of black men, and vice versa. This fact faced, … it can be seen that the history of the American Negro problem is not merely shameful, it is also something of an achievement. For even when the worst has been said, it must be added that the perpetual challenge posed by this problem was always, somehow, perpetually met. It is precisely this black–white experience which may prove of indispensable value to us in the world we face today. This world is white no longer, and it will never be white again.
>
> *(p. 175)*

As the students in the auditorium settled in, a member of the English Department rises, steps forward and says:

> The English Department of Castlemont High School is very proud to have as our guest today, the very distinguished and eminent writer, essayist, and novelist, and perhaps one of the foremost literary voices of our time. But also we are proud that he was willing to give up time from a very busy and I imagine horrendous lecture schedule to address us today.

Baldwin begins addressing the students as he addresses other audiences. That is, after "good morning" or "good afternoon," Baldwin says: "Can you all hear me?" With the tagline "Can you hear me" or a close variation, Jimmy Baldwin is in his element – relaxed, speaking frankly and passionately to people about life and living; promises and disappointments, knowing oneself individually and collectively and how such knowledge is essential to a socially just, multicultural society.

166 Students be You

From "Bearing Witness" to Teaching

Humbleness and adult respect for youth is embedded in Baldwin's caring tones that convey: "Younger brothers and sisters, I love and respect you!" I have love for the teachers who teach you. Will you, please give me a few minutes of your time. "I haven't got anything to say, really, which most of you, or all of you, don't already know" (Baldwin, 1959, p. 1). Therefore, if it's alright with you, "I'll talk for a while about the way I think and then, um, we'll have, you ask me questions, and I can find out what you think. Okay?" (p. 1).

With that introduction, Baldwin asks and answers his first question. "What is an education supposed to do and why is it necessary to become an educated person." Stating it as an obvious question and answer, Baldwin offers students reasons for their compulsory attendance at school: "The whole point of an education, in my view, is to help one learn how to live. How to live with oneself."

Understanding, that he is speaking with students, who much like himself when he was their age, consider themselves grown or almost grown; having to live with the reality of life, inasmuch as some have assumed adult responsibilities (working, providing childcare and home-making) because their parents are forced to work two or three jobs and others may think they are wise beyond their years, Baldwin offers a fact of life, that they may have overlooked, or they may have missed. Because they are overwhelmed by their day-to-day life; they are not acknowledging that their "youth" is moving on. Baldwin tells the students their parents are just other human beings, not invented for them. Therefore, they need to become educated, so their children will not have to have the adult responsibility they now have. Baldwin posits:

> It is only until much much later that the baby begins to realize that the parent on whom he depended for everything and whom he supposed held up the world, is in fact, just another human being, who is not invented for him. That is, on the most primary level, one of the meanings of an education.

Recalling the hours he spent in the library reading Dickens and other authors, learning about other societies, people and cultures; their government, day-to-day reality, including ways of raising children, Baldwin argues that education is a key to knowledge about the world and that there is much life and living outside of Oakland, California. Baldwin tells Castlemont students to read widely, and that they should read about other African Americans, in order to better understand their self and other African Americans. Baldwin posits:

> It [education] is the only way that one is enabled to enlarge the world ... when you begin to read, you discover more about the world than you knew before. You discover ... two worlds. One world is you and you have an obligation to discover whatever it is that goes on in that world.

Here, Baldwin is arguing that to become an adult and a capable person, African American students must engage with others; for it is through struggle and interaction with others that one understands and knows oneself and becomes comfortable with one's own racial skin (Badger, 1911).

And, Baldwin quickly added, you are not the only world, and "that's my problem." Baldwin's "my problem" is also "their problem," as he explains to the faces looking up at him and hanging on his every word. This too – a black, non-racialized gaze from a space of power in an auditorium, where the white gaze and voice normally dominate was not missed by Baldwin and the students. Both understood the significance. Using "I" but meaning African American children in general. The "problem" Baldwin wants African American students to understand is they have an *obligation* to discover whatever goes on in that second world, and to make that happen, they must become social. Baldwin is re-emphasizing for Castlemont students, they can't live in isolation; they must engage with life and the history of life on the other side of the Oakland Bay Bridge. The world is not Oakland. Continuing with the discourse of "I," but knowing that the students are smart, woke and following along with him, Baldwin states:

> I have got to consent to become a social animal, in order to discover and to enlarge what goes on in this world, which is all of you, and many millions of people, both living and dead, past, and to come.

Society and the role of the individual are being discussed and identity in connection to both is being argued. Baldwin is giving notice to his younger African American sisters and brothers and their teachers: that they must become educated and why. Implicit in Baldwin's comments is that their identity – self-discovery – is not only defined by Oakland, the school and/or their family members but their interactions with the larger world and the larger world's interactions with them. Their internal drive to explore the world, engage with other people and read history, Baldwin argues, will also help them to define themselves. Additionally, Baldwin is arguing that students' place and role in the world can be defined by them as they read, learn and engage with the larger world.

Karen McCurtis Witherspoon and Suzette L. Speight (2007/2009) using a Baldwinian framework argue that under natural or optimal conditions, African Americans have good thoughts of self and exhibit "self-affirmative behaviors." However, because of white supremacy "African Americans possess differing degrees of self-affirming behavior" (p. 890). Witherspoon and Speight (2009) argue that from a Baldwinian perspective:

> The basic characteristics of African self-consciousness are (a) an awareness of one's African identity and cultural heritage, valuing the pursuit of self-knowledge; b) recognition of African survival priorities and the true necessity for Afrocentric institutions to affirm Black life; (c) participation in activities

168 Students be You

that promote the survival, liberation, and proactive development of African people, defending their dignity, worth, and integrity; and (d) recognition of and opposition to the detrimental nature of racial oppression to Black survival and active resistance to it.

(p. 890)

Next, Baldwin uttered a statement based upon the lessons he learned from raising his brothers and sisters, observing black people in Europe, the time he spent in the Swiss village and traveling throughout the U.S. "bearing witness" and thinking deeply about identity, place and role. Also, about two years before coming to Castlemont, Baldwin wrote: "My revenge, I decided very early, would be to achieve a power which outlasts kingdoms ... To become a Negro man, let alone a Negro artist, one had to make oneself up as one went along" (Baldwin 1959, p. 5). Baldwin says to the students:

> The measure of one's dignity depends on one's estimate of one's self. It really does not depend, as so many people in this country now seem to believe, on someone else's estimate. It depends first of all, on what you take yourself to be, what your real standards are, what you think is right, what you think is wrong, what you think life is all about; what you think life is for.

Exercising great care, knowing that he must not come across as authoritarian, sharing wisdom he learned from parenting his brothers and sisters and speaking with college students across the country. But needing to be honest, "brutal" as he calls it; Baldwin tells the Castlemont students because their education does not occur in a vacuum, but occurs with others, in a social context, with social purposes and ends, each student has a responsibility to discover the purpose of education. In other words, Baldwin argues: becoming an educated person, brings with it the responsibility to question the purpose of education.

Continuing with education occurring within a social context, and understanding its significance to identity development, place and role in the Civil Rights era, Baldwin states:

> [Y]our education is occurring, within a given context, in a certain time in history, in a certain country ... In fact, in a very crucial time in its history ... I'll be personal about this, when I was going to school ... I began to be bugged, by the teaching of American history because ... that history had been accomplished without my presence. And this had, a very demoralizing effect, on me when I was your age and younger. It had a demoralizing effect for quite a few years after.

Teacher *Baldwin*

At this point, during his speech, Baldwin becomes "*teacher*," and the students in the audience become his students. Baldwin as teacher is concerned about the

Students be You **169**

students' development of their identity in a world that wants them to see themselves as inferior, vulnerable, powerless and frightened because of their black skin. Baldwin argues:

> speaking now as though I were your educator, as though I were your teacher, my responsibility to you would be to invest you with all of the moral that I could to prepare you for the terrible storm which is called life.

Baldwin continues:

> Terrible, and beautiful, but you must know that it is both. And you don't quite know it, and it is my responsibility to make you know it. It's my responsibility also, speaking now as your educator, to give you as true a version of your history as I can, since it is through your sense of your own history that you'll arrive at your identity.

Baldwin adds: "And no one has ever arrived at a sense of his own identity without it, this is why ancestors are important."

Baldwin's words are to the teachers in the auditorium as much as the students. He is calling on teachers to be honest and authentic. Teach African American students with rigorous, factual curriculum that considers life realities both in schools and out of schools, that will allow them to both synthesize and apply their learning in the spaces they live and, in the spaces where they will go in the future. "Go for Broke."

Baldwin's words to the students are heartfelt and sagacious. He argues that life is both hard and good. Life is what you make it; and making it depends on how you see yourself; and your understanding of your history and your commitment to deep learning and self-discovery. Contextualizing the Civil Rights movement and the racial turmoil that followed as historical and personal; and as such, significant to identity development and one's place and role, Baldwin differentiates between the aims of a society and the aims of an education.

Baldwin argues that whereas the aim of society is to provide for citizens a feeling of safety, it does not want people attempting to change the status quo or "disturb the peace." Baldwin contends that although "society" is a wonderful and beautiful creation and people cannot live without society; nevertheless, all societies have been created by men. Therefore, Baldwin argues: [T]ake nothing ... for granted ... [and] although society is under the obligation to educate all of its citizens, it is also under the obligation to discourage people from thinking too much. Now this is where all of you come in."

Not letting go of the position as their teacher, Baldwin tells students his responsibility: if he was their teacher, he would teach them to think about everything and that there is a reason for everything they do. Baldwin offers an example:

170 Students be You

> [L]et's say I was dealing with one of you who … is beginning to wonder what you were doing in school … and what waits for you outside, what good is it to be here since nothing that happened here prepared you for outside.

Baldwin continues, bringing together both the social and personal side of the problem. That is, African Americans living in a society where European Americans define the norms and standards and demand that African Americans adhere to a secondary place and role and accept themselves as inferior. Since schools do not consider African American history and do not present African Americans in important places and roles in society, other than sports and entertainment, they are not considered to have relevance and for over 400 years, schools have maintained racial stubbornness and indifferences.

To better understand, Baldwin suggests that students personalize the problems they have toward school and society, and he attempts to do so with the following illustration: "I would ask you, if you were a boy, why you dressed the way you do and if your hair is conked, (straightened, slicked back) I would ask you to ask yourself, "why?"

Here, Baldwin in not calling for, what some call "politics of respectability" (Higginbotham, 1993); he is calling out self-degadation. Baldwin tells the students the example demonstrates the wall between *society* and *thought* and that it is their responsibility to understand the standards and norms they are judged by and which they choose to judge themselves by. Baldwin posits:

> It is your responsibility as young American citizens, to understand, that the standards, by which you are confronted, and by which many of you are visibly and obviously victimized, and others of you, not so obviously, but equally victimized, are not the only standards in the world.

Baldwin continues with an example on facial features and body type and argues that there is no reason why an African American should want to look like a Greek god; for it is not the world's only standard of beauty. Today a Baldwinian perspective argues against African American girls' hair critiqued and policed (e.g., Gabby Douglas [Wilson, 2016];

Baldwin's friend, Malcolm X said the following about his experience with conked hair:

> This was my first really big step toward self-degradation: when I endured all of that pain, literally burning my flesh to have it look like a white man's hair. I had joined that multitude of Negro men and women in America who are brainwashed into believing that the black people are "inferior" — and white people "superior" — that they will even violate and mutilate their Godcreated bodies to try to look "pretty" by white standards.
>
> (pp. 61–62)

African American boys seen as mature men before their youth has run its course and the black body punished through the use of cleansing and bleaching [glutathione treatments; Hall, 2019).

Baldwin argues that the virtues Greeks adhered to were not only carried out by Greeks.

Baldwin learned from reading and "bearing witness" that habits and dispositions are not accrued because one is Greek or lives in certain places and with financial means. Baldwin states: "I come from a very poor family, and there is a vast amount of vitality, which is a very definite virtue, to be found, in those circumstances." Baldwin wants the Castlemont students to understand that, they do not have to be Greek or Greek-like to have virtue. Prudence, justice, fortitude and temperance, can be developed living in Oakland, helping their family and community and working with the Civil Rights movement.

Staying with "if I were your teacher," Baldwin tells the students, he would insist that they questioned him. Ask him, not easy questions, but questions that challenge, because they should keep in mind that he is mortal. And, although he loves them and feels responsible, the teacher is not always right. Baldwin argues that it is important that people depend on one another. Teachers depend on students; students depend on teachers; the young depend on their elders; and elders depend on youth. Baldwin crystallizes his insistence that the Castlemont students question any mortal:

> I would beg you to … to fight with me, and not let me get away with anything, no matter how I may sound, I am really only mortal, and [although] I love you very much, and feel responsible for you, I'm not always right. We depend on each other, the old and the young, to learn from each other.

Next Baldwin asserts: As your teacher, I want you to ask me about the history I teach you and the books I use. I want you to insist that I give you a full-throated, honest answer. Baldwin tells the students, you have a right to ask the most difficult questions, and as your teacher if I cannot answer your questions because I don't know, I nevertheless have the responsibility to listen to the question so I know what you are thinking about. Baldwin espousing a tone of urgency grounded in his desire that the students be assertive, says:

> I would beg you, to ask me why, for example, why history books are the way they are, and I would beg you to force me to answer, if you asked me, what relevance your education had for concrete problems, such as, getting an apartment, moving from one part of town to another. If I were you, I would force me to answer, I would put me on the spot, ask me the most difficult questions that you can, and I will not be able to answer them, but my responsibility is to hear them, and when you ask your question, any question,

172 Students be You

you begin to know more about what you really think. That's all I have to say, now you've got to ask me questions.

With that dynamic conclusion a tremendous applause erupts from the audience that lasts for several minutes. The students then settle back for the Q&A.

Questions and Answers: James Baldwin and Castlemont Students

The first question Baldwin is asked during the Q&A probably takes him back to his time in Europe observing the interactions between African Americans and black Africans and people in the Swiss village toward him – the only black man living in the village. It is during his European visit, that Baldwin discovers he is an "outsider" to Africans and European Americans living in Europe and that Europe has not shaped his culture and experience, nor does he feel a part of European culture. He understands why Castlemont students find Shakespeare and Bach boring and resist a culture that tries to control them, haunts and brutalizes them. Baldwin (1959) states:

> I know that the most crucial time in my own development came when I was forced to recognize that I was a kind of bastard of the West; when I followed the line of my past I did not find myself in Europe but in Africa. And this meant in some subtle way, in a really profound way, I brought to Shakespeare, Bach, Rembrandt, to the stones of Paris, to the cathedral at Chartres … a special attitude. These were not really my creations, they did not contain my history; I might search in them in vain forever for any reflection of myself. I was an interloper.
>
> *(pp. 6–7)*

A student asks:

> Mr. Baldwin, do you think that Black people in America should learn African history and culture to gain pride, dignity, and strength so when they are confronted by white people, we can say that we have a culture, which is at the very least equal to white people's, and at the very most, well, we don't know what it's equal to.

The question confirms for Baldwin the importance of speaking to students at Castlemont and speaking to African American students specifically. They are like him, when he was in Europe searching for his identity. The question speaks to African American students' feeling of inferiority; the beat-down they receive from white supremacy; but more importantly, it speaks to the resiliency of African Americans since 1619, not to give into, but to keep striving. African American youth as the question demonstrated, are fighters in search of a battle plan and ammunition to do

Students be You **173**

battle. Baldwin answers, "Yes" to the question but added: "be careful, find out all you can, but don't find it out with the intention of proving a point. Understand this: there is no reason for you to prove yourself to anybody, except yourself."

Baldwin next punches another hole in the armor of white supremacy, telling students when the world talks about culture, it is often a code word for power. Baldwin then addresses the heart and soul of the student's question: "Why is Africa the way that it is, poor and underdeveloped; and America and Europe, the way that they are, developed and wealthy?" Baldwin posits:

> The difference between the African cultures, which have vanished and the European cultures, which are decaying, is that Europe had the power, and that is the only difference. It is not that Europe was civilized and Africans were not, that's a lie. You understand that? And, find out all you can about what happened when you got here, but you haven't got to prove it to anybody. All you've got to do is know it. You're a man, baby!

Surprisingly, Baldwin didn't reference the students to Du Bois's (1925) "The Souls of White Folk" where he gives the historical context of European ruthless power in much of the 19th and 20th century. Du Bois (1925) writes:

> Behold little Belgium and her pitiable plight, but has the world forgotten Congo? What Belgium now suffers is not half, not even a tenth, of what she has done to black Congo since Stanley's great dream of 1880. Down the dark forests of inmost Africa sailed this modern Sir Galahad, in the name of "the noble-minded men of several nations," to introduce commerce and civilization. What came of it? "Robbery and murder, slavery in its worst form," wrote Glave in 1895.
>
> Harris declares that King Leopold's régime meant the death of twelve million natives, "but what we who were behind the scenes felt most keenly was the fact that the real catastrophe in the Congo was desolation and murder in the larger sense. The invasion of family life, the ruthless destruction of every social barrier, the shattering of every tribal law, the introduction of criminal practices which struck the chiefs of the people dumb with horror—in a word, a veritable avalanche of filth and immorality overwhelmed the Congo tribes."
>
> *(p. 6)*

Baldwin also wanted the Castlemont students, to not run from or toward their African identity, but to understand they have been born into a country with a great number of possibilities. Baldwin argues, America is a place that is not fixed; although the possibilities were wretched at their birth (Baldwin, 1959 p. 20) and remain pretty much so today. Baldwin hopes that the students will see and identify with what he is seeing, but what neither European Americans, Europeans nor Africans can see in the United States. That is, a multicultural history that has

174 Students be You

"created an entirely unprecedented people, with a unique and individual past" (Baldwin, 1955, p. 136.) that should be used to construct their identity as they move forward.

The following question tells Baldwin that the students are listening very closely to what he is saying and they have additional questions. A student asks:

"What force do you think wins out more often in this war about education? Society or thought?"

At first Baldwin bats the question around:

> Well, I don't know. It's a good question. It would seem that society wins out and in an obvious and visible way society usually does. After all, history is full of martyrs who went to various deaths because society didn't like what they had to say.

But Baldwin gathers himself and says: "[I]t s a question of what you think is most important. I'll tell you what I think. 'Thought' is most important, don't try to be safe. Nobody ever is safe."

Baldwin rarely plays it safe, an identifying characteristic is, he writes and speaks truth freely and critically. One of his more famous statements that addresses "society and thought" and pronounces his personal beliefs about America and illustrates the foundational nature of his identity and his love of the country where he was born and called home, is: "I love America more than any other country in the world, "and, exactly for this reason, I insist on the right to criticize her perpetually" (Baldwin 1955, p. 9).

Baldwin added a statement that is at the core of his identity that he wants to pass on to the students: "I want to be an honest man and a good writer" (Baldwin 1955, p. 9).

Baldwin continues, leaving the students with a final take-away, that Buccola (2017) situates: "although people do many wicked things, we cannot allow ourselves to conclude that they are, at their core wicked" (p. 136).

Baldwin posits: "the white culture has operated and is operated deliberately to demoralize all Black people." And demoralization, has, in many cases, been fatal, and in all cases, has been sinister. Because of this sinister deed, Baldwin argues: "the effort that I must make, to arrive at my identity, is mainly an opposition, to the white force of the world. Under such attention, it becomes very difficult, and under such attention, I must repeat, it becomes absolutely necessary, to deal with people as people."

Baldwin explains to the students, it is important to deal with people as people – for example, the European American shoe sale person as a person – "because you cannot spend your life … trying to be revenged for historical crimes." In other words, Baldwin is telling the students not to hold each European American they meet responsible for crimes perpetrated hundreds of years or decades ago. "If you do that," Baldwin argues,

Students be You **175**

you will destroy yourself and you will perpetuate the crime. The thing ... to aim at, this is why it is a terrible necessity to accept white people, but it is a terrible necessity on the part of white people, even harder necessity to accept Negroes because in order for white people to accept a Negro, they've got to accept their history, and something much deeper and worse than that, they got to accept, if I may be brutal and rude, but I mean this, and you must think about it, if you remember, that everything that you will do, all your life, and everything that you will say, reveals you.

Next, Baldwin utters one of the lines he is famous for:

What I call you, it doesn't say anything about you, or very rarely, but what I call you says everything about me. Now there is a very good reason which has nothing to do with Negroes, why white people call them N★★★★. It's a white invention, in order for white people to be released from this invention, they better discover where this N★★★★ really lives, and he lives inside white people, and they have to accept him, that stranger within, before they may accept anybody without. That is what I was trying to say.

The following two questions to Baldwin are about two ongoing movements: the Black Nationalist movement and the Civil Rights movement.

A student asks: "Mr. Baldwin, if I may ask you a question, what is your opinion of the Black Muslim movements and the other Black nationalist movements?

Baldwin's response as I noted above was to resist nationalist movements because he wanted to avoid categories of political, racial or cultural identity that would reify and entrap him. To the student's question, Baldwin states:

I would, oppose, with all my energy, your joining such a movement, for two reasons. If one is wary, of the adopting of white supremacy and if one is cognizant of the crimes committed in the name of this myth, one cannot possibly, now, turn the matter over, and call it black supremacy, and embark on the same terrifying road which will end up in the same place.

Continuing, Baldwin reminds the Castlemont students: "This is your country, and no matter what you call yourself, you are an American. You've been here for 400 years, your ancestors helped create this country. I don't think that you should abandon it."

Moreover, Baldwin, after attending the "Black Writers and Artists" conference in Paris in 1956 concludes that he is against "racial essentialisms" because he believes that there is an inescapable link between African and Western culture (Kramer 2001). Baldwin in *Nobody Knows My Name*, argues "For they [black writers] were all, now, whether they liked it or not, related to Europe, stained by European visions and standards, and their relation to themselves, and to each other, and to their past had changed" (1959, p. 36).

176 Students be You

For students seated before him contemplating joining the Black Muslims as a way to develop their identity, Baldwin is blunt, saying *no*! And, furthermore he argues "America is your country, fight for what is yours."

A final student asked: "Mr. Baldwin, what do you think of Dr. Martin Luther King's movement of non-violence in the south?"

To begin his response, Baldwin graciously and with sincerity acknowledges Dr. King's tremendous efforts on behalf of African American civil rights stating: "I admire Martin very much, and Reverend King's work is incredible, and I personally, am opposed to violence." At this point, Baldwin reminds the Castlemont students of his charge to them, when he said they must: question everything and everybody. Baldwin states:

> if you remember what I told you earlier, everything must be questioned. The technique of non-violence has obvious limits. It has this limit that people are not by nature, nonviolent ... and it would cost you, if you were down there now, a terrible effort, from which you might not recover. You would have to endure what you would have to endure, at the hands of those people. Therefore, your question, to be honest with you, defies me very much where you are. I think the entire strategy has got to be rethought in order to minimize damage to you. I have not yet come up with a satisfactory answer, but I will do my best, and you think about it too. Okay?

With "Okay" ... "I guess that's it." Baldwin shakes hands, accepts compliments. Thanks the English Department for inviting him and heads out of Castlemont High in Oakland, California. Arguably, he is wondering, as he has wondered since his arrival in the Bay Area, "What precisely do you say to an African American child to invest him with morale and courage which the country is determined he shan't have ... To insist that he know that he can do anything he wants to?"

Baldwin will continue to ask himself that question, even as he publicly answered the question over and over again in his essays, speeches and interviews. Not only does he answer the question – "What precisely do you say to an African American child to invest him with morale which the country is determined he shan't have" – but, the positive results of Baldwin's answers are reflected in the ways countless everyday people continue to find inspiration and a desire to act based upon his words. In addition, many African Americans: Maya Angelou, Lorraine Hansberry and Toni Morrison among others took from Baldwin's answers the moral fortitude to do the artistic craft they wished

James Baldwin and the American Schoolhouse is inspired by Baldwin's words and has used Baldwin's words to inform educators on what to do for African American students to invest them with the morals, truth, honesty, affirmation and love America resists them having. It is crucial for teachers of African American students not to treat their classrooms as disconnected from the rest of the world, but instead as a microcosm of racialized, heteronormative, have and have-not society and world. In 2014,

Students be You 177

a *New York Times* story noted Baldwin's relative absence from the curriculum of the New York City public schools that were so formative for him (and one of which bears his name). One principal quoted in the story argues for Baldwin's relevance, noting: "Many of the struggles the students face are the same: self-identity, racism, drugs, and alcohol." Yet this is an anemic rendering of Baldwin's work, especially when contrasted with Baldwin's own pedagogical vision, outlined in a lecture titled "A Talk to Teachers." Drawing upon Baldwin's passionate, honest and persuasive writings and speeches, *James Baldwin and the American Schoolhouse* presents to educators – teachers, teacher candidates, teacher educators, and deans ways they may facilitate and create spaces where they can engage in investigations of race from individual, societal, institutional and structural perspectives.

★★★

Pam's Apartment, Upper East Side, Manhattan, NY. 8pm EST

House phone ringing and ringing ... several decades before the common use of mobile phones (1983) and several more decades before the cell phone.

PAM TO HUSBAND, MICHAEL: Mike, please answer that; please, I need to finish grading my students' papers.

MIKE: It's a collect long-distance call from Ann in California. Should I accept it? That woman does some crazy things.

PAM: Give me that phone!

MA BELL OPERATOR: Hello, I have a person-to-person collect call to Pam Shorewood, from Ann Fields, in San Francisco, will you accept the charges?

PAM: Operator, how much is that a minute?

OPERATOR: Madam, that depends on if you are using Phone Plan "A," "B," or "C"; Do you know which plan you are using?

PAM: Aw, that's OK operator, I will accept the charges.

OPERATOR: Thank you Madam, go ahead ... you are connected.

PAM: Ann, Ann! Why are you calling me, and why are you calling me collect? Is anything wrong? Mike is screaming, this call will be expensive.

ANN: I just couldn't wait! I had to tell you right away, right away! Guess who I saw and heard speak today ... You will never guess ... James Baldwin. You know, that famous black guy I call "Jimmy," who was on the cover of *Time* magazine, who spoke to us at the in-service last October.

PAM: What ... What ... What are you saying ... why are you calling? James ... who? You say you saw Jimmy Stewart, the actor?

ANN: No, no! Listen, this international reading conference I am attending is so great. I am glad the school district sent me. I am sorry you didn't come. I am learning so much and I am meeting teachers from all over the U.S., and some from foreign countries. Lisa, a teacher from Oakland, CA, that I met at Conference

178 Students be You

Registration, and I have become fast friends. It is Lisa, who teaches at Castlemont High School, who invited me to go to her school with her to hear Jimmy, who was giving a speech to the High School students. I will give you all of the wherein and what for's, when I get back ... I know you are paying for this call.... But, I just had to tell you about Jimmy's talks. To begin, Jimmy had the students' devoted attention, unlike our audience, the students interrupted him several time with long applauds that lasted more than a minute or two and when he left they followed him out to the car that had come to pick him up. As he spoke, the audience was so quiet you could hear a rat pissed on cotton. Pam, they were unlike our group. Watching the clock, squirming and whispering to friends. When he was introduced, the students went crazy. They stood and applauded for several minutes, whistling and shouting ... making him smile, slightly bow and wave his hands.

ANN: Get on with it; you are repeating yourself. What did he say?

PAM: His speech was much of what he told us, however, it was directed to black students ... It was an all–Black school ... He asked them why they were in school; why were they getting an education. I took down what he said. His specific question was...

"What is an education supposed to do and why is it necessary to become an educated person?"

The answer he gave and the way he gave it, caused the students to freeze and to look at one another. The answer was not about making money or getting out of the hood; it is about developing how to live with yourself.

Jimmy said: "The whole point of an education, in my view, is help one learn how to live. How to live with oneself."

Pam, we don't talk to our students that way, we don't think about them that way and we don't challenge them that way. Our curriculum and instruction is not geared toward helping Black students morally and socially appreciate and affirm their humanity. Our pedagogy is not toward helping our students become who they are called to be and can be. We fail to communicate high academic expectations, to motivate based upon their life dream; we motivate as an obligation to pass tests so teachers and schools are not identified as failures. We don't provide our students with meaningful opportunities to achieve their dream expectations. We don't teach like positive expectations are a structure that guides behavior and that encourages students beyond their beliefs in what they can do.

Instead, our attention is toward helping them to be happy with themselves by having a minimum wage job, staying out of prison, finishing high school and perhaps going on for some college.

We are not using education as a light to illuminate the dangers they face. You talk to your son, Jack and I talk to my daughter Laura about life ... a

Students be You **179**

good life, a meaningful life as something that develops out of our possession of education, completing college, yes, but we also argue for bodily health; food, housing, clothes (external goods) and goods for the soul (knowledge, love, skills, friendship and self-esteem). What the Greeks, Aristotle called "eudaimonia." The schools our kids attend provide an education to meet the needs of the whole child.

Pam, one more thing, then, I will hang-up … also I will pay half on this call. Let me know the cost.…

Pam, the other thing is Baldwin … Jimmy … talked to the student like he really cared for them, each and every student; and cared for them as people. That Pam, I believe made them doubly excited about school as a place to pursue their dreams.

Finally, Pam the students asked him questions; of the several questions, the one that caught my attention was:

What force do you think wins out more often in this war about education? Society or thought?

Jimmy answered "thought" Pam. We need to teach black students they have big, powerful, robust brains; and throughout enslavement, up until today, African Americans have stood strong against the dedicated of a racist society in their pursuit of knowledge and education. See you on Monday, Pam. Miss you.…

MICHAEL: [to Pam] Is Ann having a good time at the conference … enjoying San Francisco?

PAM: She is having a great learning experience, if she learned and acts on what I heard her say she learned, she is going to be a much, much better teacher.

MICHAEL: Do I hear you saying you are sorry, that you didn't go with her?

PAM: Yes and no. Had I gone, Ann would not have had the dynamic learning experience she had, because I would have, probably … to be honest … blocked it. Yes, I wish I would have gone, but while there have been smart enough to follow Ann and her new fast friend, Lisa, over the Oakland Bay Bridge to Castlemont High School.

Pam sighs as her mind takes flight. She imagines what words Jimmy would have for her if she ran into him in the Harlem coffee shop close to her school.

Jimmy, I know, would offer to pay for her coffee, invite her to get a donut, along with coffee and donuts for Ann and then empathetically staring into Pam's eyes, say:

People pay for what they do, and still more for what they have allowed themselves to become. And they pay for it very simply; by the lives they lead.

180 Students be You

Bibliography

Anderson, M. (2017). African immigrant population in U.S. steadily climbs. *Fact Tank*, February. Pew Researcher Center. https://www.pewresearch.org/fact-tank/2017/02/14/african-immigrant-population-in-u-s-steadily-climbs/. 8/15/2019.

Badger, R. (1911). James Mark Baldwin: "Social Competition and Individualism". In *The Individual and Society or Psychology and Sociology*. Boston, Mass.: The Gorham Press.

Baldwin, J. (1955a). *Notes of a Native Son*. New York, NY: Beacon Press.

Baldwin, J. (1956). *Giovanni's Room*. New York, NY: Dell.

Baldwin, J. (1958/1985). *A fly in buttermilk*. In *The Price of the Ticket*. New York, NY: St. Martin's Press .

Baldwin, J. (1959). *Nobody Knows My Name*. New York, NY: Dell.

Baldwin, J. (1960). The precarious vogue of Ingmar Bergan. April 1. *Esquire* Magazine

Baldwin, J. (1961). Interview with Studs Terkel. In Fred L. Standley and Louis H. Pratt, eds., *Conversations with James Baldwin*. Jackson: University of Mississippi Press (1989). p. 17.

Baldwin, J. (1963). Living and growing in a white world. Talk with students at Castlemont High School in Oakland, California. The talk was broadcast on June 23, 1963. It is available on the Black Media Archive at wwwthebma.org.

Baldwin, J. (1993). The discovery of what it means to be an American. In *Nobody Knows My Name: More Notes of a Native Son*. New York, NY: Vintage Books. pp. 11–23.

Baldwin, J. (1998). The black boy looks at the white boy. In *Collected Essays*. New York, NY: Library of America.

Balfour, L. (2001). *The Evidence of Things Not Said: James Baldwin and the Promise of American Democracy*. Ithaca: Cornell UP.

Baraka A. (1987) James Baldwin's Eulogy. Quoted in Amiri Baraka's Eulogy of James Baldwin from 1987. 12/5/2020.

Bell, P. K. (1986). *Coming Home*. James Baldwin. Ed. Harold Bloom. New York, NY: Chelsea House.

Bone, R. A. (1965). The novels of James Baldwin. *Tri-Quarterly*, Winter, 2.

Buccola, N. (2017). What William F. Buckley Jr. did not understand about James Baldwin. In Susan J. McWilliam, Ed. *A Political Companion to James Baldwin*. Lexington, KY: University Press of Kentucky. pp. 116–150.

Cherian, A. (2014). James Baldwin's visit to Bayview Hunters Point: Racism, censorship and a vision of democracy. *SF BayView*. August 1. https://sfbayview.com/2014/08/james-baldwins-visit-to-bayview-hunters-point-racism-censorship-and-a-vision-of-democracy/. 9/13/2019.

Clair, M. (2014). A very complex thing: The battleground between James Baldwin and Norman Mailer. The Diverse Arts Project. http://www.diverseartsproject.com/reportage/2012/7/10/a-very-complex-thing-the-battleground-between-james-baldwin.html. 8/28/2019.

Cogeanu, O. (2013). James Baldwin's question of identity: The impossible community. Interculturalencounters.blog. file:///C:/Users/Carl%20Grant/Downloads/Lit0133.pdf. 8/13/2019.

Daniel, L. A. (1987). James Baldwin, eloquent writer on behalf of civil rights, is dead. *The New York Times*. https://movies2.nytimes.com/books/98/03/29/specials/baldwin-obit.html. 9/17/2020.

Douglass, F. (1845/1963). *Narrative of the Life of Frederick Douglass, an American Slave.* Garden City, NY: Doubleday.

Du Bois, W. E. B. (1903). *The Souls of Black Folks.* New York, NY: Oxford.

Du Bois, W. E. B. (1925). The souls of white folk. In *Darkwater.* New York, NY: Harcourt, Brace.

Du Bois, W. E. B. (1947) *The World and Africa.* Mansfield Centre, CT: Martino Publishing.

Entrée to Black Paris. (2010). In memoriam: James Baldwin's Paris. December, 2. http://entreetoblackparis.blogspot.com/2010/12/in-memoriam-james-baldwins-paris.html. 8/18/2019.

Gehlawat, M. (2019). Strangers in the Village: James Baldwin, Teju Cole, and Glenn Ligon. 11/13/2019.

Gyarkye, L. (2017). James Baldwin and the struggle to bear witness. *The New Republic.* February 3. 12/5/2020.

Haley, A. (1965). *The Autobiography of Malcolm.* New York, NY: Ballantine.

Hall, R. (2019). Black America's "bleaching syndrome". The Conversation. https://theconversation.com/black-americas-bleaching-syndrome-82200. 9/11/2019.

Hall, S. (1996). Introduction: Who Needs "Identity"? In *Questions of Cultural Identity*, ed. Stuart Hall and Paul du Gay. London: Sage Publications Ltd.

Henneberg, S. (2015). *James Baldwin: Groundbreaking Author and Civil Rights Activist.* New York, NY: The Rosen Publishing Group.

Heshmat, S. (2014). Basics of identity. *Psychology Today.* December. https://www.psychologytoday.com/us/blog/science-choice/201412/basics-identity. 8/15/2019.

Higginbotham, E. B. (1993). *Righteous Discontent: The Women's Movement in the Black Baptist Church, 1980–1920.* Cambridge, MA: Harvard University Press.

Jones, W. (1973). The importance of black identity to the black adolescent. *Journal of Black Studies*, 4, 1, 81–91.

Kramer, L. (2001). James Baldwin in Paris. Exile: Multiculturalism and the public intellectual. *Historical Reflections / Réflexions Historiques*, 27, 1. Spring. https://www.jstor.org/stable/41299193. 9/7/2019.

Leeming, D. (1994). *James Baldwin: A Biography.* New York, NY: Knopf.

Mabanckou, A. (2014). *Letter to Jimmy.* Paris: Editions Fayard.

Mathis, D. (2002). *Yet a Stranger: Why Black Americans Still Don't Feel at Home.* New York, NY: Grand Central Publishing.

McCrary, M. (2016). Stranger on the Seine. Identity Theory. http://www.identitytheory.com/stranger-on-the-seine-micah-mccrary/. 8/15/2019.

Morrison, T. In Chavez, M., Lavariega Monforti, J. L. and Michelson, M. R. (2015). *Living the Dream: New Immigration Policies and the Lives of Undocumented Latino Youth.* New York, NY: Taylor & Francis.

Pavlic, E. (2018,). Why James Badwin went to the South and what it meant to him. Via Brick. June 29. https://lithub.com/why-james-baldwin-went-to-the-south-and-what-it-meant-to-him/. 10/3/2019.

Pratt, L. H. (1978). *James Baldwin.* Boston, Mass.: Twayne Publishers.

Richert, S. P. (2019). What are the 4 Cardinal Virtues? Learn Religions. https://www.learnreligions.com/the-cardinal-virtues-542142. 9/12/2019.

Ricks, O. (2016). "Take this hammer": James Baldwin's radical critique of modernity. http://omarricks.blogspot.com/2016/07/take-this-hammer-james-baldwins-radical.html. 9/13/2019.

182 Students be You

Russel (1957). Civil rights. Congressional Record – Senate. Government Publishing Office's Website. July 2. p. 10771.

St. Paul. (A.D. 57–59). Letter to the Philippians. Rau, A. (2016). *Letters to the Church: Paul's Epistle to the Philippians.* https://www.biblegateway.com/blog/2016/03/letters-to-the-church-pauls-epistle-to-the-philippians/. 9/12/2019.

Washington, B. T. (1895). Booker T. Washington delivers the 1895 Atlanta Compromise speech. http://historymatters.gmu.edu/d/39/. 9/14/2019.

Wilson, j. (2016). Haters attack Gabby Douglas's hair again and Twitter promptly claps back. *Essence.* https://www.essence.com/news/gabby-douglas-hair-haters-twitter-claps-back/. 9/13/2019.

Witherspoon, K. M. and Speight, S. L. (2009). An exploration of African Americans' interests and self-efficacy beliefs in traditional and nontraditional careers. *Journal of Black Studies.* November.

Woodson, C. G. (1933). *Mis-education of the Negro.* New York, NY: The Associated Publishers.

X, Malcolm (1964). "The ballot or the bullet." King Solomon Baptist Church, Detroit Michigan. April 12. *American RadioWorks.* http://americanradioworks.publicradio.org/features/blackspeech/mx.html. 9/13/2019.

Yardley, J. (2014). A history of Paris during Nazi occupation. *The Washington Post.* https://www.washingtonpost.com/opinions/a-history-of-paris-during-nazi-occupation/2014/08/29/fce9e112-222c-11. 9/4/2019.

INDEX

1619, beginning of enslavement in the United States of America 151–152, 172; creation of American slavery and American democracy 116

16th Street Baptist Church bombing 68; Collins, Addie Mae 68; McNair Denise 68; Robertson, Carole 68; Wesley, Cynthia 68

abolitionist teaching 28

academic equity and excellence discourse 56, 96, 128, 130; hard work 130; high expectations 44, 130

African: history and culture 152–153, 163, 172–173; identity, 152–153, 167

African American achievement xiii, xx, 3, 14, 30, 32, 44, 69, 80, 119, 129

African American activism and agency xvi, xvii, 12, 24, 29, 44, 47, 68, 72, 89, 129–130; counter-narratives 113–115; letter- essay as a personal-political form 52–53, 78, 90, 121, 128–136; literacy and voice 129; pursuit of knowledge and education xviii, 167, 179; resistance and resilience i, 2, 5, 12, 19, 28, 69, 130, 168, 172

African American art and artists xix 9, 24, 43, 68, 156–159, 168, 175–176; prophets of freedom 158

African American children: agency 43; beauty 2, 133; celebration of 31–32, 52, 72; education of iii, xv–xvii, xix, 2, 6, 8, 10, 12–15, 17, 19–20, 22–23, 25, 27, 35, 37–38, 42, 48, 54–55, 63–68, 71–74, 76, 81, 84, 87, 90, 95–101, 109, 118, 137–138, 166, 179; development of identity 42; empowerment of 14, 71–74; hair 170; life importance of joy 43; murder of 123; resilience 2; resistance 14, 43

African American civil and human rights xix, xx, 2, 4, 13, 24, 32, 66, 77, 82, 116, 118, 132, 158, 61, 164–165, 176; equitable education 12

African American culture x, xi, xvii, 9–10, 14, 23, 32, 44, 51, 54, 98–99, 101, 111, 115–116, 131, 147, 150–153, 163, 165

African American empowerment i, 14, 40, 71–74, 94, 129

African American enslavement xvi, xviii, 5, 10, 13, 28, 33, 41, 42, 95, 103, 115–116, 120, 122, 129, 133, 140, 148–150, 152, 173, 179

African American experience in the United States of America: African Americans critical to economic, social, political growth and prosperity 83, 90, 123; dehumanization 15, 46, 57, 78, 85, 97, 114, 153; Emancipation 29, 46, 51, 71, 74, 80–81, 104, 129; exploitation 9, 83, 86, 90, 121, 123, 152; ghettoization 23, 52, 67, 69, 87, 92, 115, 130, 135; hospital and health care access xvi, 74, 119, 160; lynching xvi, 6, 12, 35, 44, 48,

184 Index

88, 110, 130, 144; mass incarceration xvi, 2, 6; ostracization 10, 24, 140; unequal employment 2, 10, 116, 119, 127, 161; voter suppression 11, 41, 115

African American fathers xv, 22, 52, 111–112, 116, 122, 128; counter-narratives 113–115; false narratives and stereotypes of 10–11, 116; "missing father" thesis 113–114

African American history x, xi, xiii, xv, xvii–xviii, xix, 5–6, 14, 30, 42, 44, 48, 74, 79, 101, 154, 170

African American homes and families xviii, 6, 14, 23, 32, 42, 47, 76, 111; activism and agency of families xvii; devaluing neighborhoods and properties of 115, 119, family strengths 6, 14, 32, 122–123, 128; humanity of 47, 122; letters to family, 128–129; parents 19, 32, 48, 52, 72, 76, 111–112, 122–123, 135, 137; stereotypes of 2, 99

African American humanity xvi–ii, 2, 5, 15, 31, 34, 36, 44, 47–48, 53–54, 57, 67, 78–79, 99, 101, 111, 122, 127, 133, 144–145, 150, 162–163

African American "hybridity" 151, 164–165

African American identity xv, xvi, 5, 146, 150–156, 164–165, 167–168; diasporic identity 152–153; in opposition to whiteness 174; schizophrenic 83, 111, 137; skin color 5, 28, 30–31, 36, 53, 82, 86, 93, 130, 145, 151–153, 156, 163, 167, 169

African American language xvii, 31, 35–36, 99

African American literature xx, 31–32, 50, 54, 73, 120, 138

African American mothers xv, 11, 22, 48, 52, 72, 74, 111–112, 116, 122, 149–150; childbirth injuries and death 74; false narratives of 114–116

African American music 32, 67, 79, 84, 130–131, 145, 150

African American reparation 123

African American representation in media, movies, literature, and sports entertainment 50, 93, 152

African American striving, 6, 42, 47, 53, 80, 120, 163–164, 172

African American students iii, xiii, xv, xvi, xviii, xix, 2, 6–7, 9–15, 19–21, 23, 25–26, 28–32, 40–41, 49–54, 56, 65, 67,

70–74, 77, 79–84, 86–87, 90, 92, 96, 98–102, 109–112, 115, 135, 137, 143–144, 146, 151, 155, 162–165, 167, 169, 172, 176: activism and agency 20, 82, 94, 109; in classrooms and schools that reproduce intersectional oppression 86–87, 176; critical questioning 13, 19, 110, 162, 171, 174; as "culturally deprived" 98, 100, 104, 116; empowerment 14, 40, 71–73, 129; highly capable of academic learning 162; in honors and AP classes 155; humanity xvi, 14, 72, 111; learning their contributions to history and culture 83, 138, 163–164, 172; love of self 82, 163; "miseducation" i, 13–14, 29; resistance i, xvii, 14, 115; resisting European American culture and standards 9, 10, 20, 79, 163, 172; "schizophrenic" 83, 111, 137; self-discovery 167, 169

African American teachers xix, 7, 26–35, 42, 44, 55–57, 89; activists 5, 44, 53, 65

African American women 6, 51,114; feminist agency 115; negative characterization of 114–115; violence against 51, 123

African American youth: activism and agency 29, 94; beauty 2, 133; contributions of xvii, 88, 102, 137–138; humanity xvi, 34, 130, 148–149; make freedom happen 94, positive self-image and self-worth 66, 81–83, 94; resilience 2, 5, 172

African American and European American racial relations iii, 5, 16, 29–30, 46, 50–51, 58, 66, 88, 154, 156

African and Western culture inescapably linked 154, 175

Algerian War 13

ally: the role of an 114

"Amen Corner, The" (Baldwin) 157

"American Dream Has Been Achieved At The Expense Of The American Negro" (Baldwin) 123–124, 128

American dream 10, 116; at the *expense* of African Americans 10, 121–124, 128

American exceptionalism 5, 98

American Indians: Crispus Attucks xvi, 20; genocide of 89–90, 93, 98; history 138; the only people native to the land of the United Stated of America xi, 138, representation in movies and mass entertainment, 16, 93

Index   185

Angelou, Maya 176
Another Country (Baldwin) xvii
anti-blackness i–ii, 48, 77, 115, 117, 119–120, 135; denial of 119
antiracist teaching 14
Armstrong, Emile 4
artist's duty and struggle 14, 30, 48, 58, 86, 102; "bears witness" 42–43, 159, 168; reveal reality and speak truth 48, 58, 86, 98, 102
"Artist's Struggle for Integrity, The" (Baldwin) 102
"As Much Truth as One Can Bear" (Baldwin) 102
Attucks, Crispus xvi, 20
Ayer, Gertrude Elise 66, 70, 102

Baker, Josephine 145
Baldwin-Socrates analogy 42
"Ballot or Bullet" (Malcolm X) 164
"bearing witness" 14, 27, 29, 42–43, 50, 159, 161, 166, 168,171
Beloved (Morrison) 115
Between the World and Me (Coates) 129, 135
Birmingham Children's Crusade 116 Black Arts Movement 34
"Black is Beautiful" 31, 48, 52, 78, 163
black diasporic identity 152–153
black father thesis 113–114 Black Girls Code 94
Black History Month 151
Black Intellectual Thought ii, xiii, xvii, 5, 44, 131
Black Lives Matter Movement i, 12, 17, 24, 33, 35, 44, 50, 65, 94, 134; "All Lives Matter" rejoinder 35, 119, 131; "Black Lives Matter" slogan 35, 119, 131; "Blue Lives Matter" rejoinder 119 Black Nationalist Movement 164, 175–176; black supremacy 67, 175
"Black problem" 9, 12, 23, 29, 80, 85, 158, 165 (American Negro Problem)
Black Youth Project 94
"blame the victim" 75, 99, 114, 119
Brown v. Board of Education xvi, 29, 48, 77, 117, 164
Brown, Justice Henry 96
Brown, Michael 65
Buckley Jr., William F. xix, 53, 109, 116–119, 121, 128

Cambridge Union Society at Cambridge University 116–117, 120–121, 123

Castlemont High School in Oakland, California xix, 66, 71, 143, 146, 159, 161–162, 165–168, 171–173, 175–176, 179
Chase, Secretary of the Treasury Salmon 124
civil rights xix, 1, 2, 4, 24, 32, 66, 77, 82, 100, 115–116, 120, 132, 158–160, 164, 176
Civil Rights Act of 1957 158–159
Civil Rights Act of 1964 121
Civil Rights Movement xvi, 1, 5, 13, 33, 44, 47, 50, 56, 67, 100, 116–117, 159, 161, 164–165, 169, 171, 175; Baldwin's commissioned trip to write about 159; critical role of African American youth 66, 82, 120, 161, 164–165, 171; leaders of 24, 32; protests 24, 66, 82, 120, 132, 165; racial violence against civil rights protestors 51, 158
Civil War 21, 30, 123–124; "forty acres and a mule" land distribution failure 124; U.S. soldiers of color 21, 30
Clark, Dr. Kenneth 67, 83, 110
class 42, 59, 66, 71, 79, 97–98, 119, 126–127
class oppression 87, 126–127, 149
Coates, Ta-Nehisi 54, 129, 135
Cold War 24, 68
colleges of education 7–10, 14–15, 22–23, 25, 87, 96
Collins, Addie Mae 68 color line 15, 59, 154
Congress of Racial Equality (CORE) 24, 66
Cooper, Anna Julia xiii, 5, 57, 131
Counts, Dorothy 160; father Reverend Counts 160
Counts, George 73
COVID-19 ii, 6, 11, 23, 30, 33, 40–41, 44, 48, 74, 127; higher exposure and rates of death for African American and Latinx people 23, 40, 48, 74
"Creative Process, The" (Baldwin) 102
criminal conspiracy 10–11, 19, 40, 76–77, 80–81
critical consciousness xviii, 15, 42, 58, 70, 72, 131–132
critical questioning 19, 110, 162, 174
Cuban Missile Crisis 68 Cullen, Countee 69–70, 87
cultural deprivation theorizing 99
cultural relevance in education ii, 7, 11, 28–29, 32, 56, 72, 85, 169

186 Index

culture as a code word for power 173
curriculum that miseducates 13, 42, 48, 73, 83, 144, 178; biases and omissions of African Americans xiii, 10–12, 83, 87, 144, 163, 177; Eurocentric 23, 73, 144
curriculum that centers African American students xiii, 32, 55, 88, 138; liberates African American and European American students 88, 101–102, 138

Davis, Angela 78
"determined resistance" 94, 109
deficit discourse and perspectives 15, 49, 72, 87, 98, 100, 162
Delaney, Beauford 32–33
democracy in the United States of America 2, 5, 7, 9, 14, 17, 25, 42, 46–47, 66, 86, 116, 118; becoming a true democracy 117; failings of xvi, xvii, 6, 10, 14, 58, 74, 77, 116, 135, 164; relearning of 73; protecting democracy 86 denial of truth 85
Devil Finds Work, The (Baldwin) 92 Dewey, John 56–57, 61, 73, 77
DiAngelo, Robin 124
diasporic identity 152–153
Dickens, Charles 19, 33, 133, 136, 166
"Discovery of What It Means to be an American" (Baldwin) 43, 145–146, 156
Double V social activism campaign 47, 116 Douglas, Gabby 170
Douglass, Frederick 69, 72, 131, 150
"Down at the Cross: Letters from a Region in My Mind" (Baldwin) 51, 53, 58, 90, 135
"dysconscious racism" 102

education of African Americans 80; children iii, xvi, xix, 2, 11, 25, 29, 35, 70, 100–101; critique of 11, 29, 35, 87, 100; inferior 11, 68
Eisenhower, President Dwight D. 159 Ellison, Ralph xvi, 115
Emancipation Proclamation of 1863 29, 46, 71, 74, 80–81; African Americans fulfilling their education dream 71, 80
"Encounter on the Seine: Black Meets Brown" (Baldwin) 145–146, 148–152
enslavement of African and African American people xv–xviii, 5, 10, 28, 33, 41, 44, 81, 84, 95, 98, 115–116, 120, 122, 129, 133, 149–150, 152, 173, 179

eudaimonia 179
Eurocentric curriculum 13, 23, 32
European American: critical self-reflection 57, 66; false history 154, 187; humanity 26, 67, 112; identity 22–23, 27, 52, 57, 95, 101, 105, 107, 108, 110, 133, 137–139, 146, 148–149, 151, 155, 188; language 36, 107; violence towards women, children, and people of color 51, 123, 125; moral identity 95, 151; myth of freedom 57; oppression of poor 126–127; self-worth 146; skin color 15, 51, 93, 150, 152, 163
European American race and racism problem 2, 4–6, 13, 16–18, 21, 23, 26–27, 29, 36, 41, 49, 58, 70, 74–75, 83, 89–90, 92–93, 95–96, 98, 101, 117, 124, 134, 136–139, 144, 146, 149, 151–153, 155, 161; false narratives 133; disavowing accountability for racism 98; lying about mistreatment of African Americans 84; not discussing race and racism 18, 98, 137; passive complicity 137, 151; personal responsibility to end 23; racism 137, 149, 152; white resistance 58–59, 117
European American teacher educators 19, 22, 52–53, 56
European American teachers iii, xviii–xix, 7, 9, 11–12, 14–23, 44, 51, 55, 78, 88–89, 92, 98, 101–102, 127, 137–139; examine their "dysconscious racism" 102
European American teachers of African American students xvi, xviii, 9–10, 12, 14–23
European culture 73, 153, 172–173
Evers, Medgar 68
exceptionalism 5, 98
exile xix, 147, 162
"Everybody's Protest Novel" (Baldwin) 48, 148

"factories of failure" 68, 87
feminist agency 115
Fire Next Time, The (Baldwin) xvii, 3–4, 6, 16, 28, 35, 46, 50–51, 57, 135, 162; "Down at the Cross: Letter from a Region in My Mind" 51 135; "My Dungeon Shook: Letter to My Nephew on the One Hundredth Anniversary of the Emancipation" 51
Floyd, George 6–7, 12, 17, 33, 44, lynching of 6–7, 12, 17, 33, 44 "Fly in

Buttermilk, A" (Baldwin) 159 food
deserts 74–75, 103
food insecurity xvi, 10, 48, 112, 147
"Free and the Brave, The" (Baldwin)
xx, 66
freedom iii, 2–3, 23–24, 40, 51, 58, 70, 72,
80, 83–85, 87, 89–91, 94, 110, 113, 120,
124–126, 129–130, 157–158; critical
role of African American youth
believing in 94, education and school as
vehicle of 23, 87
"freedom is never given" 70, 80
Freedom Riders 24
Freedom Train 126

Garza, Alicia 24
gay 13, 44, 59, 68, 86 See also
homosexuality and LGBTQ
gender 42, 71, 87, 97
gender inequities 48, 114–115 See sexism
"genuine teacher" 54–55
Gettysburg Address 59 Gibson Jr.,
Richard 82
Giovanni's Room (Baldwin) 3, 158
"go for broke" i, iii, ix, xix, 26, 51, 65,
68–70, 98, 108–142, 169; "go for
broke" teaching of African American
students 109–116; critical consciousness
70, 131–132
"Go for Broke" Day 108
"Go for Broke" National Education
Center 109
Go Tell it on the Mountain (Baldwin) xvii,
33–34, 36, 44, 46–47, 157–158
Golden, Harry 160
"Greensboro Four" 82, 165; Blair Jr., Ezell
82; McCain, Franklin 82; McNeil,
Joseph 82; Richmond, David 82;
Woolworth's department store in
Greensboro, North Carolina 82, 165

Hansberry, Lorraine xiv, 25, 128, 176
Harlem Renaissance 69
hate crimes 45
health care and hospital access 74–75, 112,
119, 179
Height, Dorothy 115
heteronormativity xvii, 176
hidden curriculum 54, 100
history of the Unites States of America 165,
180; multicultural 22, 45, 165, 173–174;
myths and lies 23, 32, 36, 41, 50, 52, 64,
85–86, 88–91, 96, 98, 100, 102–103,

111, 113, 123, 133, 145, 168; truthful
teaching of 19, 22–23, 30–32, 40,
42–44, 47, 43, 70, 77, 84, 86–92, 95,
97–98, 111, 143–144, 176 as the present
and carried within us 44, 48, 81, 89
History is a Weapon: They Can't Turn
Back" (Baldwin) 82, 94
Holiday, Billie 67
homosexuality xix, 47, 145, 156–157
See also gay and LGBTQ
homophobia 5
hooks, bell 42
Horne, Lena 24
housing conditions 11, 48, 74, 179
Hughes, Langston 145
human rights xix See civil rights
humanity xvii, 15, 19, 40–41, 125, 136;
appreciation of 14, 19, 72, 125, 133,
145, 162–163; 178; of African
Americans xv–xvi, 5, 15, 17, 19, 31,
34, 36, 44, 48, 53–54, 57, 67, 72, 76,
78–79, 99, 101, 111, 120, 122, 127, 130,
133, 136, 144–145, 148–150, 160,
162–163; 178; crimes against 95; "in
defense of our humanity" 24; of European
Americans 2, 15, 17, 57, 99, 125
Hurston, Zora Neale 131
hybrid cultural identities 151, 165

I Am Not Your Negro (Baldwin) 28, 35, 93
"I Have a Dream" (King Jr.) 68
identity: achieving identity 8, 19, 71, 146;
African 167, 173; critical reflection of
53; development of iii, 5, 145, 147,
168; group identity 146; literary identity
148–149; personal identity 17, 146–147,
164; plural identities 147; self-discovery
i, xix, 29, 43, 71, 143, 145–146, 148,
153, 156, 159, 161, 167, 169; teaching
identity 53; understanding of self 17; of
the United States of America 41–42,
90–91, 100, 152
"If Black English Isn't a Language, Then
Tell Me, What Is?" (Baldwin) 99
imagination 11, 28, 30; as primary agent
of resistance 28, 30; definition of 28;
moral imagination of freedom 2; in
socially constructing race and identity
51, 91, 154
imperialism xvii, 42, 120, 152
"In a Discovery of What It Means to be An
American" (Baldwin) 43, 145–146, 156
innocence. See white innocence

Innocence Project, The 94
"inspiring revolution" 72–73; in education
72–73
intergenerational conversation 129, 136
interracial solidarity 16, 22–24, 30;
boundness 23, 154; "equal respect" 23
intersectionality 33, 71, 86–87, 150
Invisible Man (Ellison) xvi, 115

James Baldwin: A Biography (Leeming) 19,
59, 128
Jeanes Teachers 54–55; curriculum, 55
Jefferson, Thomas 80–81, 83
Jim Crow 121, 125, 133
Johnson, President Andrew 125 Johnson,
President Lyndon B. 76, 114, 136

Kennedy Administration 24
Kennedy Onassis, Jacqueline 128 Kennedy,
President John F. 118, 132
Kennedy, Robert 24–25, 68
King Jr., Dr. Martin Luther 2, 4, 16, 68,
115, 121, 160, 176
King, Coretta Scott 160
Ku Klux Klan 88

land redistribution 124; failings of 124
Leeming, David 19–20, 59, 128
lens of *hope* i, 6, 73, 121, 134, 136
lens of *love* i, xvii, 2, 5, 6, 15–19, 47–48,
53, 57–58, 67, 79, 87, 95, 134–136, 166,
174, 176, 179
"Letter to My Nephew, A" (Baldwin) xix,
xx, 51–53, 109, 128–133, 136, 143, 146
"Letter from Selma, Alabama Jail" (King
Jr.) 121
LGBTQ: community 45; rights, 50
Lies My Teacher Told Me (Loewen) 88,
90, 105
Lincoln, President Abraham 124, 130
linguistic legitimacy 98
"Little Man, Little Man: A Story of
Childhood" (Baldwin) 31–32, 43
Little Rock Nine at Central High
School 165
"Living and Growing in a White World"
(Baldwin) xix, xx, 66, 143, 162
Locke, Alaine xiii
Loewen, James W. 88, 90

Malcolm X 2, 4, 29, 67, 128, 164, 170;
assassination of 128
March on Washington 58, 65

Martin, Trayvon 44, 65 mass incarceration
xvi, 2 McDonald, Laquan 44
McKenna, Natasha 65
McNair, Denise 68
media 40, 45, 95, 100, 152, operate to
support European American interest 40,
75, 100, 152
Meredith, James 132
microaggressions and macroaggressions
13, 75
Miller, Orilla "Bill" 9, 16, 18–20, 69–70
Million Hoodies 94
missing father thesis 10–11, 113–116
Montgomery, Alabama bus boycott
160, 164
Morrison, Toni xii, 7, 27–28, 31, 35, 41,
72, 95, 115, 152, 176
Moynihan Report (Moynihan, P.) 114–115
Moynihan, Patrick 114–115 multicultural
education xiii, xiv, 22–23, 28, 45, 56,
165, 173–174; multicultural social justice
teaching 28
Murry, Harold 67
"My Home on the Hill" (Gibson Jr.) 82
myth-making xix, 70, 89–91; defying iii,
xix, 3, 66, 70 myths 90–91, 103, 107,
147, 186; definition of myths 90; of
liberalism 123–124, 160; white
superiority 16, 55, 73, 120

N-word 5, 16, 25–27, 41, 52, 70, 89, 110,
127, 130, 175
*Nation at Risk, A: The Imperative for
Educational Reform* (President Ronald
Reagan's National Commission on
Excellence in Education) 55–56, 96
"National Advisory Commission on Civil
Disorders Report, The" 76, 136
National Association for the Advancement
of Colored People (NAACP) 56–57, 68
National Board for Professional Teaching
Standards 56
National Council of Negro Women 115
National "Go for Broke" Day 108
Native Son (Wright) xvi–xvii, 48, 144–145,
148–149
neoliberalism xvii, 117
New York City's Community Church 102
No Name in the Street (Baldwin) 83, 87
*Nobody Knows My Name: More Notes from
a Native Son* (Baldwin) xvii, 53, 145, 175
"Notes of a Native Son: Many Thousands
Gone" (Baldwin) 48, 84, 127, 150

Index 189

Notes of a Native Son (Baldwin) xvi–xvii, 43, 46–50, 53, 85–86, 151, 153, 158, 165

Obama, Barack 88, 113–114, 154
Ocasio-Cortez, Alexandria 76
Ole Miss riot of 1962 132; Meredith, James 132, 154
Omar, Ilhan 76
oppression iii, 3, 19, 31, 46–47, 55, 59, 65, 70, 78, 83, 109, 112, 114, 122; intersectional 33, 48, 71, 86–87
organized labor: weakening by American government and corporations 126–127

paradox of education 8, 19, 109, 162; for African American students 19, 109, 162
"Paris Essays" (1950–1961): "Encounter on the Seine: Black Meets Brown" (1950), "Stranger in the Village," (1953), "A Question of Identity," (1954), "The Discovery of What It Means to Be an American, (1959), 145–158
Pemberton, Mr. V. 66, 69
People's History of the United States, A (Zinn) 88
Philadelphia Negro, The (Du Bois) xvi
Plessy v. Ferguson in 1896 96; "separate but equal" 84, 96, 160, 164
Poitier, Sidney 93
police brutality and violence xvi, 2, 7, 11, 13, 19–20, 25, 32, 34, 41, 51, 44, 48, 65–66, 70, 77, 110, 112, 114, 122, 130, 134
policies and practices xvii, 13, 20, 29, 48, 54, 75, 77, 84, 96, 100
political innocence 97
poor housing and living conditions 11, 48, 74
Porter, Herman W. "Bill" 69–70, 87
poverty 2, 11–12, 19–20, 30, 47–48, 55, 71, 80, 96, 99, 100, 112–113, 136, 144, 146–148; in African American and urban communities 2, 11, 55, 99, 136, 144; impact on African American children, students, and families 47, 100, 112–113, 144, 146–148; of schools 12, 96; of whiteness 57, 99, 126
power 3, 5, 11, 13, 18–19, 24–25, 32, 35, 44, 47, 52–53, 55, 58–59, 70, 72, 77, 83–84, 86, 94–97, 100–101, 115, 132, 136–137, 152, 156, 159, 161–163, 167, 168, 173; European and European

American obsession and ruthlessness of 27, 52, 95, 115, 132, 136, 161, 163, 173; criminal power 53; ignorance allied with power 83; and morality relationship 13; and racial innocence 95–97, speaking truth to power 47; teachers have 11, 18–19, 70, 72, 100–101, 137; systems of 13, 24–25, 77, 84, 156
powerful innocence 97
Trump, President Donald 26, 76, 88, 119, 127; hate speech 26, 76
Pressley, Ayanna 76
privilege 44, 58, 95, 118, 122, 161
protest novel 50, 148–149, 158, 169
protests for racial justice 7, 12, 24, 29, 47, 51, 66, 82, 86–87, 109, 120, 130, 132, 138, 148–149, 158–159, 165
PS 184 in Harlem, New York 80 Public School 180 in Harlem, New York 66
purpose of education iii, 6–8, 70–74, 76–81, 83, 92, 101, 168

queerness, 86. *Also see* gay and LGBTQ
"Question of Identity, A" (Baldwin), 145–146, 155

race: investigations of 50, 177; social construction and myth of 51, 91, 154, 157
race in America 3, 14, 44, 45, 91, 151
racial activism 12, 24, 29
racial awakening i, 85, 123, 127
racial capitalism 42, 46, 69, 120
racial consciousness xviii, 2, 5, 14–15, 18, 30, 41–42, 50, 58–59, 78, 93, 111, 131–132, 137, 167–168
racial desegregation and integration 4, 28–29, 82, 119, 136, 160, 165
racial diversity 22–23
"racial essentialism" 175; inescapable link between African and Western culture 175
racial history 146; influence on identities of African Americans and European Americans 146
racial innocence 55, 58, 70, 94–99, 103, 117, 119 See also white innocence
racial oppression i, 6, 14–15, 19, 31, 33, 42–43, 46–47, 55, 59, 65, 70, 78, 83, 99, 109, 112, 122, 137, 168; intersectional reproduction 48, 86–87
racial reckoning movement 6, 17, 41, 95
racial segregation xviii, 4, 12–13, 22, 74–75, 82, 96, 112, 119, 124–127, 130,

133, 144, 149, 160, 165; de jure and de facto 75, 77, 125; negatively impacts African Americans and European Americans 125–126; occupational 127

racism: "going for broke" to fight iii, 65, 84, 109–115, 137–138; colorblindness 96, 119; in media, movies, and news stories 30, 22, 92–93, 152; microaggressions and macroaggressions 13, 75; psychological and political implications 5, 17, 27, 29, 46, 122, 160; wage gaps 48, 76; in the United States of America 2, 24, 30, 36, 44 (sins of racist country), 53, 113, 115, 145, 151

Raisin in the Sun, A (Hansberry), 25

Randolph, A. Philip, 80 Reconstruction, 33, 88, 139, 159

redlining, 77, 92

reflective teacher, 55–57, 59; critical reflection, 55, 59; reflective action, 57; routine action, 57

reflective teaching 55–57, 59; openmindedness 57–59; responsibility 58–59, 131; wholeheartedness 58–59, 131

religion and faith xix, 4, 17, 45, 94, 97, *Report to the American People on Civil Rights* (Kennedy) 118

Reparation to African Americans 123

"respectability politics" 93–94, 112, 170; definition of 93

Revolutionary War xvi, 20–21; African American soldiers 21

Roberts, Gus 160

Robertson, Carole 68

Robinson, Jackie 22, 154

Russell, Senator Richard 159 Rustin, Bayard 68, 115

Savage, Augusta 131

school funding disparities 81, 103, 119 schools as revolutionary places 70; "inspiring revolution" in education 72–73

Seale, Bobby 128

"search for truth" 77, 88, 92

Second Baptist Church in Los Angeles, California xx, 66

Selma to Montgomery March 116

"separate but equal" doctrine and schools 84, 96, 160, 164

settler colonialism 95, 108; anticolonial lens 13

sexism 48, 114–115

sexuality 42, 46, 55, 97

Sheers, Julian 160

Sherman, General William T. 124–125

Sinnette, Mrs. 69

Simone, Nina 128

Smith, Bessie 131, 156–157

"Sometimes I Feel Like a Motherless Child" 149–150

"Souls of White Folks" (Du Bois) 120, 173

"Southern strategy" 117

"Stranger in the Village" (Baldwin) 9, 27, 145–146, 153–155

speaking truth xvi, 3, 5, 14, 32, 42, 44, 47, 84, 86–87, 97, 133, 174

Special Field Order No. 15 125 *See also* Civil War: "forty acres and a mule"

stereotypes 2, 10, 41, 43, 47–48, 90; of African Americans 2, 10, 41, 47–48, 90

Stowe, Harriet Beecher 148

systemic oppression i, 19, 31, 42–43, 46, 99, 114, 122, 137 *Also* institutionalized oppression

structural racism xvii, 5, 23, 47, 112, 119, 144, 177 *See also* systemic racism

Styron, William 128

Swann v. Charlotte-Mecklenberg Board of Education 1971, 96

systemic racism, i, xvii, 19, 46, 75, 93, 99, 111, 113–114, 122, 138, 143, 152, 156, 161 *See also* structural racism.

"Talk to Teachers, A" (Baldwin) xx, 6–7, 26, 32–33, 42, 54, 67, 81, 87, 98, 101, 109, 162, 177

Take this Hammer (Baldwin) 7, 27, 161, 164

teaching truth 19, 87

teacher: as artist 14, 42–43, 48, 102, 122; "bears witness" 14, 42–43, 50, 166, 171; responsibilities and role of 48, 102

teacher candidates xviii, 6–11, 17, 22–23, 26–27, 35, 45, 47, 49–50, 53, 56, 59, 73, 88, 96, 98, 101, 177; innocence 17, 35, 45, 49, 96, 98, 101

teacher education xvi, 9, 14, 17, 27, 91, 94, 96

teacher educators iii, xvi, 7, 12, 19, 22, 29, 44–54, 56, 59, 87, 96, 177

teachers of African American children 13–15, 22, 33–34

teachers of African American students 10, 13–15, 19, 26–27, 68, 73–74, 80, 86, 101, 111, 146, 176; abandoning deficit

Index   191

discourse and thinking 15, 49, 72, 87, 98, 100, 162
"inspiring revolution" 72–73; responsibilities of 19, 21, 72, 76–77, 137, 169, 171; teaching students' history and culture xvii, 10, 14, 42, 44, 54–55, 73–74, 88, 91, 97–98, 101
"Teaching While Black" 144
Teaching to Transgress: Education as the Practice of Freedom (hooks) 42
Till, Emmett Louis xvi, 48, 164; lynching of, xvi, 48, 164
Till, Mamie 164
Tlaib, Rashida 76
transformative love 2, 5, 6, 15–18, 47–48, 87, 95, 134–136
truth as a moral principle of freedom and democracy 83–87, 92, 95, 176; digging for and telling truth 70
Tubman, Harriet 132, 158

Uncle Tom's Cabin (Stowe) 148
underfunding and closing of African American schools 114, 110, 119
under-resourced schools,81, 84
unfair labor practices 76–77, 83, 90, 123, 127–127, 163
Vietnam War 13
Voting Rights Act of 1965 116, 159
voting rights 41, 115–116, 118, 159
voter suppression 41, 115

Watts Rebellion 116
Wesley, Cynthia 68
Wheatley, Phillis 131
"white flight" 117
white fragility 16, 21, 49, 78, 124,
White Fragility: Why It's So Hard for White People to Talk about Racism (DiAngelo) 124
white innocence xvi, xvii, xix, 2, 15, 17, 18, 35, 45, 48–49, 52, 55, 58, 65–66, 70, 94–96, 98–99, 101, 117–118, 123, 153–154; definition of 98; as resistance 45, 98 *See also* racial innocence

white power 161
white privilege xvi–xvii, 2, 3, 16, 29, 44, 51, 57, 75, 78, 91, 95, 99, 111, 126, 144, 146, 161; definition of 75
white racial identity 22–23
white resistance 117; neoliberalism xvii, 117, 119; racial innocence language, 117; willful ignorance behavior, 117
white supremacy i, xvii, 2, 5, 12, 15–16, 21, 32, 44, 52, 55, 65, 73, 75, 83, 89–90, 109, 115, 122, 122, 124–125, 127, 129, 136, 155, 164, 167, 172–173, 175; calling out, 72
whiteness 15–16, 21, 32, 51, 69, 92, 98, 101, 111, 120, 149; decentering 51
willful blindness 5, 95–98, 119
willful ignorance iii, xvii–xviii, 4, 12, 15, 32, 35, 45, 50, 83, 95–98, 100, 117; as resistance 45, 98
willful innocence 15, 48–49; *See also* white innocence
Wilkins, Roy 4
Woodson, Carter G. xiii, 5, 13, 144
World and Africa, The (Du Bois) 163 World War I xvi, 153; African American soldiers xvi
World War II xvi, 47, 108, 116–117, 155, 164; African American soldiers xvi, 47, 144, 164; African American soldiers' resistance 164; American soldiers in Paris 155; Army's 442nd Regimental Combat Team (RCT) 108, 137; Nisei soldiers 108–109
Worth, Eugene 43, 144
Wright, Richard xvi, 48, 53, 144–145, 147–149

youth activists and activism 25, 29, 65, 68, 94; in Black Lives Matter 94; Black Girls Code 94; Million Hoodies 94; Black Youth Project 94; Innocence Project, The 94; make freedom happen 94

Zinn, Howard 88

Printed in the United States
by Baker & Taylor Publisher Services